Heaven Come Down

Heaven Come Down

The story of a transgender disciple

Chrissie Chevasutt

DARTON·LONGMAN+TODD

First published in 2021 by
Darton, Longman and Todd Ltd
1 Spencer Court
140 – 142 Wandsworth High Street
London SW18 4JJ

ISBN: 978-1-913657-20-8
A catalogue record for this book is available from the British Library.

Cover photographs by Katie Blakeborough
Designed and produced by Judy Linard
Printed and bound in Great Britain by Bell & Bain, Glasgow

This book is dedicated to my beautiful wife and two daughters. They provided me with the love, strength and will to not give up, to fight, survive and live again. A debt that can never be repaid.

In memory of my own father, ever the gentleman,

and to the Reverend Dennis Shepherd, spiritual father to me, and to many,

and to the thousands of transgender people who have lost their lives because of transphobia, hate and ignorance.

Contents

Foreword

It's sadly common to hear of how trans and gender non-conforming children try for years to deny their identity.

What is utterly remarkable about Chrissie Chevasutt's compelling and moving account is the lengths to which she was driven by her self-hatred.

She did everything she could to deny and conceal and repress who she is: adopting an ultra-masculine identity, running away from herself to India and the Himalayas, trying to drown out the pain of her denial through addiction to drugs and alcohol, becoming a pastor in a transphobic evangelical church, working in the macho building trade, marrying and having children.

It's all told with great vividness, great skill, and an astonishing unflinching honesty that often makes for harrowing reading.

But it's also a story of redemption; of how her remarkable partner Pam's love for her, and her own faith, brought her to accept her trans identity as a gift from God.

This makes it an inspiring and a deeply moving story of love both human and divine.

Jo Clifford
Playwright, performer, father, grandmother

Acknowledgements

It's impossible to thank all those who made this book possible, but I'd like to try and at least mention some of you. Time and space mean many are inevitably left out – but, if you have ever loved me, forgiven me and given me your time, you are part of this story. Thank you, from the depths of my heart.

I'd best start with the Three Mid-Wives who helped deliver this book, who believed in me, helped me find my voice, and taught me how to write a better story. Bebe O'Shea, Emily Garces, Carol Holden. It's not just your kind words that gave me confidence, it's very much who you are, your kindness, encouragement and love, that inspired me to dig deeper in the darkest times.

To my Three Sisters who went before me and dragged me out of a very dark place, Mia, Mel and Nikki, you are very much a part of who I am, angels all three!

Kerry Jones, this book hinges on my meeting you and the spiritual earthquake that followed. You opened up the missing chapter, and heaven came down. You are someone special, that's for sure. Thank you too, for inspiring the cover of this book!

To my own sisters, Sylvia and Sorelle. Words can never be enough. You have loved and supported me in a way that allowed me to find my wings and fly. Love that can never be repaid.

To the Sheffield massif, Nicola, Hannah, and the most irreverend Huw, who first welcomed me home (I know I've

Acknowlegements

been a pain). Nathan, Matthew and Sue, Lesley, Jane and all at Embrace, I wonder if I'd have made it this far without your constant love and encouragement.

To Mick, Toby and Mick, the Three Musketeers, your friendship was and still is inspirational, faithful and true. You've stuck by me when others have walked away. You keep my feet on the ground with your stories from the skies, and your merciless banter and kick-ass spirit. You never knew just how far you carried me, in this battlefield we call life.

To another old soldier, who has stayed true. Lawrence, thank you! You got to taste the life I longed for but couldn't quite reach. Road trip on the Somme to follow.

To my Grandad Sam, and my Gran, Florence, long gone, when words were meaningless you showed me Jesus. Without your witness, I'd be dead.

To training and racing partners over the years, not least Charlotte, Mick, Kirsty, Tony, Jez and Jules, you are living proof that the church holds no monopoly on love, and that when the church's love runs out, as it often has, there is plenty to be found elsewhere.

The Fairly boys, Jan, the Crankettes, the Groupetto, the Fast Group and Robert Millar, now Philippa York, you are all a huge part of my story. When church did not understand, you were the 'church' I belonged to, the 'church' that carried me through. A fellowship of mutual sufferings on the roads and lanes we traversed together, some of the best days, years and memories of my life.

To my English and history teachers, and my mother, who instilled in me a love for literature, books and the beauty of words; Laurie Lee, Jack Kerouac, Emily Garces, Jan Morris, V. S. Naipaul, J. A. Baker (The Peregrine), Arundhati Roy, Thomas Merton and Brother Lawrence, Bernard of Clairvaux, Siddartha Gautama, Bob Marley, Bob Dylan, Janis Joplin, the writer/s of the Gospel of John, Jim Morrison, Nelson Mandela, Justin Tanis, Tom Waites, Wilfred Owen, Wilfred Thieseger and Eric Newby, explorers, mystics, visionaries all.

To all our friends in the Vineyard Movement, and all that you meant to us, to everyone with me in YWAM Scotland and Portugal, to the saints and sinners who created and made up our Anglican church in Oxford, thank you for all you gave us.

Helen and Tom Murphy, I think I would have walked out on the church for ever, if you had not stepped into my life, led by example, scooped me up, embraced my pain and gave me hope to believe a more inclusive, affirming church is possible.

To Kathy Baldock and Reverend Tina Beardsley, your standing as spiritual mothers, pastors and teachers within our community is of great comfort and strength to so many of us. Thank you for creating and defending safe space, refuge and a place of healing and restoration.

To Wes, wherever you are, stay safe, thank you for sharing your life with me.

To Steve – we're not done yet! Thank you for being a faithful brother especially through the storms of my coming out.

To my publishers and my editor, David Moloney, I still can't believe you took this risk on me, I hope this book does not disappoint, goes far, wide, deep and lives long. Thank you for your continual encouragement and kindness of spirit.

Katie Blakeborough, you define the joy of serendipity and the creation of this book cover and so much more to come. The chemistry of a team, I'm learning loads.

To my community, the transgender community, I am sorry for all the hate, the judgement and the ugly words that Church has cursed you with. I hope you'll open your hearts again to the possibility that God is love, nothing more, nothing less. You are my tribe. Thank you for holding a safe space for me.

To the Church, my prayer is that you might listen and learn, learn to refrain from judging those whom you do not understand, and instead learn to embrace those you have oppressed and marginalised. Grace and mercy will always triumph in the end.

To my spiritual father, the late Reverend Dennis Shepherd. I never got over the loss, you showed me Christ, how the Word must become flesh. You made a mystery seem so simple. (Sheila too!)

To everyone who has battled through trauma, sufferings, depression, battles with mental health, suicidal ideation, bereavements, grief and loss, gender dysphoria and dysmorphia, or the struggle to reconcile your gender and sexuality with the world, I want to stand with you, in solidarity, refrain from all judgement and offer in my story a message of love and hope.

I've been one hundred percent honest at all times, it may not be how others remember things, or even want to remember things, it's simply life, from my point of view. Memories are seldom perfect, but they are all we have. Perhaps the hardest part of writing this book was the people I had to leave out.

The desire was to create a book, tell a story and create a safe space for all who feel weak, broken or poor and overlooked.

Come on in, take a walk in my shoes.

Footnote: Trigger Warning

If you've picked up this book and are skimming its pages, I hope you enjoy, but must forewarn that it contains themes of suicide, self-harm, violence and at times is explicit in the truth. It reflects the battles and struggles many of us face to survive in this brutal world.

1959 –1968
In the Beginning

Home was a tiny hamlet on the road to nowhere. A pub, a cobbler, an old tin mission hut and a large pond, edged by forest, nestling in the unfolding chalky white bosom of the Chiltern hills. We were miles from the nearest large town, a few homes scattered around a crossroads where the old droving roads met. Shepherds and herdsmen on their way to market once let their flocks and herds drink from the pool, which had been fed by a bubbling spring. Crayfish long since gone, the water now dark, the spring silted up.

Rich dense swathes of oak and ash, elm and beech enfold the houses, a forest stretching out for miles around. In winter months woodsmoke rises from chimneys, carried on the wind, the smell hangs over the huddle of homes, warm and inviting. Here on this crossroads, woodland gives way to downy pasturelands, rolling steeply to the river below. In summer, the scent of hedgerows, meadowland, elderflower, cut pasture and honeysuckle garland the air, a fragrance that lingers and soothes, calm, tranquil. Walking or cycling along the meandering lanes, it's a toil and labour up any one of the many long hills to reach our small community.

Ernie, the cobbler, who ran his business out of a wooden shack, nestled under the trees it was built from. He plied his trade in the pungent smell of heavy sweet rubber glues, fresh cut leather and polish. It was a magical place to sit and watch, listening to the brush polishers spinning, singing, his hands dexterous, as he cut, glued and stitched our shoes back together.

Burt, the village hobo, had worked the lumber yards of remote Canada, and toiled on the outback, desert farms of Australia, or so he said. He lived alone with his frail old father. They collected water from a well in the garden of their old flint cottage. He would appear unannounced on our doorstep, eat all our biscuits, his bad breath and the sweat-soaked smell of rural poverty lingering long after he had gone.

The Church of England had seen fit to invest in the conversion of the heathen pagan tribes, who dwelt in hamlets just like ours, and tin mission huts sprang up across the country. I don't think they had much success with us at all. Last time I passed through, the mission hall was long collapsed, rusted and buried in the soil, beneath a thicket of bramble. Wild dog rose and fern growing, luxuriously and resplendent, stood rejoicing over its decaying frame. The community lived on its life, devoid of religious concerns.

The village had its own tragic stories to tell. It was a close and closed community. The woods hemmed us in, seeped history, the ghosts of the past. I loved to count, with bated breath, the rings of oak stumps, long since felled, one hundred, two hundred, three hundred years old. They whispered their stories to me. I could hear them as I laid my head down on the mighty old trunks to listen. How many lives, both human and animal had sheltered beneath these mighty trees, shadowed by their branches? Now they lay buried beneath the leaves, undisturbed in the rich, dark soil at my feet.

We lived in an age where phones and televisions were scarce. Our phone number had only three digits, and calls were connected through an operator by hand. We had our first television installed in time for me to see the blurry black and white images of a man taking his first steps on the moon. Cars were few, wheezing rattling buses occasional. I remember an old woman out of Goring who would bring vegetables for sale with her ancient cart and horse. Winters we often got snowed in for weeks at a time, the phone our only link to family who lived aeons away. We were stuck in a living time capsule. The years rolled by and nothing ever seemed to change. The world seemed a far away and distant place.

Everyone knew each other, and as we went about our business it was hard to keep our lives a secret. There were few kids in the village; a gaggle of children from the council house close. A small tribe of angry, noisy boys who bullied and harassed the quiet, lonely, over-sensitive child that I was. They swarmed about me like wasps. I could not understand their language or their ways, they were smelly, rough, callous things, who would regularly dump me in the prickly hawthorn hedge, then strut and prance away in rumbustious glee, smirking, belly laughing, happy. I would pull myself out, and slink home defeated, crushed, feeling useless, mocked, rejected, stung by their bitter jibes.

I had an older sister, Sylvia, whom I adored. My only friends, the two young sisters who lived next door. We grew up together, like peas in a pod, seldom apart. Between our newly-built homes, dad had planted young sapling hedges. We walked between the young plants, not noticing the division between our homes. Neither did I see the distinction between boy and girl, male or female. We were really just sisters. Together, we played, and sang, and laughed, did all the things that innocent children do. Make-believe and imagination filled our days. We chased each other round the gardens, horses one moment, birds the next, to collapse in giggles, exhausted in each other's arms.

We spent long summers bathing in the sun, our bodies turned brown and golden. Cooling ourselves under hosepipes or buckets of water flung, screaming, squealing, not knowing if we really wanted the cold-water shock on our skin, laughing and drunk in the excitement of being chased then soaked.

We sucked on home-made ice lollies, and savoured bottles of pop, like queens drinking champagne. Winters we curled up cosy in blankets by the open fire, roasting chestnuts gathered from the woods, or buttered toast on long sooty forks. We dressed up, in beautiful, fairy dresses and stole their mothers make-up. These sisters were my life, they took away my crushing loneliness. We lost and found ourselves so many times, snuggled together, gazing into the flames, a peace and calm, a comfort and a solace we never found in the world of television that was to come.

Mum had left home shortly after I was born. She went to work in Singapore with a friend. This gaping, aching void of absence hurt, but I was oblivious to what it really was. In my early years it did not even register that I was supposed to have a mother. The neighbours adopted me into their family and were sensitive enough not to raise the subject of my missing mother.

Dad was everything to me. He was a father of such warmth and affection, I felt as if I lacked nothing. He ran a design business from a small studio he had built on the side of our home. Being a single working dad, he left us to our own devices, to entertain ourselves, but I was secure in the knowledge dad was always there for me, whenever I needed him. If he was too busy, he would give me reams of paper, pencils, pens and leave me to draw and dream, write and create at one of his desks.

His cooking skills were basic, simple, plain, his repertoire dish was sausage, egg, beans and chips. Chips fresh cut and fried in a pan of boiling oil on the weary blackened stove. Seems like every other week the pan would explode into flames that licked the ceiling, and he would dramatically leap across the kitchen and smother it, in a flourish, with wet tea towels.

Dad was a natural comic, with a lovely warm, mischievous sense of humour. Ever the practical joker, he'd balance pillows, tubs of water and open bags of flour, painstakingly balanced on rulers, over doors left ajar, and laugh out loud as victims screamed and shrieked, after being hit in the dark or soaked in shock, as they walked under his booby traps.

So, we survived – this broken family, with a stream of au-pairs, nannies, cleaners and the occasional girlfriend. Dad carried a world of pain in his heart, but he tried to never let it show. Motherless, I was miserable, and never knew why, I never thought my unhappiness was because I didn't have a mum. Melancholy clung to me like an unwanted bad smell. I've never seen a photograph of me smiling as a child, and there are many; instead a deep, haunting loneliness filled my eyes. Sylvia had battles of her own, and she rebelled, hard and fast, and drifted further and further from home, vulnerable and bewildered at the cards life had dealt her. Neither of us knew how to communicate our pain. We began, increasingly, to exist in our own separate lives and our loneliness increased.

Dad would wake me early before his work began, and we would go mushrooming, armed with buckets, the dew on long grass sparkled, spraying and soaking our boots. Returning home with buckets full of huge field mushrooms, we'd share them with our neighbours. We cooked them up, one saucer sized mushroom, dripping in butter, on huge wedges of toast.

Rising with the dawn, wrapped in warm layers, drab coats, dull colours, sneaking out into the frosty morning. We'd stash fishing rods in the car and idle quietly down the hill to the river. Parking up in a hidden spot, climbing the gate, we would slink along hedgerows, camouflaged, and settle by this most beautiful, enchanting of rivers. Hunkered down in the shadows, trying to remain hidden from the searching eyes of the water bailiffs, without a word, we would hook a worm each and drop it in the clear flowing crystal waters, waiting patiently, sat still, motionless in an eternity, praying for the trout to bite.

More than once we got chased by the bailiffs in their Land Rover. We would leap the streams and culverts and run for our lives. Dad would hide our coats and the small fishing rods beneath the rear seat, and the trout wrapped in paper, in a pile of rubbish in the boot. After stealing our fish from the river, we cruised through the sleepy little town, stopping by the bakers for a loaf of fresh bread. Nothing ever tasted quite so good as those exquisite, gorgeous shimmering brown trout, lightly dusted with flour and butter and fried gently, lightly in a pan.

Dad had permission from the local farmers, to shoot the rabbits that devastated their crops. At dawn and dusk, he shot and stole their pheasants too. He reasoned out loud, 'No one can own the fish in the river, or the birds in the air.'

He would take me out, dawn and dusk, to poach pheasants. I guess my father was trying to initiate me into his male world, me his only son, but it was too late, even then, for I was already me. What I saw, what I felt, what I breathed in those early years spent with him, was not the masculine pursuit of sport, or hunting, daring, or proving our skills and stealth. What I loved was being immersed in the world of nature that mesmerised me with its beauty. I forgot all my melancholy, all my loneliness and misery. This world breathed over me a peace and I breathed it in, I drank it in, I could not get enough of all the glory I saw, heard and felt.

☆

The greatest earthly treasure my dad ever bequeathed me was his prized collection of birds' eggs. Eggs which he had gathered from his earliest years before and during the war. One of those hobbies certain boys did to escape the harsh bleakness of life in the grim, grey and dull mining village. It helped him forget the fears of war and the bombs being dropped. He scoured the hedges, woods and fields, waiting, watching and tracking these flighty elusive birds to their nests. On rare trips to the seaside, he would disappear, not interested in arcades, the beach or building sandcastles. Instead he climbed cliffs and scoured sand dunes for birds, nests and eggs. Eggs, that to the other boys in the village, were exotic and rare; seagulls' eggs, terns and oyster catchers.

Every spring and early summer I explored further and further into the woodlands, hedgerows and the pathways, through the meadows and pastureland. Wandering under wide open vast skies that echoed with skylarks as they sang, tumbled and fell from their soaring in the heavens. Drunk with the beauty of it all, I would lay on my back, soaking in summer's sun, gazing giddy into the floating clouds, feeling the gentle breeze upon my skin, my heart filled with the song of myriad larks carried on the wind. I never did find that skylark's nest, hidden in the long grass.

Trembling with joy and anticipation, pushing through a thick brush of thorn and brambles to find a tiny nest so intricately, delicately woven. My legs, arms and face scratched and torn by the brambles and thorns, bloodied even, I scarcely felt a thing, the beauty of a cluster of eggs was so wonderful, so miraculous, it took my breath away. Carefully, I would pick one, and only ever one – my father's only rule. Wrapping it in cotton wool, I placed it lovingly in its small tin coffin to carefully carry home. Retreating as quickly, as quietly and as carefully as I could, to sit and wait, some distance off, patiently, until the mother came, squawking, alarmed, clicking, scolding and circled her nest. Only when she had settled in and nestled down once more upon her eggs, could I depart, but even then, I felt pangs of pain, the knowing dread, that in my pocket, I held her tiny chick in egg. Murderer that I was. I wondered how she felt, the mother on her nest? Did she know, could she sense? She had lost a child.

Unpacking the egg, colours so soft, mottled, hued, small as my little fingernail, so delicate and fragile, so wondrous, exquisite. They were the most beautiful things I had ever seen or held. Pricking each end of the egg with a pin, I would blow, pushing air through the tiny hole with all the force my lungs could muster, lips pursed, cheeks bellowing, as I sweated from the effort. Get it wrong, blow too hard, or clutch the egg too tight, and weeks of patient searching would be wasted, the egg crushed. Eventually, drip by drip, this life would bleed down the sink, this same blood that pumped through my veins, that sometimes I had seen, in shock spill out – I realised I was no different from the incredible tiny life, yolk cum bird in egg, that I had just ended. I could die just like that, if all my blood escaped. Holding the fragile blown egg, seeing its bloody contents, a life, disappearing down the plug hole, I had stumbled upon the secret that all life is sacred. I understood fully the eggshell fragility of my own life.

Gently washing the egg, I dried it and tenderly placed it in my treasure box, labelled in the neatest script I could muster. Sitting on my bed, with the box on my lap, holding each egg in the palm of my hand, I would remember their stories, when and where I, or my father, as a boy, had found each one. Then I would place the box beneath my pillow, lie back content, and dream.

That I did not have a mother was a consciousness that only dawned on me very gradually, with the passing years, and with that awareness came the increasing knowledge that something both inside and outside of me was wrong, very wrong. Sylvia started school, and the closeness we once enjoyed seemed to fade as she found a world of her own. For two short years I lived almost inseparable from the two sisters next door. Dad worked in the studio and I would slip through the thickening hedge to inhabit their women's world. I loved their company, and forgot about my worries, my emptiness and loneliness. I was just one of the girls, doing all the things that young girls do with their mum.

My sisters next door started school. I was sent to school in another village. They soon lost all interest in me, a smelly 'boy' and we drifted apart. Starting school, totally alone and isolated, I had no friends to hide amongst. The loss of my two sisters next door, and the loss of my own sister to other schools, devastated me. Boys were an entirely alien species, I did not understand them at all. School was a threatening place and a deep despair and fear settled in heavy clouds upon my heart.

My first term at school was spent clinging to the skirt of my form teacher, every breaktime I would dissolve and sob, deep and genuine tears into her lap, I was totally lost in a strange harsh new world. Infant school playground was a bleak and brutal world. It was hard enough in the classroom, under a teacher's watchful eye. Outside in the playground the bullying, the mocking, the jeering and the continual rejections began. For some reason I did not understand I was somehow other, an outsider.

One of the few memories I have, is of one of my paintings taking first prize in my year's art exhibition. All the boys had drawn and painted soldiers, guns, cars, castles, trains and tanks, I had painted a huge single iris, like some huge vulva, shocking stamens, throat and petals resplendent in soft feminine pastel hues. I remember feeling so proud as my father held my hand and looked up at my painting, taking centre stage, pride of place.

With no friends in the tiny hamlet my solace was found wandering the paths, fields and woods. Whilst dad worked, I was free to roam, so I grew up feral, no rules or laws to contain me. Making dens, hidden in bushes, on a bed of ferns, leaves and grass, I would lie still and silent, till the woods closed in around me, and the creatures settled back into the rhythm I had disturbed. Foxes, rabbits, squirrels and deer would pass me by, often stopping, staring sullenly into my eyes, asking me what I was doing on their patch. They got used to me, familiar. Our eyes would meet and we would engage in short unspoken conversation, till they would turn, bored of me, and carry on their way. I talked to spiders weaving webs, and watched caterpillars crawl branches and spin cocoons as they hung beneath the leaves. I hunted snakes in summertime, glow worms, grass snakes, even the adder, as they sat and basked at the edge of fields, south side of hedges and woods, on the warm sun-baked earth.

As long as I was back for lunch or tea, this hidden, secret world was all mine, I didn't have to share it with anyone. It was where I escaped to, to leave my pain behind, where I hid from boys, and where I felt I belonged. Of towns and cities, I knew nothing. Of hedgerows, fields and woodland, I was but a small part of the sumptuous whole.

From an early age I suffered violent dreams – yet was I even asleep? Where they came from, I did not know. Endless nightmares of being hunted down. A shadowy figure, a vapour, a stench of evil, that visited me and left me shivering and dripping with the cold sweat of fear. It was a visitation, a terror in the night, that left me traumatised. Too frightened to turn off the lights, I would read books into the early hours till I fell, exhausted, into sleep. The fear would cling to me for days, weeks – an oppressive crushing force. How, where and why it lifted off again, I have no idea. Life would return to being bearable, but the nightmares tormented me for many years. It was my first encounter with evil, and where that evil dwelt, I could not tell. It filled me with a worrying, crippling doubt about life, that all was not entirely as it seemed, or certainly not like the adults made out.

Mum and dad divorced, and whatever faith they had went underground, so Sylvia and I grew up free of the shackles of religion. My sisters next door were sent to church in the mission hall on Sunday mornings, so that mum and dad could spend a morning lazing, reading the papers, drinking tea and canoodling in bed. The girls' attendance was reason enough for me to tag along behind, to sit between them and soak in the childhood bonds that held us tight. The Sunday School teacher would walk the two miles from her home in the neighbouring village, to teach us in the ways of God. She would hike in her stiletto heels and summer frocks, all scent of a woman, and we would kneel like lambs at her feet.

My only abiding memory of this church was one of shame and humiliation. One winter for the nativity, I was forced into sack cloth, a tea-towel rammed upon my head and was told I had to be a shepherd, then they paraded me at the front of church. For the insecure, shy and deeply introverted child I was, this was a form of torture. I vowed never to return through the doors of the old tin mission hut, cursing its very existence. So it was that I learnt, at such an early age, to hate church and Christians for their domineering ways. Was I humiliated because they made me perform in front of the crowd as a boy? All I ever wanted, even at that tender age, was to be a girl, like Mary, and the angels, my 'sisters' from next door.

Our only other brush with religion was with one of the au-pairs who came to look after us. She was a devout

Christian. Friday nights, dad and his business partner would drive into Reading and drink at the Boar's Head, which they had renamed, the 'Whore's Bed'. Invariably they would stagger home drunk, to find the au-pair, on her knees, preaching the Bible to them through the letter-box, refusing to let them in until they had repented, and were 'truly sorry for all their sins'. She did not last long. Her demise, I think, was not because of my father's judgements, he was far too laid back, but maybe because of hers?

For one of my birthdays, I think I was seven or eight years old, dad offered me the opportunity of my first big birthday party. I invited my best friends. About a dozen girls came; my neighbours with their girl-friends and a few girls from my class at school, and one boy. The boy went home early, in tears. I remember feeling for once, a profound happiness, to be surrounded by my closest friends, all girls. Perhaps my father realised, for the first time, that I had a problem. It was the only time as a child that I ever really celebrated my birthday. I never felt happy as a boy, and birthdays only seemed to rub the wound even harder. Christmas was an equally miserable time, without a mother.

As a single parent, dad had to keep working, earning, to pay the bills and keep us warm and fed. For the long summer, Easter, and Christmas holidays Sylvia and I were packed up and sent off to stay with grandparents. These vacations were wonderful long days of unspoilt leisure in the warmth, richness and routine of a family home. Retired and available, we had their undivided attention, and we wore them out. Summers spent picking hedgerow fruits for Grandad to transform into homemade wines. Blackberry, elderflower, sloes and dandelions. Grandma made quince, crab apple and blackberry jams and jellies, and rosehip syrup. We feasted and gorged ourselves. We were even allowed to sip the sacred wines and savour each year, Rhubarb '58, Elderflower '63, Blackberry '65, written in a delicate script on home-made labels. I was intoxicated on flavours and smells that sunk beneath our skin. Even in the harshest winters, we breathed and smelt summer all over again, it seemed as if Grandad was a magician.

Evenings in front of the coal-fired range (even in summer, the stove was never allowed to go out – it heated the water for the house), I would sit curled up on Grandad's knees, or nestled into his side. He would tell me of his childhood, spent growing up on the farm his father worked. As a young boy he was stable hand to a team of mighty, gentle shire horses, who pulled and ploughed, carried and carted across the county. Seventy years old and he could still roll off their names, a man who loved his charges and missed them even now, after all those years. I would shut my eyes and see these magnificent horses, and touch the sheen on their coats and feel their groomed manes and tails, smell their warm breath and the musty stable floor.

In 1916, only eighteen, barely more than a boy, Grandad signed up and was sent into the trenches on the Somme. Returning eighteen months later, he was a crippled, broken man with a body riddled with shrapnel from an exploding shell, and a soul that had tasted and seen hell.

The farm turned to mechanisation, all the innovations and benefits of war, whilst his horses lay slaughtered in Flanders' fields of mud, never to return. This country boy, this gentle-man, was broken hearted by the ravages of war, and the relentless grinding wheels of 'progress'. The Great Recession hit. Forced to turn his back on the life he loved, Sam went to work in the mines.

The hell of the trenches did not diminish his faith, if anything it deepened his love and longing for God. His compassion for, and his cynicism of mankind remained. He had a smile that lit up the darkest room, but his eyes carried a sorrow for a past he could never share, and there it lay, buried in his heart, like the shrapnel lodged deep in his body, a grief and pain that he could neither extinguish nor let out.

He was devout in church attendance, so we sadly got dragged along. The church stood on a hill, in the old village, apart from the new village and mining community that grew around the pit, the distance between, symbolic of a wider divide.

The dark stone Victorian Gothic building rose up around its ancient Anglo-Saxon skeleton, and was as grim as the mining houses down below. It felt gloomy, foreboding as death. Maybe the loss and grief of two world wars and too many pit disasters had seeped into its cold stone walls. The warmth of the mining community was strangely missing. The vicar's artificial, pious voice droned, only alienating me further – he never spoke like that when he saw us in the village. The services and hymns, we were forced to endure, me behaving as the model 'boy'. It all felt and sounded like some forlorn dirge. I hated church.

All I longed for was to be free, to walk the fields and hedgerows, lanes and paths. I protested so stubbornly and so defiantly against going to church, that the only option they had was to bribe me. I must have been such a terrible disappointment to them, but they never let it show. This bribe, the veritable sum of half a crown, was more money than I had ever held. A deal was struck; I would go to church only on the most important days. The rest of the time, I was skint.

The miners were not on the whole a God bothering community; the Legion and the pubs were their church, but if they did, their preferred religion was practised in the chapel, 't'other side village'.

On Sundays when I was spared from church, left free to wander, I would often pass the little chapel on my way down to the stream in the valley, and wonder at the rich harmonies that swelled and rose from the open doors. There was a joy in their song that sounded to me, like the birdsong in the hedgerows, woods and fields that beckoned me, but as a shy child I was far too nervous to ever step inside alone.

One summer's day, having to run an errand for Grandad, to buy some stamps and post his letters at the post office, I ran into the village boys. The miners' kids were a rough lot, used to beatings, violence, the macho world of hard-working, hard-drinking men. This hypersensitive kid from down south was spotted, a stranger, a soft target for their own pent-up angers, and they descended on me in an unruly gang, ready to rough me up, turn me upside down and empty my pockets, bloody my nose and send me home.

They grabbed the letters, and jostling, one boy suggested ripping them open. Someone turned one over and read my Grandad's name and return address on the back. In a sober tone he told his mates shut up, and held up the envelope, passing it round for all to see. They hushed, then silently parted company and let me through. They escorted me, like a guard of honour to the post office, and waited outside for me to come out. Shaking like an autumn leaf in an October wind, I fell out the door, not knowing what to expect. Someone offered me a sweet, another slapped me on the back.

'Your grandad's a legend, an a 'ero, he saved ma fathers life.'

He spoke the words with a defiant pride. Others nodded, and murmured their assent. Grandad's work in the village coal mine was as a first responder, a medic. In the event of accidents and pit tragedies, which were not infrequent, when shafts collapsed and men got buried alive, he would be amongst the first to reach them. Some thirty or forty men were killed in the pit in the many years he served the community there. He had seen it all, and carried them out, on stretchers, some dead, some crippled, others, over his shoulders, or weeping in his arms.

It was this one encounter with these boys that so deepened my already profound admiration and respect for this old soldier, warrior and saint. At the same time, it only deepened my shame, that I could not be a man like him, or a boy like them.

Mother returned into our lives as suddenly and silently as she had disappeared. One day she reappeared, to take us out for the day. She stood there in the doorway, a tanned tall amazon of a woman, with raven black hair, dark tanned skin, clothed in cycling shorts and a silk racing jersey, defiantly celebrating every ounce of her womanhood. I never knew why mum had left us. I didn't know why she had returned. Fierce and independent, physically as strong as any man, yet, as I would soon discover – emotionally and mentally she had the strength of a summer flower in a hailstorm. Her temper quick, her anger flashed, eyes blazing she raged – like some wounded animal, tears, screams and shouting poured forth. I was both drawn to her and frightened of her – of when the next storm would come.

She quickly struck up a relationship with a young man who was working as an apprentice, a draughtsman, for my dad. They met whilst racing on the track at Reading. John's real talent lay in racing bikes. He had already won national championships and was only just beginning his racing career.

John treated me harshly, mockingly, maybe he saw my gentleness and sensitivity as weakness and was trying, like my father, to help toughen me up. He would push me around physically and rough me up, it was more than play, it hurt. His manner to me both domineering and bullying, I disliked, feared and resented him from day one. Mum married John. The hatred and animosity they showed my father made me miserable. I was torn in my loyalties, mum seemed desperately bitter and unhappy. I ended up leaving my dad to live with them.

Memories of standing in court, before a judge, as a nine-year old young boy, being questioned about who I wanted to live with, left me feeling entirely lost. Feelings of being manipulated and controlled, that I could not even begin, or dare to articulate. The utter misery at being torn between two parents. Dad did not fight, there was nothing he could do. I watched him let me go, I was filled with grief at being pulled away from someone who had loved me with all his heart. He was a peaceful, loving father, a gentle man. My mum? Maybe, I thought, I could make her happy, maybe I thought it was my job to do just that?

Within weeks of moving to live with mum and John, with a bullying manipulative 'persuasion', they stopped me from seeing my father. They left me feeling as if the choice should be mine. It seemed as if in the short space of a year since my mum's return, I had been torn from a home of peace into one of emotional violence. If I was miserable in my own skin before I left my father, it now felt like the eggshell fragility of my life was being crushed between ugly fingers, but I didn't know whose hands they were that were slowly breaking me.

Moving into a new junior school for the last eighteen months, I was once again the outsider with no friends. My path into the school was set by an elderly lady who taught maths. She seemed barely taller than we were, but what she lacked in size she made up for with a fierce and bitter temper. For some reason, perhaps my hopeless dyscalculia, I became her punchbag. I was neither rebellious nor a trouble to her, but she perceived me as dumb. More than once I remember her shouting at me to come and stand at the front, there she would scold me and pick me up by one ear, in a vice like grip. I marvelled at her strength, given her age and sparrow like frailty. There she would hold me up until, to relieve the pain, I was balanced, quivering on tiptoe.

She knew what she was doing; my legs would cramp, and it would feel like my ear was being ripped from my head. Tears would roll silently down my cheeks, the boys would snigger, until she would drop me suddenly, I almost fell to the floor. I never dared tell anyone, even my mother, about this repeated ordeal. She was a senior and respected teacher, and I was abysmally hopeless at maths, who would ever listen to me or believe me, a child?

Straight away, the boys despised me as a weakling, whilst the girls showered me with sympathy, which opened into close friendships. As ever, the boys in this school were unwelcoming, I was shy, timid and they acted like thugs and bullies – bawdy, crass, pompous and full of spite. I couldn't relate to a single one. The girls welcomed me into their midst with open arms. We played hopscotch, skipping, and netball. In summer we would sit on the playing fields and make daisy chains and talk of our dreams, our homes and families. I had a new-born baby step-brother, whom I adored. With mum working, daytime, I was his primary carer. We bonded close.

Ever since those early childhood days with my two sisters next door, I had secretly carried on dressing as female. I didn't know why. I knew it was 'wrong', but it also felt right, natural, like being safe and snug at home; it was me. It expressed who I was far better than any of the male clothes I had ever worn. In boys' clothes I felt uncomfortable and awkward, like some fake or imposter. Being a girl I felt peaceful, happy and not jaded, weary or ancient. Yet the aftermath of dressing as female, was a bitter poison in my soul. I would plunge into despair, knowing myself to be a freak, hating myself because I was not a boy, a man. My soul pulled one way, the world the other, I was slowly being torn in two.

Had anyone questioned me to any depth, I think they would have recognised I was battling with depression and despair even as an eleven-year old. My feminine soul was mocked, ridiculed, hated, despised, so I buried it, hid it, denied it. I pulled on the mask of being a boy, the loneliest boy in the world. I found it impossible to be like other boys, or make friends with them. The last year of junior school, I became withdrawn, even from the girls. I played truant as often as I dared, forging sick notes from my mother. My inner, feminine being wanted so desperately to run away and escape, to be released, free. I felt like a bird, trapped in a cage.

Leaving the housing estate my school was on, I had to risk walking the alley, or make the much longer detour home. My heart would always be in my mouth whenever I entered the alley. Older boys would loiter, use their muscle and size and make me run a gauntlet of mockery, they picked on anyone who was, younger, smaller or vulnerable. They emptied pockets, pushed us around. Standing our ground was inviting them to give us a kicking, a black eye, a swollen lip, torn blazer or have our shoes taken and hurled over fences or telegraph wires. I always walked home alone, the only boy from our hamlet.

I don't know why I did it really. I turned into the alley and just pushed on through, ignoring all the usual taunts,

'Poof, Pansy! Sissy! Faggot! Gay! Queer!'

I shoulder barged back for the first time in my life. I stood my ground and took the kicking. I got the swollen lip, the black eye, torn blazer and bruised ribs. I left the alley to taunts and catcalls, whistles and jeers. Tears rolled down my cheeks, but inside, I was seething white hot rage. I hated men, I hated boys. Everything in me turned to hate. Never again would I allow myself to be so humiliated.

My body was turning against me, as puberty made itself known. An Adam's apple grew a hard lump in my neck, causing my voice to drop and deepen. I could not bear the harsh sounds I heard coming from my own mouth. It caused me to mumble and speak quietly, softly. The androgynous feminine me was lost as my body muscled out, shoulders broadened, my jaw squared and nose seemed far too big for a girl's; so it was I began to loathe and detest my own body. Soft downy stubble grew from my chin, and my chest, legs and arms covered in body hair. At nights I lay awake for endless hours, tortured by a body I did not want, it hardly felt like mine anymore. I plucked my body hair with fingers and thumb, until they were worn, red and sore and the bedlinen covered in clumps of hair. My genitals, this ugly bag of balls and this flaccid penis that hung like some ugly awkward appendage – a scarecrow, it seemed so out of place. I began to self-mutilate. This was the torment and the horror I tasted in the ugliness of my metamorphosing body.

Then the suicide attempts began. I would try and suffocate myself with anything at hand, I tried hanging myself. Yet something in me must have been too terrified to die, I was clinging onto life, hanging by a thread, and too often, convulsing and close to black out, blood draining from my brain and oxygen from my lungs, I would claw and fight to undo knots that I had pulled so tight. The feeling of life slipping away and the frantic struggle to breathe again, left me exhausted, spent, dangling between this world and the next. The physical, mental violence of this self-hatred raped my childhood innocence. Bitterness and misery took firm root in my soul. Each time, in the aftermath, I would have to emerge from my room, the garage or the house, go to school, or eat my dinner at the table, and act like nothing was wrong. My tongue was tied, I could tell no one. No one would ever understand.

'God, I never asked to be born! – I never asked for this!'

If there was ever a God as the adults pretended there was, then I hated this God with all my heart. I was being punished, and this was hell. Childhood had evaporated, disappeared and left me with a life and a body I could not bear. Inwardly I was dying, my outer life a charade. All I could do was pretend. I was not yet even twelve. I had lost my father, my grandad and grandma. The once familiar, wandering, undulating lanes and roads that led back home to my father's house felt distant, forgotten. I longed to revisit them, to walk down the lane and knock on his door. Everything seemed to have been washed away like mud in the rain. I felt like an eggshell broken, the life seeping away.

1968 – 1976
Running Away

My salvation came in the form of a bicycle. A birthday present from mum and John. Maybe it was a gift to soften the blow of being torn from my father's side and love. A handmade, scaled down to fit me, lightweight racing bike, equipped with light wheels and tyres and a five-speed derailleur, it was a thing of beauty, a work of art. I cherished, polished and loved it. This bike became my life, my escape from everything and everyone. It opened up my world and gave me the wings on which I could disappear.

I had grown up surrounded by bikes, by cyclists, and I loved the world of two wheels. Club rides dropped in regularly on my father's home, emptying our larder of biscuits, cake, tea, milk and sugar. None of us minded in the slightest. On cold or wet, winter days they would sit round our open fireplace enjoying the blaze and roar, warming themselves before the ride back home. In the summer they sprawled across the garden lawn soaking in the sun.

I loved these 'uncles and aunts', their fit, tanned, lean bodies, they were bursting with life and energy. The women were stunningly beautiful, in a most ordinary way. They shone with a vitality and health that was just delicious, I loved them with all my being, I looked up to them as my big sisters and friends. A wild, riotous bunch, full of high-jinks, bawdy humour and practical jokes, I looked forward to their visits, a high point in my quiet solitary, secluded life. Their camaraderie was warm, inclusive and infectious,

I wanted to be part of their family, and they accepted me wholly, never made me feel unwelcome or different to them in any way. They were family friends, who swelled dad's infamous parties and lit up proceedings. They threw each other's clothes and shoes on our roof, they drank freely, loved abundantly and veered towards a riotous excess that filled me with happiness.

Mum had never learnt to drive, instead she cycled, everywhere. She would think nothing of cycling a hundred-mile round trip to visit friends and family, or to watch John race. I got dragged along, with cramping, aching, screaming muscles and my bum, raw and sore, unused to so long on a saddle. We would visit mum's mother, fifty hilly arduous miles away. By the time we arrived I was shattered, broken by the ordeal, but I would collapse and fall asleep, my young body pumped with endorphins, adrenaline and testosterone. I came to realise that I was happier, my other pains pushed away, forgotten, purged, whenever I had done a long ride. I began to ride my bike more and more, every day.

The more I rode, the more I seemed able to forget, to leave behind the crushing despair and suicidal battles I was going through. Exploring quiet lanes, travelling further and further afield, going as far as I could in the time allowed. I covered huge distances, returning home exhausted but ecstatic. The countryside in which we lived was breath-taking, exhilarating. Twisting windy lanes, hills – long, steep and fast. New horizons unfolded, endless before my wheels, the roads and lanes stretching out into the distance, inviting me, calling me to explore them.

Riding at dawn and dusk was wondrous. Gliding silently round wooded leafy lanes to come face to face with badgers, deer, foxes, owls, and hawks. Often, I would slow to a halt and we would watch each other for precious moments before they would disappear into hedgerows, sky and field. Once more I was immersed in the world I loved, free and able to forget myself, if only for a few hours or days. Riding forced me to live in the moment, absorbed and able to leave behind the war that raged within. On the bike I was genderless, I existed outside of society, free. The road, the bike, became my home, my peace, my freedom and even, in the midst of my raging inner conflict, a place of innocence and wonder once more, even joy.

Moving to live with my mother and my step-father, I was plunged from a home of love into a family life of bitter acrimony. They were embittered and vengeful against my father and his very young, pretty new wife, but they also seemed to be bitter and hurtful with each other. Mother's long dark moods, unspoken depressions, and the violent emotional storms that erupted as she clashed with my step-father reduced the home to a scary, unsafe place for my new baby brother and I. John had a volcanic temper that seemed to teeter on the brink of physical violence. Plates got smashed and cups shattered, tins got hurled like missiles across the kitchen. Shouting matches and rows shuddered around the house as my brother and I hid, cowering upstairs, pretending everything was just fine. John seemed mighty angry at the injustices in his life. It seemed that I, and my mother, were a big part of what he suffered.

Unforgiveness and vengefulness was the flavour and taste that permeated our family life, it enveloped the home, rose up the stairs, seeped beneath our closed doors, and I imbibed it even as I hid beneath the sheets, lying in my bed. Fear, bitterness, hatred and unforgiveness, began to run in my veins. In all my years living with mum and John, I cannot remember a single apology, to each other, or to either my brother or me. The angers built up and festered, like cancers.

We did have happy days together; Mum had many beautiful qualities. She loved us, cared for us and gave us her time. She spent hours reading to us, she spent days taking us out, spoiling us with treats and always looked after us. She was incredibly compassionate, and overly sensitive to any suffering. She hurt when others hurt. She gave me a love for so many things. These days and moments of happiness were small oases in the storm.

The entire holiday before Senior school I spent in trepidation, trembling and dread. I was worried about the beatings that would surely come. Ever the outsider, bullying was bound to happen. All summer my stomach was either tied in knots or turned to acid. It was a miserable anxiety that even the bike could not free me from.

I landed in a concrete jungle of over a thousand children, crippled with fear and hypersensitive. The boys were all ego, bravado and swagger, keen and quick to prove their worth, with fists and feet, with quick wit and sharp tongues. I was just a dumb ass by comparison, a poor boy from the backwoods, I had not developed a sense of humour; I'd never needed one, living as a loner. Where other boys began walking and talking like their fathers and filling their trousers, I shrank away from my own masculinity, repulsed by it.

I cut myself off from all female friendships, I didn't want to be beaten up anymore. I don't think I had ever been effeminate, and certainly wasn't camp, but being one of the girls got me labelled as 'Pansy, poof, sissy, faggot, gay and queer', so I walked out on my tribe, my female 'family', my friends. I was frightened to even be seen with them. The bullies who had beaten me in Junior school were now entrenched as second and third-year pupils. I felt lost, I was lost, I put on a brave face, tried not to look anyone in the eye. Stay out of trouble and maybe I might survive.

'The Lone Ranger!' Wherever I went the whistle and taunt would follow me.

'Hi ho, Silver.'

'Hey where's Tonto!' Sniggering followed behind me.

They were singling me out for treatment because I stood alone. I didn't know any boys, and certainly had none who I could call friends. They thought I was aloof, a middle-class snob – a poof. I was scared and we were poor. We could not afford a television, a car, or holidays, we rode our bikes instead. My school tie and blazer second hand, free from the school's charity hand downs. It was this frayed tie and worn out blazer that got me my first beating.

'Can't afford a decent tie?!'

I looked at the boy, in his smart, shiny new uniform. Without even thinking, I retorted,

'Can't afford to get your teeth stuck in!'

He had buck teeth. Anger must have roused my wit from its slumber. I wasn't going to be bullied anymore. He waded in fists flailing. His mates gathered round, laughing, goading shoving. The usual game – kids gathered and swelled the crowd, deliberately, to hide the fight and stop the teachers being able to get to us and stop it. It was no fight. My body was all legs, puny arms, I couldn't punch my way out of a wet paper bag. My temperament of gentleness, reduced my punches to feeble flops that only made my attacker bolder and more confident. I hated fighting. I hated violence. I had never hit anyone or anything and didn't ever want to.

Our home was a couple of miles of serious uphill from school. I had an old, battered bike to get to school. I would sail down in the mornings. Every home time I would race past everyone in front. The older boys did not like being overtaken, but my heart would not back down, I wanted, oh so wanted, to rub their faces in the dirt. I had the legs to shut their mouths up.

School held little interest for me, it was something to be endured, till the bell at the end of the day, the weekend, or the next school holiday. English lessons were the one exception, here my love of books and words and stories held me, fed me, nourished me. I got lost in the magic of Thomas Hardy, Laurie Lee, Wordsworth, poetry and anything that evoked the countryside that was my place of peace. In *Cider with Rosie*, I found a magical world that mirrored my own, except I identified not with Laurie, but with his beautiful sisters, and with Rosie. Here in the English lessons my inner and outer worlds conjoined and merged in a temporal and short-lived escape. My appetite for reading was voracious, I fuelled it by begging, borrowing and 'adopting' books, wherever I could find reading matter that filled the void in me. I was disconnected, even from myself. My truth, and my true self were buried beneath a fragile mask of pretence; being a boy in a world that could let me be no other.

Subjects that I either disliked or was no good at, I gave up on. I didn't even pretend to engage or learn. Lesson after lesson I spent staring out the window, planning my next rides, or else wrestling deep down inside with this feeling of being a freak, someone who did not belong. I'd watch as the rain beat against the windows on dreary, miserable days. On such mindless days, my inner world would surface, and I would wonder how I came to have this male body, when everything in me was so feminine? It was a question that hung over me, haunting me, mocking me. Then I would be jolted back into the classroom by an angry teacher or a flying piece of chalk, or a heavy wooden board rubber.

Where could I find an answer to this split personality that I dare not acknowledge, even to myself? It was my deepest question, the only question that I wanted answering, a question I could not even put into words. It was a subconscious unuttered question, but it still troubled and haunted me, like a fleeting ghost. Every and any other question was simply insignificant, for those questions did not trouble me, torment me and wrack my body, mind and emotions and leave me feeling like a damp rag, hung out to dry, waiting to be used again, to soak up all the pain, despair and misery of life.

Not the Encyclopaedia Britannica, the Library, not even David Bowie could tell me anything about myself, 'my condition'. At home we didn't have a TV. Mum and John worked so hard just to survive, or else they'd be riding their bikes, they did not have time to vegetate in front of a screen, they both hated TV, so asking for one was never an option. Instead mum and John listened to the radio. I would overhear programmes about mental health, or debates about social issues. Interviews with famous people or talks on history, politics, and the canned comedy of the day. The only thing gained from these meagre pickings was the profound fear that I was schizophrenic. It's the only thing I ever heard that seemed to describe the struggles and pain I felt.

This newfound knowledge terrified me. There was no one, absolutely no one with whom I could share my dark secret. A chill cold fear hung over me, the fear of suicide or being placed in a mental asylum. I passed by the town's mental hospital, every day, on the way to and from school. It was a mean grey oppressive place, with bars on the windows and great heavy wooden doors. If you hung about outside, you could hear people wailing and screaming. It made my blood run cold. Occasionally you might see residents being taken for a walk. They looked like ghosts with pallid, jaundiced skin, sunken eyes and thousand-yard stares, shuffling along with stuttering flicks of the feet. Would my life end in a place like that? I always passed by the place as quickly as possible, with an involuntary shudder.

☆

It was inevitable, living with someone whose life revolved around one thing – cycle racing – that I should want to race too. John had raced as a professional. He had represented Great Britain and won so many national championships that almost everyone but his closest rivals, held him in awe. John was old school, he believed it was wrong to push the body too hard, too young. He made it plain, loud and clear – he did not want me to race until I had finished school and my studies, but I was in angry rebellion. If I couldn't race, I would train so hard it would become pointless me not racing.

The frustration and anger I had once vented at an impotent invisible God, begging to be given the body I so ached and longed for, now poured itself out on the bike. I had given up any thought of God. My anger now channelled through the pedals and onto the road. I kicked them so hard. I poured out the fury, anguish and agony of my inner life and the pain of life at home.

For speed training I had no access to a moped or motorbike, so I jumped the local buses between towns. Glued to their rear bumper, no helmet and pathetic brakes, I would get sucked along at thirty miles an hour, I taught myself to suffer and spin the big gears at a high cadence. Every day, riding to and from school, I slip-streamed these buses. At first, I lasted only a few hundred yards behind them, before getting blown away, but gradually I grew strong enough to hold on all the way between the villages and stops. It was a dangerous, potentially lethal game, but I could only see the benefits as my ability to ride at high speed was getting better and better.

Ignoring my step-father, I entered races, in defiance of his ban. My first year of racing was nothing special. I was only fourteen. Results were average and the disappointment raw, but I was hooked, I knew exactly what I wanted to do with my life. From hopelessness and despair, now there was a way out, a hope and the dream of success and happiness. My fate was made by one of John's teammates. He had seen my mediocre results and ridiculed me in an ugly way. It cut me to my core and lit a fire of rage in me. The following winter I trained, harder than anything I'd ever done in my life before. My vision fixed on one sole purpose, an anger so deep – he was going to have to eat his own words – and I was going to ram them down his throat, so hard, until he choked on them. Revenge took root in my heart.

The perversity of my own self-hatred, my hatred for men – drove me out in all weathers. During summer I had trained in the scorching heat in the middle of the day. I relished the sweat that poured like rivers into my eyes and stung. If it was bitterly cold, raining or even in snow and ice, I felt somehow invincible, the cold and rain only increased my sense of purifying weakness and feminine identity from my soul. The more it hurt, the better I felt. Smashing the pedals to ease my inner pain, I became so obsessed, so driven, absorbed and focused, that the suicide attempts began to subside and my torment abate. I was self-harming; I had become addicted to the bike and what it gave me. Without realising it, I had quickly become dependent on the endorphins, adrenaline and testosterone that coursed through my body after every training session or long ride, they formed a potent powerful drug to a growing body and tortured soul. Decades would pass before I would recognise this addiction and begin to untangle the warped motivations that sustained me.

The burning anger I felt towards men and the deep, very real and conscious resentment against my step-father, fuelled me with a fire no one needed to stoke. It was the beginnings of a toxic masculine-self, the defence shield I needed to protect myself from the world's hate. Anger was my strength on the bike, it was barely visible on the outside, I still wore the same mask, the quiet, over sensitive, introverted little squirt. Training now, I no longer noticed the countryside in which I rode. I no longer felt at home and free in the solitude and wonder of nature. Instead all I saw were the times of my training rides, the improvements, my next bit of lightweight racing kit, and how I could grow stronger.

Another junior rider that I trained with suggested we join the boxing club. We joined, not to box or spar, but to train with them, doing their circuits once or twice a week. It was the most insane training I ever did, tired already from a week of intensity on the bike. The boys were uber fit and mean. It fitted the image I was unconsciously creating for myself. Wrapping myself in ultra-macho physical activities to create a 'male' persona, like other kids wore clothes and played with fashion. I had another motive, a secret motive; I wanted to learn how to punch, to punch hard.

My second year of racing was a little better than the first, but the results to me, still seemed average. The only books I read now were cycling books, gleaning how better to train, race and look after my bike. At school I had started out as one of the weak ones, one of the vulnerable ones, ripe for bullying, teasing and mockery. I dreaded sports. I was a loner. In the changing rooms, where, if you showed any sign of weakness, you got whipped with wet towels, the boys ganged together, even a small penis got you a mountain of grief. It was ugly, nasty normal schooldays childhood stuff.

At football I was hopeless, but in rugby I found relief; on the rugby pitch you could legitimately bring down the bullies. I hurled myself at the biggest and the strongest, delighted when they hit the ground. It got me bloody noses, black eyes and split lips, but compared to the self-inflicted pain on a bike, it was nothing. More than that, it earnt me begrudging respect. I wasn't one of the glory boys who scored the tries, but I was no longer seen as entirely soft, weak or girl-like. Slowly I was being accepted as one of the boys, even if I did not enjoy their friendships. It suited me well, like an aura or defence shield around the feminine soul I could not kill.

Starting the next year's racing, and turning sixteen, I now qualified as a first-year junior. My favourite distance was the ten-mile time trial, and that is what I had trained and specialised for. What I loved, what I was hooked on, was speed on a bike, the feeling was like no other. All I wanted was to ride as hard and fast as possible. A ten-mile time trial was twenty minutes of pure pain if you got it right. Lungs bleeding, legs screaming, heart about to explode out your chest stuff. Riding at almost maximum effort for twenty minutes was like walking a tight rope of cut glass, overexert and you could blow up, and lose more time recovering than you could ever regain. Too little effort and pain meant losing altogether. You had to empty the tank completely, so that over the line you only had the energy left to avoid crashing the bike. It's like a sprint but a sprint with no end, the pace is blistering. Losing was not an option for me, I was obsessed with winning. Bust or die, ride hard or go home.

Those first few races and straight away it was obvious my body had matured; my times came tumbling down each race, and my position in the results climbed higher. I had developed a smooth supple style, spinning big gears with relative ease. That season I demolished a lot of local riders. The teammate of my step-father – who had put me down so callously, was one of the first scalps I would claim. It barely abated my anger and its rampage. I won several open events, beating not just the juniors, but the seniors as well. Locally as a junior I was almost unbeatable. In both the Junior National Twenty-five Mile time trial, and the National Best All-Rounder competition I placed twelfth. I was only 16 and competing against mature 18-year olds, I had another two years to mature and compete as a junior.

At the end of the season my best time for ten miles was now twenty-two minutes dead, the equivalent of twenty-eight miles an hour, something beyond my wildest dreams. It was faster and quicker than most men's times. Not so far off the National Senior record. Neither was it a one-off fluke on a fast course. I was churning out twenty-two-minute tens, nearly every week on my local course, which was not known for producing quick times. All those hours spent sucking in the exhaust fumes of buses had done the trick. I finished the season buzzing. I was only sixteen, fast and flying high. I had done everything I had set out to achieve and more. Could I, could I, possibly pull it off and turn professional for a big team? That was the question that hung over me in my dreams.

Training and racing was all about pain management. How much pain could you inflict on yourself before you 'backed off'? The pain of racing and training, the pain in my legs and body was nothing, compared to the pain in my heart, the pain of family, the pain in my soul of feeling trapped. Subconsciously I hated myself as a male, I hated myself for being feminine. Feeling pain on the bike bought me relief from the pain of my life; I was trying to flee from my own inner reality, a gender incongruence that tormented me, but I could not see it; I was lost in chasing glory.

Mum and John's marriage was falling apart. They bickered continually, the atmosphere in the home was permanently heavy, ugly, tense and oppressive. Full-scale arguments broke out frequently and descended into bitter emotional, verbal and even physical violence. I wept for my kid step-brother, and longed to run away, to escape the bitterness, the conflict and the misery. My step-father seemed to resent my very existence, as I hated his. If I moved out, maybe love and peace would return to them? There was so much conflict raging within myself, I had no capacity to help or cope with theirs. Was I the cause of all their unhappiness? I threatened to leave if they could not stop their continual bickering and rows, but they were stuck in a rut so deep, and I had no place to go. I hadn't seen dad in nearly five years and it was breaking my heart. My only escape was my bike.

A small group of lads in the village was always antagonising me, calling me names, jeering me whenever they saw me riding. One day as I was racing past, they whistled, mocked and spat at me. I was so tired of their abuse, something in me broke, snapped. Seeing red I slammed on the brakes, flicked the bike around and rode up to where they stood. Four against one is not healthy odds, but I really, badly wanted to hurt them, to cause them damage, wound them. I hit home hard, again and again, I went berserk in their midst. My face was split open and my ribs sore as hell, before they eased off and we stood there glaring at each other, bloodied noses, winded, wounded, trying to catch our breath, hatred in my eyes. Then one of them, the eldest and the gang leader reached out and extended his hand,

'Fair play mate, I'm sorry we got you so pissed.'

I had beaten them and they knew it. The two of us ended up friends, I was known as the 'crazy fucker'. I was pleased; my male disguise was pretty complete. I was slipping deeper and deeper into anger and violence.

One day I found myself beating a guy from school up, just because he had bad mouthed a girl who liked me. I was instinctively protective of the fairer, gentler sex. Listening to the words he had called my 'girl-friend', who was not in fact my girlfriend – the red mist descended over my head and heart. I hunted him down. Punching him, over and over again in the stomach and face, relishing every strike into his soft flesh. My inner pain and hate came boiling, bubbling out, a molten lava of suppressed rage against every male who had mocked, crushed and beaten me. I stopped mid flow, shocked at myself, like someone waking from a nightmare, and walked away, stunned. I had become everything I once despised.

Our training routines as junior riders were pretty spontaneous, random, wild and ill-disciplined. We would sprint for every village, town and county sign. Village signs earnt you three points, a town sign, five, and a county sign, a princely ten points. It meant constant, quick witted thinking and ambushing each other with constant attacks. Whoever was in front chose the route. I tried to keep us on the flat, my mates tried to keep us in the hills, where they could 'put me on the ropes'. We honed our bike handling and racing skills. We gave each other awful beatings. Defeat only made us go away, train harder and come back for more.

Bobby, one of my training partners, and I had just been for an end of season spin, we were coming back into Maidenhead from Bray. I couldn't resist jumping him for the town sign and the five points. I came at him from behind and passed a good few-miles an hour faster. Bobby was by far the better sprinter. Side by side, we passed the town sign at a good thirty miles an hour. I grabbed the brakes – nothing happened, I barely slowed. Only yards in front was a stationary queue of traffic waiting to join the main road. It was rush hour.

There was a stationary van straight in front of me. Face planting at thirty miles an hour into the back of it, with no helmet, was not going to work. I skewed the bike down the kerb side of the van and sailed through, smashing the wing mirror on my shoulder, and skidded headlong into the oncoming traffic.

I hit the car full on, catapulted onto the bonnet, I was watching in slow motion as horror crossed the woman's face. The car screeched and juddered suddenly to a halt, I was thrown onto the road on my side, still strapped to the bike, and slid for yards, tarmac tearing into my flesh. I could taste blood, metal and excruciating pain. Adrenaline pumping furiously, unstrapping from the pedals, I got unsteadily to my feet, looked down at my bike, my pride and joy – destroyed, before I collapsed, unconscious. An ambulance whisked me away. Someone delivered my bike to the police station. I survived with only minor injuries. By rights I should have broken both legs and have a shattered pelvis or broken my back at the very least. The steel bike frame between my legs had been folded and cut clean in half, like paper by a knife. I was still strapped into the pedals as I impacted the car. God only knows what the impact speed had been.

In time I healed up, but as soon as I climbed on my new bike and pressed the pedals in anger, I knew something was badly, seriously wrong. I couldn't put any power through the pedals without a crippling pain in my lower back. I was crocked. Limping through the winter and spring, I trained as best I could. My head was in denial, and my heart would not quit. I was dosed up on pain killers, but it made no difference.

First race of the season, a ten, an important race on my local course. I hurt myself like never before, ignoring the spasms of pain stabbing me in my back, shooting up my spine, exploding in my brain. For the five miles to the halfway turn I spent myself, legs pumping like pistons, heart maxed out and my lungs searing. At the halfway turn roundabout, glancing at my stopwatch to check, I was already a minute slower than my best. I sat up, tears welled uncontrollably and rolled down my face. All my dreams disappeared into nothing, I could feel the suffocating waves of despair settling down on me, an oppressive cloud. I limped back to the finish, pulled off my number and pedalled slowly home. My racing career was over. Maybe if I weren't battling with my inner life of chaos, I could have sought out specialist medical help, truth is, I think my anger had burnt me out, my head and heart more wrecked than my body.

Fifth Form, my last year of school. Growing in confidence, gained in racing and rugby, I had relaxed a little, but I was still a total loner. A boy called Lawrence and I found ourselves in the same classes regularly, we enjoyed the same music and bands. We had a similar view on school sports and the same weary indifference to so many of our teachers. The endless conflict between teachers and classes fused us into a tag team of mild anarchy. To us it was harmless fun, joking and a relief to the drudgery of learning by rote. The teachers must have hated and dreaded us. Neither of us was really intent on learning, or being locked in a classroom, we'd rather be outside in the big bad world. We were restless, bursting with unchanneled energy, too easily tempted to riot. I was disciplined by the Head several times, told to rein myself in or face expulsion.

Lawrence was quiet, self-contained, a distinct individual, confident and sure of himself, a security that gave me confidence. Our friendship gave me hope, maybe I could be a man after all. Our paths had barely crossed in the first years of school, but once we started our exam years, our lot fell together. Lawrence wasn't part of the gangs that revolved around the bullies of school. For that I respected him immensely. You had to be a certain kind of cool to stand apart. Where most stood apart and were visible for their quirky differences, Lawrence was camouflaged in the crowd. He was a man's man, solid and dependable. Liking him was not difficult, he had a quick wit and dry humour that made me laugh inside. We were in the same Scouts group that met near my village. We hiked, went mountain climbing and abseiling, we canoed, caved and cycled together. Our mutual love of being outdoors and adrenaline-fuelled exercise and sports, cemented our friendship.

In my last years at school I got chased by a girl who refused to be put off by my cold shoulder and withdrawn nature. I was still so insecure in my masculine image that I could not bring myself to get close to girls. It raised too many painful questions about who I was and my secret, hopeless inadequacies as male. I was frightened of too close a friendship, of intimacy with a girl, for fear of being 'found out', being exposed as a failure of a man, but she liked me, flirted, and would not take my 'No' as an answer. It was a strange but good feeling to be chased. We fell, as only adolescents can, head over heels in love. We explored the forbidden treasures of unbridled love and passion. It was electric, blissful and we got drunk, fully satiated.

Walking her home late at night, making sure she always got home safe, I acted the chivalrous male. Then I would turn and run into the dark, until my lungs felt like they might explode. I ran until I couldn't breathe and was forced to a standstill. I would drink in the still night air like someone drowning, gasping for air, and cry. Loving this girl, only left me in a state of torment, confused still further as to who I really was. It did not make me feel more masculine, if anything, I felt all the more a fraud. In physical love, my whole being knew only one thing; I was instinctively, intuitively, inherently feminine. My male parts felt like a dumb appendage, a sham, an awkward intruder into our physical love and relationship. If I shared who I truly was, our relationship, this love, would be over, gone and I would feel robbed, cheated, once more. She had taught me love, sexual intimacy, physical gentleness and kindness.

Alone in my bed the tears would stream down my face and soak the pillow, night after night. It was at its worst whenever we had slept together. Frightened of who I was, unable to understand, swamped by feelings of such poverty and failure. To try and ease the pain, I would bite into the flesh of my own arms, like a bulldog in full fight, my jaws would lock, until I punctured the skin and drew blood. The pain was excruciating, the bruising would last for days. I hid the scars. It propelled me further into inner chaos and despair.

The bike accident and end of my racing, the death of my hopes and dreams hit me hard, my outward personality became moody, unstable, emotional and violent. Fits of anger and rage that flowed from my own self-loathing spilt out frequently, forcing her away from me. After a wonderful two years of intimate and trusting love she left me, and rightly so. I was a mess and plunged yet again, into grief and despair. My warring parents, the loss of my girlfriend, no more training and racing, no more endorphins, adrenaline or testosterone, no more hope of escape, left me with crushing emptiness, a total hopelessness. At weekends, desperate to escape homelife, I started disappearing to my sister's in London, drinking heavily and smoking dope.

Our final exams were over, summer fast approaching, Lawrence and I wondered what we should do with our lives. My racing and training life now over, it seemed like my life was heading in all the wrong directions. Lawrence and I had taken to drinking in the pubs in Cookham, where we were not known or recognised as school kids. Talk of joining the army began to feature in our pub crawls. The army appealed to us both; we were both born for the outdoors life, we both craved and thrived on intense physical exercise, adrenaline activities and ridiculous, outrageous physical risk and challenge.

Unsure of ourselves we started sixth form. It was a mistake. Neither of us was academic, in any way. That winter we quit school. Lawrence took a job in a carpet shop in town, and I began an unofficial apprenticeship as an illustrator, in a late attempt to gain some skills and earn some money to buy beer and pay off my bike debts. Boredom was killing Lawrence in the shop, and mum and John were making my life hell at home. More drinks in a lot more pubs. We agreed that the army would probably be a repetition of school, the carpet shop and home; more than either of us could cope with. That narrowed our choice down to the Royal Marines or the Parachute Regiment – the elite. Physical toughness, high risk, higher chance of action and danger. The challenge appealed to us both.

The Army recruiting office was just along the road from Lawrence's shop. We polished our best shoes, ironed our Levi's and got a hair-cut. The Recruiting Sergeant tried his best to intimidate us, but we were desperate to sign up. A trip to the barracks at Aldershot followed. A day of assault courses, mud, classrooms and firing guns. It was nothing special, but it pointed us in the right direction. We knew it was right for us. We sent off our applications for the Royal Marines.

Returning home, I was filled with pride and a newly found sense of purpose and hope; I was going to become a Royal Marine. I was excited. When I told family my plans, they tore into me, verbally and emotionally, viciously, with every accusation and argument they could muster. Even my dad, whom I had secretly begun seeing again, railed against me with a bitterness and anger I had not expected. Sylvia could barely talk to me – that I could think of putting on a uniform and be paid to kill people made me her enemy. I was devastated by the total rejection of my family. I didn't have much in life, but my family, no matter what the problems, were part of me. Losing my sister's love and respect was more than I could bear. Inside I crumpled, yet again my hopes and dreams crushed. I hated myself all the more, if I really were a man, I figured, I would have told them I didn't care what they thought, I was going anyway.

I knew I was too soft, too weak, too caring, too kind, too sensitive to think of hurting them, how did I ever hope to survive as a Marine? My self-loathing intensified.

The atmosphere in the home between mum and John, and now between me and them, deteriorated still further. I was bitterly resentful at their lack of self-control and lack of love. I no longer attempted to hide my hatred of John. My anger and aggression began to spill out against them both. Hostility was now open, easily sparked.

Lawrence had gone, joined the Marines. He was my only close friend. There was nothing and no one tying me to home any more. I delivered an ultimatum, either they sort out their differences, stop the violent rows, or I would leave home.

I wasn't even seventeen. Who was I?

The next evening, a big row kicked off. I packed a few clothes in my racing kit bag, snuck down the stairs, and quietly closed the door behind me. I slunk off into the night, feeling like a robber and a thief. Walking down the lane, a huge surge of relief swept through me. I was free at last. Then came an equally overwhelming burden of guilt. Running away and leaving my young brother in such a bitter, unhappy home felt cowardly, like I had betrayed his trust in me, and I guess I had. He had been a source of so much happiness to me, his childish innocence and seeming oblivion to the war between his parents, had bonded us closely. I had doted on him and loved him as best I possibly could. I cried as I walked away from him, fearing for him and his future.

Feelings and thoughts of both dread and hope flooded in. On the road, walking through the dark, the three miles into town and the railway station, I was in turmoil, I was still a kid. I felt broken and exhausted, driven out.

1976 – 1980
The Big Smoke

With nothing but a bag of clothes and an empty wallet, I embarked on a new life. Arriving exhausted in the city, late at night – I sat on the deserted underground train as it rattled, jolted, sparked and squealed, over-ground to Wimbledon. Wired, wide awake, cold and ravenously hungry I climbed off the train, and made my way out of the empty station. Even in the city, I was alone. Cars flashed past. Streetlights cast dim pools of light. Walking slowly past the large suburban houses, wondering and uncertain, would I be welcome, this boy who had wanted to become a soldier, a killer, a Marine, a keeper of peace and a maker of war?

My heart felt strangely empty, the relief of running away, sneaking noiselessly out the door, was overshadowed by a deep, profound sense of utter desolation. My thoughts and feelings tumbling and raging, conflicted, as I knocked on my sister's door in the dead of night. Music pulsed from the house, everyone was still up, very much wide awake, wine and beer flowed and joints were being passed round. Sylvia embraced me and welcomed me home. She put a glass of wine in my hand, we munched on toast and she listened as I poured out my heart. I slept in a spare room. The sleep of the dead. I think she'd seen this coming all along.

The hope of becoming a professional cyclist was gone. Injury meant forgetting the dream, and I was free from home – the bird had flown. In quieter moments, when I had the time and space, and dared to reflect, the sense of loss was total. The broken dreams of a life on the road, riding a bike every day, travelling, being part of a team, with a purpose and goals; winning – they were thoughts and feelings that cut me apart. I had built my whole life around the bike, and everything it represented. It was easier not to think about it, not to indulge regret, and try to create a new life. My whole identity had been wrapped up in my cycling success, the bike had been my only safe place, it had become everything to me, without the bike I felt like a nothing and a nobody, with no future.

'If I wasn't to be a pro cyclist, who was I?'

The emptiness cycling left in my life, was like petrol on the fire of my consumption of alcohol and drugs. All I wanted to do was de-stress, let off steam, and find myself. My athletic self-discipline had evaporated overnight. I had made myself sick, driving, punishing, beating myself into exhaustion in training and racing. Now I was being propelled by a force of nature far greater than me, I'd yet to learn that nature abhors a vacuum. I had no idea that I was an addict, or what it was I was running from. Where once my body and soul had been dependent upon adrenaline, endorphins and testosterone, and craved them as much as the obsession of training and winning, now they craved for something to fill the void and stave off the physical and emotional violence of withdrawals.

With nothing to live for, I was the rebel without a cause, the drink and drug abuse spiralled rapidly out of control. The suicidal ideation returned with a vengeance, but it had morphed from childish attempts to kill myself, into the unspoken death wish of the hopeless, but I was unable to recognise its voice, or see its power over me. I lived in a state of permanent denial and delusion as to the extent and reality of my feminine self, yet it was this pain I was constantly trying to obliterate.

Life in London moved to an unbroken, continual, soundtrack of music. My sister's home was a bohemian, diverse collection of students, post grads, musicians, artists, art teachers and friends, passing through on their travels or studies. The huge house with its many rambling rooms was seldom silent for long. Jazz, punk, reggae, rock, blues and classical all blended and mixed, like cocktails at the best bars. There was a humour, a wit and a wisdom in themes and juxtapositions that played out in the house. For me, this eclectic wall of sound was a stimulating and rich education.

It was an awakening to another world. I spent my first earnings on drugs and albums; Led Zeppelin, The Doors, Cream, Dylan and so many more, I was drawn in by the passion and the fire. Jim Morrison, Jimi Hendrix and Janis Joplin seemed to stand apart, an unholy trinity, archangels, they moved the very depths of my being. Their early deaths, their mortality, and their voices, touched a deep chord in me that resonated and reverberated and echoed around the empty chambers of my soul, I bonded with them, to them.

'Live fast, die young.'

Their voices, their music, ran in my veins and was manna for my soul. Their creative genius and chemistry seemed sublime, unsurpassed. It was a transcendent and spiritual experience even without the drugs. White youth, high on anything and everything they could lay their hands on, had exploded the blues into another realm, another stratosphere. For me, the 'hippie era' transcended music, it was a life force, I signed up in the rebellion. Music and drugs had become my life.

Soaking up the biographies of Hendrix, Joplin, Morrison and many others, I was absorbed. Music, musicians, had reawakened my appetite to learn. My love of books renewed. I bought books, borrowed books and liberated books from dusty musty shelves and read voraciously. These singers plunged me into the worlds of Jean Paul Sartre, Simone de Beauvoir, Camus, Hermann Hesse and Nietzsche, of Carlos Castaneda and Aldous Huxley, Dostoevsky and so many others. Wordsworth, Keats and Kerouac, I even found a much-quoted copy of Thomas de Quincey's, *Confessions of an Opium Eater*. My head and heart found itself immersed and absorbed in philosophy.

I understood existentialism and its rallying call for authenticity, but the nature of the prison I lived in, my own dark secret, meant authenticity; being real, honest and true to oneself, was a virtue that escaped me, one that I could not realise. I could not bring the inner being I so hated and was ashamed of, into the stone-cold sober light of day. My soul remained divided, in denial, my truth buried, hidden from everyone, I even deceived myself, my macho-mask remained complete, but my stubborn pride and arrogant mind was being prised open, like some vulnerable fleshy clam, to new ways of thinking and seeing. Music was turning me on, turning me onto the possible existence of a spiritual realm and world. Music and drugs led me into meditation, reflection, contemplation.

Once I had shunned learning, now I took it up with all the commitment of the most diligent student about to sit exams. I was craving knowledge, cramming everything in. I read for the sheer joy of it, I read because I was desperately searching, I knew not what for. I just knew that I would know when I had found it.

I read all about Ken Kesey, he of *One Flew Over the Cuckoo's Nest* fame, a film that was to haunt me and stalk me through the coming years. Kesey who had fired up the original 'Magic Bus', driven into the unknown night, to Woodstock, and a decade of experiments with LSD, exploring the human psyche, and the spirit realm. Using drugs only added to the appeal for me. In those early days of exploration, I vowed to myself that I could have no taboos. If I was to find my freedom and happiness, then I had to be willing to open myself up to whatever it was I most feared. In London, anonymous, I had the freedom to find myself. It gave me hope to hold on and start my life over again.

Alone, when the drinking and partying was over, everyone gone, coming down off the highs, waiting for the hangover to clear, it felt like I'd been beaten up by a gang of thugs, my body felt wrecked, bruised and battered, all out of kilter with my brain. My head pounded like it had a jack hammer in it. Daylight was too bright, light slashing at my eyeballs. Darkness gave me no focus and the room would spin again. Wrung out and sick, in those bleak and rare moments of introspection, undealt-with traumas of childhood and adolescence would rise to the surface from the depths of my subconscious where I'd tried to bury and drown them. The ugliness of those comedowns and the emotional emptiness and aftermath only served to make me want to shut these things out for ever, and I'd get wasted all over again.

This feminine soul was screaming for escape, for life, for hope, but the masculine, ugly dominant side of me controlled everything. My identity so rigidly split into two separate warring parts. I despised myself. The suicide attempts may have stopped, abated, but it felt like my life was, as the moth to the candle, caught in a deadly flame. All I desired was to drink and take drugs, more and harder than anyone else, just to lose consciousness. So, I did, and I forgot these brief moments and times of lucid self-awareness, and rammed them down even harder behind the mask of a self-contained alpha male gone wild. I wasn't even eighteen.

I had arrived in London the same time as punk broke on the scene, but I was more drawn to the rising phenomenon of reggae, Rastafari and its sacred herb. We lived in south west London, Brixton was on our doorstep and access to chill sounds and spliff was easy.

My interest in music had been awakened by my step-father's vast collection of jazz and blues albums. Apart from his bikes, his vinyl was his only other passion. On first moving to live with mum and John, my heart had leapt when I first heard the blues playing through his enormous hi-fi speakers. Goosebumps rose on my arms, the hairs at the back of my neck stood on end, and it felt like something electric was flowing through me. My heart and soul, connected, bonded with the blues. The blues had been one of my few areas of study in all my school years, I knew the music, I researched the history and stumbled upon the story of black slavery. I had become familiar with the Civil Rights Movement and read the stories of Martin Luther King and Malcom X. Muhammad Ali was one of my teenage heroes. I didn't know what the connection was to this black music and history, but I had connected, big time.

Now, in London, I related to the Rasta poets, prophets, artists and musicians like Marley, Burning Spear, Linton Kwesi Johnson and Peter Tosh. In searching for the answer to my deepest question, not just that of my tormented identity, but also of my purpose in life, these songs drew me in. Rastafari was a spiritual movement of protest, hope and the promise of a better life. They shared my growing hatred of Christianity, capitalism, mammon and the politics of Thatcher. Their music had a mellow, uplifting, chilled and happy vibe about it, I loved spliff, and so I settled in for the journey.

☆

Finding friends of my own, I moved on from my sister's and joined them in a large squat in Roehampton. The first time I saw Lizzy, she was sat in her bed, a huge king-size mattress laid on the floor, like the Queen of Sheba, surrounded with silks and fabrics full of gorgeous colour. She had a magpie's eye for jewels and treasures, art and beauty. Her schoolbooks strewn about and a joint in her hands, Joplin's voice soared from two huge speakers that dominated the room, and I fell, instantly, in love.

Lizzy was in her last year at school, unhappy with her boyfriend, who would use her and then disappear. We formed a friendship that ran deep and wide. I had tasted love before, but never so complete as this. We would talk for hours on end, into the early hours of the morning. We would laugh so much, so often, till the tears streaked down our faces and our bellies hurt. Shutting the door on the world, and all the pain in our lives, we would make love in endless waves till exhaustion would pull us into sleep.

Lizzy's ex had started to bad-mouth her, and my protective nature seethed with anger. One evening I found him standing some way from the pub with a friend. Out of sight, I wasted no time. I slammed my fists into his stomach. He doubled over, to protect himself. I grabbed his long hair, slammed his head down, brought my knee up hard into his face and watched him crumple to the ground. I walked away, not bothering to look back.

The consumption of drugs left me with zero boredom tolerance; I changed jobs regularly, but managed to keep a decent income. Buying more dope than we needed, I sold small amounts and made a little money on the side. It was easy, and I liked helping friends out by creating an easy supply. I gave people dope, I loved sharing the happiness it gave us. With money coming in, no rent to pay, we could enjoy a decent quality of life.

Lizzy and I hitchhiked down to Stonehenge for the music festival to see Hawkwind. The Stones and Zeppelin played Knebworth so we dragged ourselves there and slept under the stars in each other's arms. Springsteen at Wembley Arena, Tina Turner on her first solo tour – God, she tore the roof off! Peter Tosh at the Palais, Bob Marley at Crystal Palace. Music, literature and the arts took centre place in our lives.

Jeff was one of the 'elders' in the squats that we made and left as battles with Councils and police were won and lost. He was a calming voice of reason, and for his age seemed, at least in some areas of his and our lives, to hold a lot of wisdom. In others ways he was hopeless, a victim to heroin addiction, which at times would suck all life and sense from his mind and eyes. Jeff was a seasoned traveller, worldly wise, with travels all over Europe and India already under his belt. He wheeled and dealt, freewheeled and disappeared for months on end. No one would know where he was. India, or prison, dead, or living in a van down on the south coast?

Lizzy and I had devoured the Beat classic, Kerouac's *On the Road*. Hungry, starving for adventure, we saved up and bought one-way tickets on the Magic Bus for Athens. The Magic Bus Company ran the cheapest means of travelling across Europe. We took our spliff and boarded the Magic Bus, to get out of the heat of London, the riots and search our white souls, wondering at the deepest levels, just where we were headed. Jeff joined us with his long-time girlfriend and fellow junkie, Mary.

In Athens, we slept on the hotel roofs for fifty pence a night, with little more than a sleeping bag, toothbrush and a handful of books. We hung out with other hippies in Athens, drinking the heavy sweet retsina and smoking hashish late into the night, flip-flopping incredulous around the Acropolis and other ancient sites. We got chased and beaten up by the police as they descended on the market squares to break up and bust the Greek youth. Our generation was turning to riots in their protest against the harsh austerity of a corrupt regime. We lapped it all up, and came back for more.

Boarding a ferry, we began to island hop across the azure Aegean Sea, dolphins and porpoise surfing the waves of our wake. Surrounded by this blue ocean, eating in sleepy tavernas on local produce and the endless supply of fresh fish, drinking cold beer and cheap local wine we would talk late into the night. When the bars closed, we would slip quietly away, avoiding the few island police, and roll our mats and sleeping bags out on the beach, beneath the vast and endless skies. Night turned the heavens into a bejewelled display of such extravagance it took our breath away. The waves breaking gently on the glistening sands, a hundred yards from where we lay.

Over bottles and spliffs we would share our hearts, our thoughts and our ever-searching souls, discussing Buddha, Rastafari, yoga, Kerouac, philosophy and faith. I was finally wide open to a spiritual life, a spiritual world and what might lie beyond the human eye.

I had absorbed the nihilism of the existential writers and philosophers, as they searched for authenticity, but whilst I loved their ruthless honesty, the hopelessness of their existentialism left me in despair. I took their values of personal honesty and authenticity but junked the bleak nihilism and hopelessness, the meaninglessness of their school. For years I had wanted out, a way out – death. Now I was not so sure. With Lizzy I'd tasted a real love, a love that sparked hope, her hunger and lust for life soaked into my soul. I still wanted to riot, burn out and not fade away, to go out early with a loud celebratory bang, but the search for meaning and a purpose to live for, went on. I did not subscribe to the fundamental tenets of Rastafari, but I took hold of its hope and protest, the hope of a better life was comfort for my soul.

On these-peace filled beaches, empty of tourists, only the occasional family coming down to bathe, under the blazing heat of day, we talked most of all about India, its brutal poverty, and experiencing life and death, up close, on a daily basis. Jeff talked for hours about the Himalaya and the overwhelming power they exert upon the soul, of getting high on nothing but clean mountain air and bathing in freezing cold crystal-clear waters. A solitude, purity and freedom unobtainable for most of us in the West. He was a natural born storyteller, easy to listen to, serious, funny, charming, erudite, clever.

Every now and then we'd go and dive beneath the blue waters and snorkel and gaze at fish, cooling our bodies down, and return and lie beneath wet towels that steamed in the heat of mid-day. Our skin turned the colour of walnuts, our hair grew down over our shoulders. We dined for free on the figs, tomatoes and oranges that grew along the lanes that led down to the sea. We supplemented them with freshly-made yoghurt, honey and bread from the baker's, a white cottage that looked just the same as all the others, save for the large oven in the front room. The village of white painted stone, sat above us, spread eagled in winding passages upon the hill overlooking the sea. The elderly sun-wrinkled locals seemed to like us. The police in turn, for a small bribe, looked the other way and let us stay, so we lived and slept on the beaches for weeks, for free.

To talk of India we would return again and again, as I pumped Jeff for knowledge about the best ways to travel, what to avoid and where to stay. A seed of an idea had lodged in the crevices of my mind. From this sun-scorched beach, the Himalaya called, mystery and wonder beckoned from snow-capped peaks of indescribable splendour. Jeff had cast a spell. He was a follower of Buddha, practised yoga and read extensively. To him, it was not a religion, just a way of life, I liked that uncluttered simplicity. No rules, only compassion and charity and a letting go of all the earthly attachments that held us captive.

Jeff and Mary returned to Athens to get a slow boat, via Egypt, to India. Lizzy and I remained, living alone on the beach. We soaked in the sun and felt our souls unwind. We read Kerouacs, The Dharma Bums, Hermann Hesse's *Siddhartha* and *Narcissus and Goldmund*. In the evenings we would swim the surf and make long slow lingering love, our bodies one and a feeling of bliss would fall over us as we looked around at our island paradise. For once life tasted sweet, it was a love and a peace I had never known before.

Nothing lasts forever, and our paradise fizzled out with the unpleasant realization; even though it was costing us next to nothing to live, we were running out of money. Packing our small ruck-sacks we hit the road. These islands were so hard to leave.

The journey home was a perilous, at times almost miraculous, hitch-hike across Europe. We calculated we had only enough money to buy a banana and a Mars bar a day, everything else we would have to beg or steal. We slept in a railway siding by the docks, in derelict houses, on a motorway embankment, and by the side of the road. We begged the money for ferries to Italy and England. We got robbed of everything we had left. Hitch-hiking, we tasted the exhilaration of relief when someone was kind, and the crushing weight of despair, stranded at the sides of roaring motorways and dual-carriageways for days at a time, in blazing heat and freezing rains, at times on the brink of hypothermia. Exhaustion, hunger and the sense of total brokenness in our bodies was new to us both. We were malnourished, dirty, dishevelled almost beyond recognition. To those driving by it must have looked like we'd walked out of an apocalypse.

One Italian man picked us up as we stood shaking and shivering in icy rain, and drove us half the length of Italy. When he dropped us off at a motorway services near Turin, he stuffed bank notes worth thousands of Lire into our grateful hands and pointed to the motel. We turned around to move away but were immediately set upon by a gang of Italian fascists. I think they thought we were Romanies or thieves. I was blinded by both anger and fear and stood my ground as they prodded and provoked. I was only saved from a beating by Lizzy, who dragged me forcibly into the reception of the motel. She threw the pile of notes at the receptionist and demanded a bed for the night.

Our bodies wrecked, our spirits heavy, we had walked some twenty miles, high into the Alpine pass that led into France. No one was stopping to pick us up. Our cheap beach flip flops were disintegrating and falling off our feet. Starving and dehydrated, we wept tears of relief when a young French couple took pity on us. We collapsed into unconscious sleep in the back of their car. They took us to their home in Grenoble and fed us with horse steaks and a fine red wine. They gave us their spare room for the night. When we climbed out of it, their bath it was ringed with a thick black grime we could not clean off, we felt both ashamed and overwhelmed by their kindness. In the morning they drove us out to the edge of the city and dropped us by the road for Paris.

For the first time in both our lives we had experienced good and evil that had broken our hearts open and shaken us to the core. We had encountered angels and demons and kindness too powerful to describe. It had been a roller coaster, helter-skelter ride that we never wanted to repeat, but wouldn't ever have wanted to miss out on. We both felt changed forever, by our short time on the road.

Lizzy and I had been together a couple of years now. I lived for nothing and no one else. She gave me peace and hope. My distress, the battles within myself and the feminine part of me, that I tried so hard to hide, were made easier in Lizzy's presence. I felt safe, comfortable, secure, happy and relaxed with her. In my sexuality I felt far more female than I could ever admit, even to Lizzy. As a male I felt impotent, my male parts an awkward, ridiculous, appendage. As androgynous, I felt free to love with my whole being.

There was still a part of me that felt like it was in self-destruct mode. The subliminal death wish, the mantra of live fast, die young, continued to play in my heart and mind. The sense of inevitability about the oncoming carnage, was a palpable dread within me. I knew it was an inescapable reality that felt ever closer as the months rolled by. Something within me knew that I was going to die young, and the fatalism of that made me even more abandoned to drink and drugs. Any sane reasonable person might have stepped back from the brink, the only thing I knew was to walk into it.

My chosen, favourite method of annihilating myself, and anyone who dared to join me, was Tequila, laced, marinated with a couple of tabs of acid, and as much spliff, coke and amphetamines as I could afford. We smoked spliff like most folks smoked cigarettes. I was disintegrating, mentally and emotionally. My gender confusion whilst secret, was staring me in the face and it was reaching crisis point, causing me to become volatile and unpredictably violent, my usual denial no longer possible. I was beginning to fall apart. Emotionally I was becoming more and more unstable as the drugs took their toll. I was burnt, frazzled mentally, from too many bad trips, hallucinations that didn't always stop, from the amphetamine crashes and the cocaine. Paranoia stalked the hallways of my imagination. Lizzy and I talked about India, both of us wanted to go, and I was desperate for a new start. I was dealing full-time to raise the funds.

South London had taken to the streets; the rioting in Brixton had spread. The voices of the dreadlocks against the Babylon system of the Thatcher government helped fuel the anger in the black communities. They had already suffered too much discrimination, continual police harassment and social prejudice. The rioting was spreading to other communities and areas of London. The police did not know where next might erupt. Black Marias parked up on every street corner. Police stood in full riot gear under clear blue skies, heat rose off pavements and roads and bounced off walls and glass. They stood, sweltering, and melted in their uniforms. The atmosphere was charged, electric with a static, surrounded by a kindling of simmering resentments that threatened at any moment to ignite. The police were frightened, and so their only defence was to be more aggressive and threatening. The mood in this part of South West London was ugly beyond words. Cars were overturned and set on fire, shops looted, ransacked and left with empty shelves. You could cut the tension with a knife. Fear hung in the still, humid, muggy air and came out of your pores as sweat. It was a tinder box, a powder keg, waiting to explode. Just one, small, spark was all it took.

If I had become emotionally and intellectually bonded to the black artists who sang the blues, then Rastafari cemented my spiritual, emotional, psychological and intellectual oneness with black identity, black theology and politics. I knew intimately the history of slavery, segregation, the Civil Rights movement, apartheid and the simmering racial tensions in my own back yard. I totally got the philosophy and theology of Rasta; I was white, but I knew I was also 'other', different in my soul. I knew instinctively that I was a reject in white and Christian ideologies. I felt like a slave. My hatred of Christians, Christianity and the entire Babylon System was rooted in this bonding to the blues, to Rastafari and the slavery in which Christianity had been so active and complicit. It felt like one step from war on the street, a war I believed in.

I believed no black person would be likely to understand this soul bond in me, a secret, self-hating white skinned transvestite. I didn't understand it myself, but I related entirely with the black plight and fight for freedom, I had become part of it. I watched daily the prejudice of systematic and institutional racism, as the late seventies and early eighties seethed with tensions between white policing and black communities like Brixton – a place I hung out and passed through, being a part of my south west London 'patch'. Thatcher stood for the white ruling elite, the institutional racism and the oppression of the poor, she stood for all that was Christian in my eyes. I hated Thatcher and I loathed and detested Christianity as a religion. The only Christians I saw, were in the Sunday best parade to church, they didn't hang out with people like us. The love of my Christian grandparents, from whom I was now estranged, through my own shame, was forgotten.

I was carrying within me, all the bitterness, all the unforgiveness and all the desire for revenge I had learnt at home. Unforgiveness was a trait to be proud of, revenge a pleasure. The bitterness? When you are already poisoned, you don't even taste it.

Saturday morning, to save money and to avoid being caught with drugs on the underground, where there was no place to run, I borrowed Lizzy's battered old bike. Putting the saddle up high as it would go, I set off pedalling slowly through Wimbledon down to Earlsfield, across to Streatham Park,

Tooting, Balham and up past Brixton Hill. Once into Brixton, gangs of black youths and men stood on street corners, almost urging, beckoning, provoking the police with loud music blaring from open windows. The police stood, in full riot gear, at the other end of the street, keeping their distance, close to their vans, should they need to run, or charge, whichever way the next battle went. With my heart in my mouth I weaved my way through traffic, my pulse racing and the sweat dripping off me in rivers of dread, waiting to be stopped, by either police or yardies, a stranger on their turf.

My contact was waiting for me. We shared a cold beer, and I handed him my cash. We rolled a spliff before business, and I sucked it down, greedy long tokes, trying to relax after the fraught journey. I was wired. Disappearing, he came back a few moments later with two bulging large supermarket carrier bags, and dumped them on the table in front of me.

'There you go man.'

I could see large clusters of grass seeds pressing through the flimsy plastic bag, screaming, 'look at me!' A conspicuous display that could get me pulled.

I was shaking with fear and rage.

'How do you expect me to carry that through the middle of Brixton, crawling with cops?!'

'S'all I got. Take it or leave it. No one's forcing you.'

His cool, a deliberate bait, a provocation, daring me to buy, or walk away chicken. I stared him out, giving him the 'evil eye', trying to burn a hole in his cretinous skull. If I went back empty handed, in the mood I was in, I would blow the two hundred pounds in one weekend on one almighty binge of drinking, LSD, cocaine and dope. Grabbing two more carriers, I did my best to stuff the grass inside the double layer of flimsy plastic bags. Slamming the pub door behind me, I stuffed one bag up the front of my t-sheet like an expectant mother, and hung the other over the handlebars.

My biggest problem was that the brakes on Lizzy's bike

did not exist, they had worn out long ago, it was a bike we never used, so no one ever thought to keep it roadworthy. Now I had to negotiate Brixton Hill, endless traffic lights and the possibility of a policeman or gang stepping into the road to stop me. Fear pulsed through me and adrenaline had me jittering like a boxer before his fight. I was pumped. My senses on overload. Everything in me was preparing for disaster; getting jumped by a gang, or busted by the police, either way I knew I was in for a serious kicking, and prison without question if I was stopped. Prison for a long time. I was just praying that no one would look at the carrier bag swinging from my handlebars, or the bag of grass stuffed up my t-shirt. I felt heavily pregnant!

Back home in our squat I was wrung out like a wet paper bag, physically and mentally exhausted, paranoia was stalking me, haunting me in an unstoppable nightmare. Total dehydration and my head pounded with the stress of blood pressure gone through the roof. I had had 'bad trips' before but never one like this, it was the worst trip on dope I'd ever known. Lizzy sponged me down as I lay, shaking on our bed; I had just taken the scariest journey of my life. After four cold beers I began to calm down.

Monday morning, I went to the bank, asked for a couple of hundred plastic change bags. Then I dug out every 35mm film canister I could find. We weighed out the grass, separating the seeds, grass in the change bags, seeds into the film canisters, enough to grow a bumper crop next summer. For a few years I lived my life a rizla paper thin gap between my dealing and prison. The stress, fear, drugs and paranoia ground me down, fuelling both a deep internal violence, and the charade of physical violence to protect myself.

Lizzy had undoubtedly slowed my self-destruction down. In her presence I was happy, peaceful and fulfilled, content. Like a bee nestled in the heart of a flower, there was nowhere else I wanted to go. Away from Lizzy I was becoming increasingly volatile, unpredictable as the battle raged in my soul. Lou Reed's album *Transformer* played on my deck, often. 'Walk on the Wild Side' taunted me, tempted me. It was the only reference point I had in a wilderness of any real information about why I was miserable as a male. This feminine self wanted expression, wanted freedom, to escape the prison of self-loathing. Maybe that is all I was – a transvestite.

Secretly I had begun to buy female clothes and make-up. I washed out my matted dreadlocks and washed them till they fell, thick and luscious tresses, on my shoulders. When I was away, or when everyone was out, I would get drunk enough to lose my inhibitions and dress, even walk out, late at night. This taste of being free, split me only deeper in two. I wanted to run away, start my life all over again and live as female in this skin. To Lizzy I daren't say a word, I was frightened of losing her love, the only constant in my life.

I had always had a compulsion for stealing, for theft, even as a child. Something I did not understand or analyse, perhaps it was born of necessity in the poverty of my mother's marriage. Now in London my sticky fingers led me into petty crime. I had no license, no insurance, but my driving, even in London, was plenty good enough to be safe. Learning to drive in London was easy, my only problem was evading the police.

One night I needed to get back to my mum's village, forty miles from London, for a deal. In a 'borrowed car', I headed out of London. It was a big chunky Fiat two litre, that guzzled fuel and liked being driven fast. Running late, rain hammering on the windscreen, stereo blasting and wipers keeping to the beat, I gunned the car into the services slip road to refuel. It was hard to see through the sheeting rain and spray coming off the motorway. The slick of oil and rubber, left by heavy lorries, washed into a lather by the rain, caused the car to spin out and pirouette beneath me. I released my grip on the wheel, there was nothing I could do. Way too fast, the car hit the kerb, flipped into the air and slewed across the grass with unstoppable force. My body instinctively flinched and tensed waiting for the inevitable crash, my brain already kicking into panic. The thought of an ambulance, which of course meant the police, and the police spelled prison for me.

The car slewed to a graceful stop. I slumped, sweat poured from my forehead and body, relief slowly sinking in. Using every ounce of skill, I managed to limp the car, sliding, wheel spinning, off the sodden grass. I was expecting a burst tire, broken shocks, but to my surprise we were in one piece and driveable, just an awful lot of mud. There were too many other similar episodes as I ran my life outside the law, living on the edge, often wasted, often high. If I couldn't borrow a car, I'd jump the barriers and free ride the tube to Hammersmith, and hitch-hike back to mum's. Otherwise it meant catching the train, but by this time I was scared of catching the train.

Something quite terrifying was beginning to overtake me, an uncontrollable desire to kill myself, to end this mess of a life. Back then, the trains usually had one long, open compartment, each section of a dozen seats had its own single door on each side of the carriage. You could only open these doors manually, by pulling down the window, turning the old brass handle to alight on the platform. Every time I got on the train to travel in and out of London with my haul of drugs or pockets full of cash, my whole being was screaming at me to open the carriage door, step out and end my life.

These journeys became the most fearful white-knuckle rides, as I gripped my seat in terror, or chain smoked my way through the hour-long ordeal. Sweat would pour from me, even in the middle of winter. If everyone got out of the train and left my carriage empty, the inner voices telling me to kill myself, became deafening. I was begging myself to end the nightmare I had become caught in. I would rock and shake, almost whimpering, trying to hold myself together. It was a part of me, a pathetic part that I could not bring myself to tell anyone about. I was a single step from oblivion, and I knew it. Perhaps the fear of failing in suicide kept me from trying? Having to live, crippled, staring out from a paralysed body at a world that I could have no control in, seemed even worse than the prospect of death.

My self-destruction was now fully manifest, I couldn't push the envelope of excess any further, I was visibly falling apart. Balancing on a knife edge that all my friends could see was crazy beyond words. I was damaged goods and out of control. One night, returning from Soho on the train, high on tequila and acid, seething and raging inside, my reason distorted, just to shock my friends from their complacent slumber, I had set fire to my own hair, the greasy dreadlocks exploding instantly. Only quick thinking on the part of my friends, smothering my head in their jackets saved me from getting badly burnt. That was how evil acid could be. Acid and self-hatred, a lethal combination. I was mad at the world, mad with everyone, mad at myself.

Everyone but me could see the state I was in. Most people recognised me for what I was; unhinged, crazy, and they would walk away, preferring to keep their skin intact and out of A &E. I was dangerous to be around. Even my close friends began to give me an ever-wider berth. To Lizzy I must have been an insufferable mess, a liability of monster proportions, way too much for a young girl to have to live with. Blinded by my own narcissistic obsession, the desire to obliterate myself, I could not even see the pain and misery I was causing her.

I was living on a fault line in my own soul, an inner life that was crumbling apart and threatened a quake off any scale. My personality was fragmenting, splitting apart. Unable to hold the pretence and lie any longer, I broke down and told Lizzy my secret. For the first time ever, I heard myself speak out the dreaded word, 'I'm a transvestite.' Describing myself, admitting, to anyone, even myself, for the first time in my life, that I was a transvestite. I dare not tell her that I also feared that I was schizophrenic.

Winter 1980
Red Lights

Stumbling through the door, into the warmth of the big old house on Kingston Road, our squat, our refuge and our home, felt like coming in from the storm. It had been another terrifying train journey home, battling with the suicidal urge to throw myself out of the train. I was drained, spent. All was still, dark and quiet as I climbed the stairs to our bedroom on the third floor. Opening the door, I looked at our bed in quiet disbelief. Jeff and Lizzy lay there, naked, half covered by sheets they quickly gathered around themselves, staring at me in shock. I was frozen for a moment by the power of a homicidal white-hot rage, it hit me like a thunderbolt. My only question, in those short milli-seconds of horror, was,

'Who is going out the window, me or him, or the two of us?'

I looked again at Lizzy, and my heart shattered into a million exploding pieces, like a bomb going off in my hall of mirrors. Shards of shattered fragmenting dreams ripped into my emotional turmoil and confusion. The woman I loved and adored had turned her back on me. A strange calm returned as quickly as the rage had taken over. Turning on my heels, I walked out and quietly, gently, closed the door behind me. I could do nothing, would do nothing, to hurt or harm her. In that instant, I knew I had already caused her pain enough.

Stunned, shell-shocked, concussed, I descended the three flights of stairs in a daze, and walked out into the night. A tidal wave of despair swept over me; I was drowning. My emptiness was total, beyond tears, I was numb, and more than that, I was afraid for my own life.

In the darkness under the stars I wandered aimlessly, a dead man walking, not knowing what to do. Maybe now was the time to run away and try and start my life all over again. Thoughts of being able to live as female played out in my mind, I had no one I loved left to hide from, but the thought left me feeling sick with self-loathing. Every female I had ever loved had rejected me. I could only conclude that I was an abject failure of a man. It felt like the darkest night of my life. Wishing I only had the courage to end it all, in the early hours of the morning I returned to the house, let myself quietly in, took a bottle of wine from the fridge and emptied it in minutes. Popping a couple of Valium, I crashed out on a mattress in the tiny spare bedroom on the second floor. I watched the fragile eggshell of my life, broken, crushed, the yolk spilled out upon the floor in the dirt. So, this was it. What could you do with a broken egg yolk, covered in filth?

Days drifted by, I was disorientated, lost. Emptiness and hopelessness had sucked all the energy from me. Unable to face anyone, hiding in this bare, hollow room, I chain smoked joints and stared for hours at the ceiling. At night after everyone had gone to bed, I got dressed, put on my make-up and walked the streets, hiding from the kerb crawling cars, running if I thought someone was watching me. All I wanted was to be female, and alone, yet I was aching for someone who could understand me and make sense of this mess of a life. It was as if this sickness had consumed my whole life, some sick joke. Hell seemed all too real, hell was no future threat, I was living it in the here and now.

People were passing through the house all the time, friends and friends of friends, looking for a bed for the night, or a place to stay whilst they saved some cash, in order to rent a place of their own. As a household we loved to offer folks a refuge, as long as they paid their way, contributed to the bills, sharing in maintenance and the buying and cooking food. We had always been a big, extended and happy family. Now it felt like I was a cancer in their midst, and I could not shake the feelings off. Mary had disappeared, and a young guy had moved into Jeff and Mary's old room.

Chris was gay – and a transvestite. I had never met, or been friends with anyone who was openly transvestite or gay. I couldn't think of anyone who I even suspected of being transvestite, except myself. Was I gay? One night we sat down together in his room and started to talk, I admired his naked honesty, his confidence, his unashamed joy in being a queen. He even seemed to like himself. I had watched him, mesmerised as he applied his make-up, wig and clothes. He – or she – would go out to the pub and parties, with seemingly not a care in the world. All I could find within was a deep hatred of my own feminine self.

Sitting and talking, rolling joints and knocking back wine not by the glass, but by the bottle, as if it were beer, we both knew what was coming. I let my last vestiges of self-control go, I fell into his arms and bed. I didn't know who I was anymore, I let go of the struggle of hiding my 'otherness'. Instantly, the moment we lay there and he started to make love to me, I knew I was not gay. The thoughts that I might be gay had tormented me for years, but now, the force of the discomfort and repulsion I felt lying with him was overwhelming; I hated my own genitals; in puberty I had pathetically tried to cut them off, now I realised I hated all male bodies. I was flooded with panic and nausea. With tears and apologies, I fled to the bathroom, locked the door behind me and collapsed over the toilet to be sick.

The house watched me sinking into a black hole of despair, Jeff reached out trying to patch up our devastated friendship. Maybe his concern was genuine. Where once I had a genuine love, affection and respect for him, now all I felt was loathing and contempt. Though he was an addict, he had never offered me gear, we all knew the score, too well. He was on the gear once more. I didn't know if he'd got Lizzy doing smack, but if he had, I would kill him. Now, I asked him for some. I tried my first heroin; it was evil. A boil, the size of an egg came up on the side of my face the next morning. I looked sick and ugly as hell. The nurse in Outpatients refused to deal with the thing. I came back to the squat, boiled some water, sterilised a needle and lanced it myself. Another day in paradise.

I had to get away from this house. Being close to Lizzy was destroying me. Depression, numbness and despair had set in. I no longer felt anything. I would rather be dead than stay here. The cheapest rooms I could find were all in a few streets close together in Earls Court.

The door opened and an old man looked at me, he was casually but smartly dressed, his gold watch, tailored shirt, and hand-made leather shoes, the not so subtle power play, the show-off wealth of the filthy rich. Silently I followed him up five flights of stairs. I was assailed with the stench of sweaty bodies, dirty laundry, oppressive poverty and musty stinking carpets. The smell of cooking impregnated the walls and fabric of the place. A door opened and I caught sight of a family. Vietnamese? Too many to number quickly, crammed into one small room. The place was a maze, a rabbit warren of corridors and flimsy walls and cheap cardboard lined doors. Every large and originally spacious, once beautiful room had been divided into two, and even three, small bedsits. They were hovels. It was little better than a slum. I kidded myself, in denial.

My room was on the top floor. The old man opened the door, and showed me the room. It measured six foot by ten. A narrow single bed with a grubby mattress, a small fridge with a Baby Belling two-ring stove perched on top. A hand basin, battered writing desk and a large broken wardrobe. Everything clearly thirdhand. I threw my bag on the bed. I asked where the bathroom was. He walked me across the corridor and opened another cheap cardboard lined door. A grimy tiny shower and a dirty toilet.

One month's rent in advance and a month's deposit against damages, was all he said. I unrolled a wad of notes and counted out his due. He pulled a tiny notebook from his pocket and pencilled in my cash. Rent due on the first of each month was all he said. I closed the door behind him. A moment later there was a polite knock on the door.

'No overnight "guests".' With that he disappeared and I never saw him again.

I didn't care about the squalor, the noise or the smell. It was a roof, a room, somewhere to live, I had escaped the house and felt better for it. A single thought now occupied my mind, the seed Jeff had planted in my heart, back on the beach in Greece, now became my hope and goal. India beckoned me, the Himalaya called out to me. I needed to get out, before I killed myself. I would go to India and try and sort my life out, turn a new leaf, write a fresh chapter, a new blank page, start over again with a clean slate. I would take up yoga, study the life of Buddha and emerge a new person, healthy, strong, wiser and kinder. Maybe, like the man said, all our sufferings were rooted in our attachments. I was already practising yoga, meditation and letting go of everything and everyone.

Killing myself was not something I wanted, but I was scared. Scared at the loss of all my feelings. Scared of the continual suicidal thoughts when I was alone and not preoccupied. It felt like a race against time, I had always believed that I would die young. I had to get away and find some peace. Having the goal of India gave me a focus. Ever since puberty had destroyed my life, I had wanted to die, but now, ten years on, I was genuinely scared of dying.

I converted my possessions into cash, my cash into drugs. Doubling my money dealing was easy. The money lay hidden, stashed in hiding holes in my room. I was running up huge overdrafts on my two bank accounts, I refused to break into my cash savings; I used the bank whenever I wanted to buy food, books, and drink. If I spent anything, it was always the bank's money, never my own. The huge overdrafts didn't worry me, I wasn't planning on coming back anytime soon.

In the last few months before I went to India my understanding of spiritual things took a strange twist. Back home in the village where my mother lived, I had taken to staying with one of my old friends, Paul. We trawled the pubs, I sold my gear, then we would return to his place and get as high as we possibly could. One night doing our rounds of the pubs, we passed a party going down. Steve said he knew these people, maybe we should gate-crash. I remember very little – except getting outrageously drunk.

The following weekend on my return, I discovered to my horror, that Paul and Steve were going out with two of the girls from the party. Paul was going out with a vicar's daughter, Steve with a girl who sang in the choir. I was disgusted. Paul started attending church, and became 'one of the family'. He hadn't become a Christian, but he had bought the book. Whenever I came back for the weekend, we always ended up back at Paul's, sat around getting wasted. Paul would read huge chunks of Bible to me. I found it mind-numbingly incomprehensible.

It was a heady mix. Our love for Rastafari philosophy, its understanding of the western world, slavery, capitalism, materialism and mammon, all got jumbled up with the teachings of Moses and Christ. Whenever Paul went off on one of his long preaches, wrapping up Marley, Marcus Garvey, Jesus, Dylan and Burning Spear, with a bit of Moses for good measure (Bob Dylan had just gotten himself 'saved' – it was bitter news to me), I would roll the biggest, fattest, longest joints you have ever seen, and try with all my evil skills to get Paul as wasted as I could. I'd drop tabs of acid in the bottle of Tequila and watch him slowly keel over and collapse, incoherent and babbling. My revenge was always sweet.

For a few short months he explored and exploded the Bible and pondered at the contradictions of religion. The biblical roots of Rastafari fascinated me. Christianity left me feeling cold. That Christianity had enforced and condoned slavery, apartheid and segregation with biblical texts was unforgiveable. The Bible left me even more convinced than ever, that I wanted nothing to do with church or Christians. Their God commanded genocide and child sacrifice. From my perspective as an outsider it looked like Christianity, materialism, capitalism and mammon were all inextricably rolled into one, each reinforcing and consolidating the other.

TV evangelists, in their private jets, climbing the Christian capitalist consumer ladder, to the mantra of more, bigger, better, latest. Prosperity gospel was booming business, its preachers superstars. I had never met or heard of any Christians on the downwardly mobile steps into the dirt of the slums and poverty. The Tories always played the Christian card, a trick that killed Jesus all over again as far as I was concerned; their politics regarding the poor seemed the exact opposite of Jesus' own example and teaching. Their capitalism always exploited and oppressed the poor and the weakest in society. I saw that, first-hand, every day in London. My hatred of Christians stopped just short of violence.

On one of my last visits back to the village to sell drugs, it was Christmas Eve. Paul and Steve dragged me on a pub crawl, I didn't mind, it meant more customers. On the way home they insisted on hitting church for the Midnight Mass. I was furious; they were drunk, and all I wanted was one last drink in our local, before going back to Paul's to start a night of dope.

They crashed upstairs to join their girlfriends in the balcony. I was so angry with them for pulling me into church. I could've said no, but part of the anger in me wanted to wreck the service. I stood just inside the doorway, ignoring the suit who looked more like a bouncer than a welcome. I folded my arms, swore at him profusely and told him to get lost, I was going nowhere. The cold blasted in behind me, I was raging.

The vicar stood in the centre of the aisle at the front of church, directly in front of me. He was clothed in the usual religious garb; black cassock, dog-collar and white flowing surplice. His hair was pure white, not silver grey, but pure white. He had a huge smile, that shone like a lighthouse in the storm. All the anger, rage and bitterness in me boiled. I stared straight into his eyes, with all the hate that I felt towards Christians, The Church, The Babylon System. I put the evil eye on him and cursed him to hell.

He welcomed everyone warmly, and invited me in.

I stood there, cold as ice.

The service started, a hymn was sung. I looked up at my two friends in the balcony, gave them the finger, smiled, turned on my heels and went to the pub to wait for them there.

My room looked out onto the eight underground lines that ran into Earls Court Underground Station a few hundred yards away. Here, below my room, all the tracks came above ground. The noise was constant, with trains running most of the day and night, there never seemed to be a gap of more than a couple of minutes between them. The squealing, grinding, clanking wailing rumble of trains seemed to dominate the streets around the station. The crockery that I sat on my tiny table would judder and vibrate as a train rolled in, and if I left them long enough, they would shake themselves across the table and fall to the floor. The foundations of the whole street lay feet from the railways tracks and all the buildings shook and the windows reverberated and rattled in their frames when a train passed.

My old friends never came to Earls Court and I never went to see them. I cut myself off from my past and withdrew deep inside myself, nursing addiction and depression as best I could. My yoga was becoming my way of trying to get a handle on the depression, that and an increasing consumption of drugs. There was no one I knew that gave me any sense of belonging, or even bearings, from which to orientate my life. I sold my drugs, made my money and tried to keep from killing myself. The train journeys back to my mum's home were the thing that worried me most, the voices in my head, screaming at me to kill myself, throw myself out the doors and onto the tracks, were violent and relentless.

My days and routine settled into something of a rhythm. Usually a line or two of coke for breakfast, and a smoke of whatever dope I had to hand. I had to avoid taking acid, I was no longer able to cope with the mind-bending hallucinations, the highs, lows, paranoia and ugly come downs. Acid could be good, but it was wild, unpredictable, and for me now, mostly evil. I'd ridden the highs that made you think you could fly, walk on water and walk across roof tops like Marvel Comic heroes. I'd seen it kill a few of our friends.

My chores were few. Nothing but a hand washing sink and a small electric water heater, one small saucepan, a plate, bowl and knife, fork and spoon. Once a week or so I'd go and sit in the launderette and read, or roll a small joint if it wasn't busy. Here I met the girls who worked the streets adjacent to the tube station. One of them noticed my bras and pants, and my embarrassment as she watched me pull them out the washing machine and bundle them into the drier. She said not a word, reaching out and offered me a cigarette. The girls knew who I was. You couldn't work on the street and not notice anyone who walked the block more than once. That is how you survived, with the eyes of a sparrow, ever alert for predators. They accepted me as one of their own. We sang to each other when the hawks were hovering.

'What's your name?' she asked in a kindly way.

'Paul', I said, somewhat sheepishly.

She laughed, a small, friendly chuckle.

'No, your "other" name?' Her friend chipped in.

'Erm … I don't really have one …'

I liked these women, a lot. They were fiercely protective of each other, they were sharp, quick witted and funny. There was a warmth in their friendships that pulled me in, they embraced me into their midst. They seemed to survive without the pimps and parasites that controlled so many of the women on this patch of turf.

Lunchtimes were spent in the pub. Afternoons I'd sleep or wander round London, trying not to spend. In the evening I'd sit in the pub with the prostitutes I'd met in the launderette.

'It's the girl with no name!' they would call out to me whenever they saw me walk through the door.

'Shift your arse, Yvonne, make a space for Legs.'

They would squeeze up and create a space at their table. These women took me in and looked after me. They took trouble from no one. They were a friendly welcoming bunch. We would get outrageously drunk until closing time and being thrown out. I guess, for each of us, we were just trying to numb the pain, the hurt of whatever was eating away at us from the inside. All of us had a story that had led us into this place of human dereliction. In my broken state I was so glad of human warmth and kindness, over the months I lived in Earls Court, it felt like I belonged with them. I'm pretty sure their love and friendship saved me from tipping over the edge and suicide. They watched out for me when I was on the street. Parting company as we spilled out the pub, we gave each other a hug and a quick kiss on the cheeks.

A young couple, backpackers from Australia, lived in the next-door room. They were always friendly, I kept them supplied with cannabis and coke. At night, sometimes even in the middle of the day, through the flimsy uninsulated walls, I could hear them noisily and extravagantly, passionately, making love. It severely messed with my heart and head, rubbing raw the wound of my own inability to make women happy. Failure felt like my middle name. I didn't feel guilty listening to them, there was nothing else I could do, this was slum life. Other times I'd put the headphones on and crank up the volume, mostly Lou Reed, *Transformer*.

'Take a walk on the wild side.' It seemed to sum up my life and where I'd landed. The room shook, the needle scratched, and the record would get stuck on repeat, and all the coloured girls sang, 'Do da doo, da doo, da doo, da doo, da doo.'

Sometimes listening to them making love was too much pain for me to bear, the pain of love lost and destroyed, it drove me out and I would walk the streets en-femme. Longing for friendship, company, acceptance, love. After the pubs shut and I'd said goodbye to the girls, I'd wander home and skin a joint and drink another bottle of wine, or glasses of Tequila, snort a line of coke if I had it, till I was high and didn't care about anything anymore. Then I'd put on a dress, stockings, heels and do my make-up. Here I was, a transvestite, caught fast, like the fly in a spider's web. Transvestite, it was the only label, language or understanding of myself that I had, it's the only thing that seemed to describe my life.

Too often I found myself out on the streets in the early hours. Sometimes I'd come to, wake from the trip, the high, the drunkenness and realise I couldn't remember how I'd even got dressed up, let alone out the door and down five flights of stairs in my heels. I had no idea why I was even here. It was just good to be out, at night, in the dark, where I felt safest, to be me, to be free.

Self-control is not something you have much of when the drugs have taken over and despair holds you in its vice-like grip. Drink and drugs had reduced me to a shell, broken me and mashed my insides to a pulp. The loneliness left me with a craving for love, a thirst to be with someone, anyone who might understand me, instinctively I knew I was in the wrong place, but another part of me told me that being on the street was all I was worth. This was the bottom – or so I thought. I was flirting with death and didn't care any longer. I wanted to die, I wanted this hell to end.

After closing-time the prostitutes would gather in groups, for safety, on the street corners. They would look at me and wave, or smile, welcome me over. 'Hi chick.'

I could see their pimps eyeing me. It made me shiver. I never did stop; the girls never did ask why. They left me be, so I walked the streets alone, trying to stay in the shadows. Cars would cruise and crawl by, windows tinted, occasionally to stop and money would be exchanged, packages change hands, and you knew, everywhere flesh was for sale. If I saw a gang, I'd cross the street and find a crowd, or a shop doorway to hide in.

The takeaways and restaurants did a roaring all-night trade. This small square about the station, with perhaps the cheapest, most squalid housing in all of London, was home to a multitude, poor immigrants, refugees, addicts, prostitutes, back-packers travelling the world on the cheap. Anyone down on their luck, or desperate enough, got sucked into the cracks here. Neon signs and red lights.

The alcoholics and dossers, the homeless and the addicts would sit outside the hotels and kitchens beneath the ventilation grills and warm themselves from the cold. Smells of cooking, clouds of steam would waft out and surround these huddles who sat at the bottom of the human food chain. I wondered how long before I joined them. Everyone got to know everyone and the locals looked out for one another, and for me. A hundred eyes seemed always to be watching. I was anonymous but far from alone. This was the fabric of an underworld, that even in my dealing I had not touched. This was life on the street, a place of lawlessness but not without a code.

The police kept a low but visible presence, passing through in their cars every now and then. We were a long way from Brixton. Sometimes you'd see a couple on the beat and I'd be grateful for their smile, a smile that signalled they were sympathetic and friendly, I knew they would protect me and tried to keep me safe. Others looked at me as if I were a disease, a dangerous threat to humanity. I knew it best to get out their way as quick as possible. Good cop, bad cop. All the while it felt like I was surrounded by predators, perverts, rapists, pimps. The ugliness of the male species oozed from the very eyes that watched me like prey. The fear of violence, rape, clung to me and made my skin crawl, my body physically shudder.

I got followed home. A young man from the far east, Malaysia or Indonesia, I couldn't tell. As I neared my home, he drew close, walking up, right behind me. He whispered in my ear, 'Can I come in with you?'

I had become a prostitute. I was too wasted, too far gone now to care. I opened the door to the house and wearily let him in. Sat in my room I poured two glasses of wine and rolled a joint. He looked pleasant enough, a nice guy, gentle, even kind? There were no nasty vibes. I was stunned, shocked at myself, and sat watching myself. Was it really as easy as this? I wasn't in need of money. I didn't need money. I was desperate for company, for love, for touch, for understanding and not this never-ending eternal loneliness that was threatening to snuff me out.

My bed was hardly big enough for one. I lay down. I was taunt with fear and adrenaline. Not a shred of sexual arousal or attraction, was this what business felt like? It was as if I was watching myself, looking down at myself from outside of my own skin, an out of body experience. He climbed on top of me and undid his trousers, fumbling, nervous and in haste. The sight of his bare flesh, his penis brought me back to myself with a jolt, and I felt the old nausea wash through me. I pushed him off, got quickly up and opened the door, showing him that I wanted him out. He seemed to sense my total distress, and quietly, quickly he tucked himself in and left. What had I become? I despised, loathed myself, in my own eyes I was a worthless bag of dirt. But God, I hated men.

Crumpling onto the bed, I shook, with fear, with helplessness, with suicidal rage. I had been lucky, I dreaded to think what could have happened. No tears would come, I was drained, numb, unable to feel those emotions I had long since buried. There was just an emptiness inside of me, a total desolation. Hope had no meaning. Finishing the bottle of wine, I took a couple of Valium and sank into sleep. Every night I had been taking the Valium, it was the only way I was able to sleep. Nights without Valium led me into a sleepless hell.

The morning came with merciless glare. Wakened by the shaking house, the rattling glass and thunderous noise of each passing train, I lay and looked at myself in the mirror. No hatred could be more complete. It was time to leave, time to run, time to escape the life I had fallen into. Maybe I could save myself yet. I sold the hi-fi, my last few records, gave my last few clothes to the charity shop on the corner and gathered the few things I would take to India. I transferred the bulk of my cash to Travellers Cheques. The cheapest flight I could find was Afghan Airways, via Moscow and Kabul to Delhi. I pocketed the money set aside for rent, and headed for the airport, a large lump of dope in my pocket.

Spring 1981
India

S tretching out across the runway, a long line of women, dressed in beautiful saris, a myriad of bright colours, yellows, reds, greens, blues and purples, incandescent like a peacock's plumage. Bangles and rings of silver and gold, wrapped round ankles and wrists, from fierce proud necks, and nostrils that flared as they carried the wicker baskets on their heads. They walked with a stately grace, a lithe ease, a dignity that betrayed the loads of earth they balanced on their heads. This human female line of earth movers snaked into the distance. They were moving earth for some construction, but they might just as well have been building the Pyramids. I had landed in another world and another time.

Heat, a blasting wall – like entering a furnace – hit me with the force of a huge wave, as I stepped out of the air-conditioned comfort of the plane. It was thirty degrees or more. Heat rose shimmering from the runways, distorting vision and creating mirages.

'Welcome to India.'

The air was dry, still and heavy. My shirt to clung to my skin, wet with sweat, before I'd even cleared the customs hall.

'Welcome to India.' The Customs Officer watched me with cool efficiency from beneath dark brows, like a hawk, his eyes skewered me to the floor like a knife.

'How much money do you have? Your visa is for six months.'

I was worried about the large lump of dope in the bottom of my rucksack, I showed him my Travellers Cheques – several hundred pounds worth. Glancing at my passport, he waved me through.

I walked out of the airport, onto the street, into the chaos. Taxi drivers hit their horns, the noise of which was like nothing I'd ever heard before. It was a constant barrage of sound that assailed the ears. Dozens of hotel boys, street kids and touts surrounded me and begged, demanded and cajoled. I felt like the centre in a rugby scrum, about to get buried in the maul.

'Baksheesh.' 'Baksheesh.' 'Baksheesh!'

'You come my hotel meester.'

'My hotel best hotel whole of India.'

'You want hashish?'

'You have eenglish cigarettes?'

'You have biro?'

'Baksheesh, baksheesh!'

'My hotel best in all of Delhi!'

Fighting my way through the scrum, I boarded a 'put-put' and asked for Connaught Circus. Sat in the little three wheeled open-air taxi, skimming through the city, weaving, horn blaring, dodging thundering lorries, swerving the sauntering holy cows, buses bearing down on us, driving straight at pedestrians as they scattered before us, it was a wonderful feeling to finally be here. England and all my struggles, all of a sudden, felt a long way away.

'Hit the road Jack!' I sang happily to myself.

My rucksack was as light as I could make it. No clothes, no camera, just a diary, pencils and sketch book. I didn't want to take photos, or even leave footprints. I wanted to disappear, become invisible, live every day to the full, to absorb this country into my blood and take it back as part of me. I had no home, no material possessions or belongings, nothing, even back in England. I had sold everything I owned, free at last. No ties, no plan, no timetable, no agenda, no attachments,

I was following after Siddhartha, the Buddha. This was the clean sheet, blank canvas, new chapter, the fresh start I had craved for so long.

I found a hotel. Western rock music blared from numerous 'ghetto-blasters'. The hotel's roof dwellers were junkies, addicts, casual drug takers and kids away from home for the first time, people living on the cheap, trying to stretch their money out. It was an enclave, a bubble, 'home from home'. Dealers descended on me like flies. I retreated into a self-contained space of non-communication, I was scared of myself, my lack of self-control, but for the first time since Lizzie had left me, I felt positive, hopeful. I was world weary, street-wise, and only twenty-one.

The barber's 'shop' was a piece of pavement on the wide boulevard. Squatting down in the scant shade of a cherry tree in blossom, beneath a blazing sun, the street kids came to gawp and jape, point fingers, giggle and flirt. My long hair fell away. He chewed on paan, crimson, like blood. Now and then, he would stop his work, and ceremoniously spit a spray of paan into the gutter behind me. He slid his razor deftly over my throat.

He had nothing to say. Instead he looked, steadily, unwaveringly into my soul. It felt neither intrusive nor rude, a silent conversation, of mutual respect. It was a form of communication, the follies of language laid aside, that I learnt to enjoy. He was, I realised, reading me – he was discerning what I was made of; love or hate, hope or fear?

It was here, from this barber, that I started to learn how to read people, studying their eyes, expressions, countenance and posture, the joy of reading souls like others read books. Holding the other's gaze, without staring or looking away, something we baulked at in the west. His wizened, wrinkled old face creased and a smile lit up his eyes and shone from his face, a deep well of peace, a serenity and a charity that emanated from within.

For a few pence he had left me feeling clean and fresh, but more, he had kindled a spark in my soul; the emptiness and meaninglessness of so much superficial language and communication, compared to the depth and beauty of his silence. I walked away sad, calculating his daily income, wondering in which cardboard box city he lived, and who he struggled to feed? I had landed in a world of karma, reincarnation and a million gods I could not fathom.

Street map in hand I searched the streets around the hotel for a tailor. An old man, smart in shalwar kameez and a Nehru cap, told me the best thing I could do was go to the tailors' quarter in Chandni Chowk Bazaar, Old Delhi.

'Take a rickshaw to Jain Temple, opposite Jama Masjid, you can walk from there, you will find the tailors' quarter easily.'

The bazaars' alleyways and thoroughfares were crowded, jostled and noisy as shopkeepers shouting at one another across the way, every now and then a holy cow would saunter slowly through, nosing in the gutters, foraging for anything to eat from the debris that lay there. You had to watch where you landed your flip flops. Everywhere the singsong litany of beggars, a background noise of poverty and grief. I fed on the sights and sounds, I loved the cacophony of voices and noises that ebbed and flowed from one street corner to the next.

Every street brought fresh and delightful surprises. A street of shops that only sold flowers, garlands of puja. Around the next corner would be some kind of temple. The dingy streets were awash with colour like the palette of an artist painting in the midst of a summer's garden. Every hue and tone, every shade and shadow dancing with life and the play of light. I had barely touched the lump of hashish that I had smuggled into this hippies' paradise, I was in love, for the first time in a long time I was in love with life, in love with the place, in love with the people.

Finding the tailors' quarters after a few delicious detours and cul de sacs, I browsed and tried to look disinterested, but everywhere shopkeepers and tailors were desperate to part me from my money.

'Where are you from?'

'When did you arrive?'

'Where is your wife?'

'How are you liking Delhi?'

'Are you wanting for anything in particular?'

'Sir, what is your line of job?'

All this information, they related to one another in their singsong mother tongues, back and forth across the street, the merchant at the end of the street would know all about me before I had even reached his shop.

'Welcome to India.'

Haggling and bartering for goods was an artform, a skill, a theatre that provided everyone with a subject for gossip and review. Westerners: prized customers to be fought over, their lack of subtle, nuanced bargaining skills providing a tragi-comedy for the merchants to direct, and star in, shop fronts a stage for the whole neighbourhood. The merchants fleeced them together, and laughed about it afterwards. Muslims and Hindus united in commerce. Urdu, Hindi, Punjabi, Gujarati and Kashmiri all tumbled and fell in the hubbub and blended music of a thousand voices.

When it came to haggling, it wasn't that I wanted something cheap, I was willing to pay a fair price, but I wanted to learn how to gain and win respect, I wanted to live in India as long as I could make my money last. I had the one thing so many tourists lacked, I could take as long as it took. The merchants in turn responded to my lack of haste, they sensed my patience, determination and respect. They were reading me.

The majority of India's population, on or below the poverty line, do not read books, they read people. The street is their entertainment, their life, and many would not survive if they could not read. I was learning to read, without the aid of language. The ability to read people was survival. It felt like we had grown fat and blind in the West, and lost this basic survival instinct, a sixth sense, most of us lived and slept, safe and secure at night. India was a nation of ever-watching eyes.

A quiet Kashmiri tailor invited me to have a seat. A boy brought us tea. We chatted the usual stuff, small talk, pleasantries. He was keen to secure my custom. He wasn't unpleasant, far from it, he was charming, genteel.

'Is he charming because that's just the way he is, or is he charming because it helps him make money?'

He certainly wasn't poor like the barber on the pavement, but nor did he have an ounce of the tranquillity that the barber had exuded. He measured me up. I left him a part payment and he told me to come back in a couple of days.

Everywhere the beggars watched. One, a solitary old man, gaunt and silent with arm outstretched, motionless as a heron standing midstream waiting for lunch to come swimming past on the tide. Children, maimed, disfigured, some said deliberately so. They clung at my clothes with a plaintive cry, 'Baksheesh, baksheesh', and dared me to look them in the eye. The lepers, their hands, limbs, faces and eyes eaten away by accident and disease, sometimes open wounds crawling with maggots. I gave one a coin, another a piece of fruit and then a deluge of beggars descended on me clamouring for more. I was desperate to get rid of these western clothes.

Selling my rucksack and sleeping bag to travellers on the hotel roof, I rolled my few belongings, a diary, pencils, a Hindi phrase book, into a blanket, held by one long webbing strap. I collected my new shalwar kameez. They were the deep burgundy colour of the Tibetan Buddhist monks. With the advantage of skin that turned dark brown, I looked less like a rich tourist and might even blend into the heaving throng. India was used to a myriad skin colours and racial types travelling for pilgrimage, business and love.

Rich was a relative word.

'You have biro meester?' a regular cry from kids on the street.

They would sell it for a rupee, that made them rich.

I didn't even have a biro.

I spent a few weeks exploring Delhi, Old and New. I marvelled in the Jama Masjid; I took a train and spent a couple of weeks soaking in Jaipur, Agra and the desert of Rajastan. I was blown away by the love affair of the Taj Mahal. I was in love with India. I bought a stone chillum and some dark hashish. My favourite pastime was to squat on my haunches, bum just off the floor, like the native boys. There in the shade, I'd light my chillum, and watch the world pass by, some days, for hours on end, absorbed in the midst of all the beauty and squalor I observed.

The Himalaya were beckoning. I wanted to travel as cheaply as possible, not to save money, but because I wanted to immerse myself in the country and people. My money could stop me experiencing the simplicity of poverty, I craved simplicity and freedom from desires; I would live on as little as I could each day, eat local food, stay away from the tourist trail, travel with the poor. Watching India, its poverty and its daily scenes of death and the dying, from behind the windows of air-conditioned hotels and coaches, felt like a form of voyeurism to me.

I was trying to put my Buddhist understanding

into practice; I didn't want to cling to comforts, but I was experiencing the fear of 'letting go'. Siddhartha called it 'attachment' – the root of our sufferings. I did not want to be attached to anything or anyone. Love, as I knew it, had broken my heart too many times. What lay beyond, beyond love and loss?

The biggest battle in me had always been between my male and female selves. My longing now was to escape them both, to let go of all attachment to either, because they were the cause of my suffering and torment. To be honest, I was so absorbed in this new daily life, in seeing and learning all that India could teach me, that I had all but forgotten this inner battle. For now, it receded, lay dormant, sleeping.

Practising yoga every day, was creating a rhythm to my days. Learning to sift through my thoughts and lay aside worries, irritations, resentments and distractions was a Herculean effort surrounded by so many people and so much noise. If I could do it here, in the heart of the city, then I knew I would be able to go much deeper in the mountains. Would this newfound peace, enable me to leave the drugs behind forever?

The lies of materialism were too obvious and held no attraction to me. The intellectual arrogance of my science and atheism had left me empty. The claim I had once spouted, that there is no 'God', no other realm for humanity to explore, now seemed shallow and unconvincing.

What was love?

What was hope?

What was faith – everyone had faith in something, or someone?

Were we just bags of dirt, waiting to die, ashes to ashes and dust to dust?

What or where was Nirvana – a life beyond earthly, fleshly attachments? Was it a paradise within, or someplace else?

We didn't even know how the human brain worked! As far as I was concerned, where science ended, the spirit realm began, as yet untapped by science, an unknown, elusive mystery. There was mystery and there was wonder, I had come to India to explore this unknown. Could there be something beyond the rational, knowable world of our senses? Christianity and science both claimed to hold the answers, but both clung to materialism like drowning men. The churches' ugly display of wealth and the clinging to power betrayed its teacher.

'Yuppies' was the label of these times. 'Young and upwardly mobile'; 'Living the Dream', the goal. My instincts told me the truth was probably to be found amongst the poor, the ordinary, the un-noticed, the oppressed and insignificant – downwardly mobile would be my direction of travel and entry into the life of India. Attachment to the comforts of western life and privilege seemed the most urgent to let go of. The way of Buddha; simplicity, poverty, charity, compassion, meditation, stillness, reflection. Letting go of the things we put our trust in. Things that were, so often, illusions of security, things like bank balances and relationships. I was searching for something else. Searching for the jewel in the lotus.

Plunging into the swirling morass of India's poor, I bought a third-class rail ticket to Pathankot. My western white impatience was reluctant to die as I squatted in the vast concourse of the station. Perched amongst the villagers, the farmers, the rural poor, as they sat on piles of sacks, bedding and battered cases and trunks, I watched the frantic milieu of city dwellers dressed in western brightly 'notice me'

coloured garb, pushing and barging through the throng, cursing, elbowing their way to the front of the queues.

The poor sat, waiting patiently for the rush hour to pass them by. The men squatted, some gently rocking on their heels, they smoked, chatted and argued. The women sat or stood in village and family huddles, watching, laughing, bantering and gossiping away the time, whilst children played and cried or slept exhausted, wrapped enveloped in a mother's bosom beneath a sari or snugged up in mountainous piles of luggage.

The women's clothes, saris, shawls, shalwar kameez, their panche, skirts and choli were brilliant, dazzling colours, incandescent, shimmers of silk and cotton. It was a chorus, an anthem, a symphony of colours. They wore their wealth in gold and silver bangles, family heirlooms and hand me downs. To me, there is no more beautiful sight in the world than India's women, even the poorest, dressed like queens. The riot of colour, the sheer exuberance and visual feast of their feminine expression gave me a deep-down happiness. It was as if they were chasing misery away with joy, defying the dull seeping danger of famine, disease and poverty. The colours danced before me, even as they moved slowly in the drab crowds.

The flies hovered and swarmed and lingered round my face and uncovered arms. Flies, always the flies. Goading, tempting and cajoling my self-control to cave in and my anger to lash out in exasperated fury at their buzzing relentless torment. I had tried keeping fastidiously clean, but sweating and smelling and tasting the sweetness of sweat upon the lips was impossible to avoid, the flies homed in on me. Searching for the cavities of ears and eyes and nose. The women just dropped their shawls over their faces and babies.

This journey into the heart of India was as much about the inward journey of discovering myself and seeking to find a better, wiser, stronger me. India was the mirror in which to take a long hard look at myself. It started here, sitting with the poor, sweating in the dirt, swarmed by flies, letting go of my impatience, my privilege and the power of money. I tried to nonchalantly fan myself with a newspaper and keep the flies at bay.

I browsed, fascinated, through the pages of my fan and read the short articles tucked away as asides. In the Himalaya foothills in the state of Uttar Pradesh a bus had been held up by dacoits, the highwaymen who appeared like ghosts in remote and un-policed places to rob the vulnerable. The passengers had managed to turn the tables on their assailants and had locked them on the bus. They torched the bus, dacoits and all. Justice had been done.

Welcome to India. India was beautiful, India was huge, but India, at every level was brutal. It was a land immersed in religion and the quest for eternal peace, but it could turn to violence and lethal force in seconds, then equally quickly, fall back into the slumber and rhythm of life, survival. Life and death its daily currency, life was cheap, death ever present, India fascinated me, India scared the hell out of me. Here I was, launching out solo; lone white 'male', a target for every goonda, thug and pickpocket in every overcrowded town and backwater village.

As the train rolled in, the platform was already full. Goats, children, chicken. Red suited porters, burly, well tipped and over-fed, cursed, shouting and barging through the throng. Bags were hurled at windows, where miraculously a family member had already arrived. People were boarding the train before it was even in the station, running, jumping and heaving themselves in like finely tuned athletes. A crush of fighting bodies at every door. I shouldered my bedroll and waded in. A hand reached out, grabbed my arm and helped pull me up. A wiry, thin, muscular fellow beamed at me and grinned. We pushed through the corridor and he squeezed a way into one of the compartments already packed with bodies wedged from wall to wall.

Proudly the man barked at his family and begrudgingly they formed a space in the middle bunk. He motioned for me to join them; all nervous smiles and polite 'hellos', I practised my sparse Hindi. Then began the long arduous process of interview, the influence of the Raj still holding sway, English still the lingua franca, the language of all India's commerce and interstate communication. Hindi was known by some, but often local languages prevail.

'Where is wife?'

'Where are you coming from?'

'What is your name?'

'You are having many children?'

Underneath it all was a warmth, a sense of fun, a childlike curiosity. Whether you wake, or sleep, a hundred eyes are always watching you, reading you, from this, there was no escape. This is the lot of the poor. Most of India is poor – personal space is a privilege of the rich, or else only found in remote rural India, and even there it seems the walls and trees, rivers and mountains have eyes. You exist only in the context of someone else's sight. I sensed the thieves and predators watching me too.

'The wonder of a transparent soul with nothing to hide.'

The human morass of life on the platform rapidly formed into villages, tribes, clans and families on the train. The hawkers, the beggars and the wallahs magically appeared. Goods were paraded outside each window, cash changed hands and newspapers, cigarettes, sweets, food and chai were all taken on board. There were six bunks in the small compartment. Each bunk, more suited to holding one, held an entire family, whilst other family members took it in turns, cast out from their nest, sitting on the floor, or standing in the corridor, or tried to sleep, sandwiched against the back of the bunk. Small children sat legs dangling on the top bunk. A large matronly woman filled half of the bottom bunk. A young husband and wife occupied another with their three young children.

The train slowly rumbled out the station. Non-paying passengers waited at the platform ends and in the sidings and as the train lumbered by, gradually gathering speed, they ran, sprinted and jumped, hanging onto the glassless window's steel bars, clinging like limpets to the side of the train, arms hooked through the steel barred open windows, into the compartment, their faces peered in, watching us, the lucky ones. Others jumped onto the footplates at each doorway and wedged themselves in a cluster, four, five and more, hanging onto each other for their lives. They were jumping the train, a free ride, maybe one or two stations on their daily commute to work, or they were beggars, thieves and wanderers, changing town. There were already dozens camped upon the roofs of the carriages. Every now and then a hand would appear at the window from above and help haul another stow-away onto the train's roof.

The train journey north was twenty-four hours on this local, stopping train. About 130 miles north to Ambala across the dusty heartlands of the Punjab. Even the place names excited me. Rudyard Kipling's Kim was a childhood friend of mine, and now I was travelling in his footsteps. About two hundred miles to Ludhiana, and then another slow hundred up to Pathankot. The scenery rolled by my window, I was mesmerised by the beauty, the low, flat plains of Haryana and on into the Punjab. Mile after endless mile of dusty farmlands, low built villages and the occasional bustling town. White painted houses, squat, thatched hovels spread out on either side. Oxen ploughing fields, a land in which time seemed to stand still, stretching away into an infinite horizon. Heat haze and morning mists added to the ethereal magic.

Mealtimes and each bunk came alive from slumber and boredom. The careful ritual of sharing out the precious food. Most families had food stashed in stacks of 'tiffin' cans, or rolls of cloth and paper that were opened up to reveal a mouth-watering array of simple Indian fare; rice and vegetables, chapattis and sweetmeats. I was made to feel at home, at one with every family, the hospitality of India poured into my lap, the joy of karma, of kindness that can never be repaid. These cycles of re-incarnation permeated the smallest details of daily life. Washing, prayers, food, rest, worship. I felt ashamed with my packet of biscuits, and meekly passed them round.

Dusk fell over the rural scene as the train trundled slowly, steadily through. The fields and houses seemed bathed in a translucent glow. Night drew in, the train stops grew more frequent, pulled up in some siding, out in the country, waiting for what seemed like hours for the next express or mile long freight train to come thundering, clattering, roaring by. Passing by rivers and marsh-land a deafening chorus as hundreds of giant bullfrogs, filled the night air with a competing, bellowing, roaring, croaking amorous cacophony, louder than even the rattling train.

Pulling into the sleepy midnight stations, I watched as passengers awoke under the flickering lights, the tune of the chai wallahs sang out, even before the train had stopped, welcoming it in.

'Chinni, chinni, chai.' 'Chinni chai.'

Their song echoed to the chinking, chiming accompaniment of dozens of spoons as they rang them in the glass cups – once heard, a sound you never forgot. The air thick with diesel, cooking oil, woodsmoke, spices and pungent foods. Hands thrust through our window and money exchanged for food, cigarettes, lighters, newspapers and chai. I bought chai, hot sweet steaming chai. Chai, the strong tea brewed in an abundance of warm milk, lots of sugar and cinnamon, it tasted as perfect as the finest of wines to me.

The train decanted its precious cargo and a few lonely souls clambered on board. Fat porters and thin sinewy gnarled old men threw baggage back and forth. The human mass was thinning out as we moved further and further north.

The Himalaya

In Pathankot, the crowd spewed out, relieved and stretching, scratching and coughing from the train, into the transit, frontier, trading town. Sikhs rubbed shoulders with Pathans, Afghans, Muslims and the Hindus of the lowlands. I could have carried on by train, all the way through to Jammu, but I wanted to slow down. Anyway, Kim had stopped by here. Next; by bus up into the mountain foothills.

The town was teeming with lorries coming and going from the manufacturing cities of the plains and the remote mountain regions. Searching for the bus station, happy to stretch my legs and walk, I came across a huge sprawling lorry park full of hundreds of colourful painted wagons. Lorries that pumped the life blood of food and goods along the arterial roads that wound deep into mountain valleys hidden high above. The place was bursting with life. It was a seedy, dirty place. Not just grease and oil, but dirty ramshackle huts that sold everything from food, fruit, cigarettes to cheap, counterfeit, bootleg booze. Over everything hung the sound of Bollywood soundtracks pumping out. The prostitutes would not be far away.

There were dozens of tin shack garages. Mechanics, drivers and their henchmen hefted huge crowbars, slung tyres and beat at the lorry's insides with lump hammers and wrenches. It was as if India's automobile industry was still transitioning from the agricultural age. The drivers were a cut-throat, shifty looking army with weary blood-shot eyes, and tired, oil smeared clothes. They lounged in the restaurant shacks and spilled out into the roads, sprawled on rickety chairs and charpoys. Some sat playing backgammon in their underwear, others pulled on large communal hookahs, getting stoned and shooting the breeze.

Stopping at a grubby chai stall, I ordered and sat down. From my rucksack pocket I dug out my tobacco, the last of my lump of dope, and skinned up a joint. I was doing what I loved the most, just watching, musing, drinking in the sights and sounds, the faces and the fascinating unfolding drama of another ordinary yet magical day in India.

A sinewy, sallow skinned man sidled over and rapid fired an order at the proprietor. He sat down opposite me without a word, and began to read me. His eyes slits, from a life spent outside under the glare of the sun. He was as typical as any northern frontier driver gets. A mountain man, unkempt, unshaven, a ragged turban on his head. His eyes were the eyes of the hashish consumer. Large brown irises looked unwaveringly, deep into mine, his pupils dilated down to tiny pin pricks. His face wrinkled, etched with myriad lines like the mountains and ravines he carved his way through. No doubt he smuggled dope, hashish, heroin, opium.

He sniffed the air and smelt my joint. 'Hasheesh good?'

I passed it to him for a toke.

'You want hashish, heroin, opium?'

He rolled out a cloth and placed a large lump of shiny black opium on the tabletop. He told me the cost. I couldn't believe the price. I unrolled a few rupee notes from my top pocket and handed them over. I'd only ever once seen a lump like this in London, and could never have afforded it then. He cracked a toothy, lopsided grin. His teeth were yellow, few and far between. I passed him the joint again, and he took a long, deep drag, filling his lungs. He closed his eyes, leant back, and slowly exhaled the smoke.

'Hashish good.' He grinned. It was cheap, Lebanese.

We drank our chai, and he described his routes.

'Jammu, Islamabad, Peshawar, Khyber Pass, Jalabad, Kabul.'

He was driving the frontier towns.

'I am making much money, all the way.'

'Afghan?'

He nodded and grinned.

'Soviet Russia?' I probed.

His face hardened and frowned. He spat viciously to the side and drew his thumb across his neck in one fast, slashing swipe.

'I sell them much hashish, heroin, opium. Soviet fucked!'

We finished our chai and shook hands. I liked this wiry little hand grenade of a man full of nervous energy. The proprietor placed a plate of rice and meat on the table in front of him. He slid it towards me and passed me one of his chapattis. I tore the bread and scooped up a mouthful. I wasn't sure quite what it was, maybe goat? Probably goat, chewy, hard and lean. He wolfed down the lion's share. I skinned up another joint, sprinkling in small lumps of the opium. I sensed he could kill me, just as easily as he had fed me.

We sat back and ordered another chai. I lit the joint and passed it to 'hand grenade'. He closed his eyes, leant back and inhaled, deep, long, hard. I pulled on the joint, a long deep toke. Slowly the opium began to roll through my body and mind. I could feel myself relaxing and feel all the nervous tension and excitement of the days and weeks subsiding away. I shut my eyes and let the peace roll over me. I was tired, exhausted.

'Challo, challo.'

The Human Hand grenade stood over me.

'Very good, very good.'

I stood up, and shook his hand.

'Thank you, safe driving, and maybe see you again somewhere on the road.'

He drew his forefinger across his throat, his eyes glinted as he turned on his heels and disappeared into the ramshackle mess of huts. He was even happier making money selling opium and hashish to Russian soldiers, than he was selling it to me. Afghanistan was Russia's Vietnam.

'Challo, challo,' he said as he walked away.

'Let's go, let's go.'

I remembered Ken Kesey on the original hippie bus. The early experiments with acid, opening wide the doors of perception. Break on through to the other side.

'You're either on the bus, or off the bus, there ain't no half way!'

Stoned, I found the coach station and bought a ticket on a local, slow bus up to Jammu. I was on the road, free at last.

It was a long day's drive up to Jammu. Occasionally we would hit open freeway and the driver would gun the engine and hurl the bus out into the middle of the road forcing cars to scatter and lorries to swerve. Sometimes he got it wrong, pulling out at just the wrong time, then slamming hard down on the brakes with all his weight, swerving inline again, his vicious curses mingled liberally with, 'Inshalla!'

The highway was littered with skeletons of wrecked lorries, cars, even a twisted, mangled, rusting bus. We passed an ox cart that had been hit, the carcass lay dismembered in the road, the tarmac crimson red like betel juice on concrete. People stood, stared, scratching their heads and backsides as we roared by. It was best not to look ahead, but watch out the side windows at the passing countryside and pray the pagan prayer, *'I don't want to die'*. For the first time in years I was anticipating the future, looking forwards to what was around every corner along the way. The road began to climb steadily up, winding, twisting, turning. Huge bushes of marijuana grew by the sides of the road, I could lean and out and pluck leaves as we passed. The engine groaned, screamed and laboured as we overtook the slow, over laden lorries that blocked our path as we climbed higher into the foothills.

In Jammu I transferred to another local bus bound for Srinagar. I avoided the fast tourist coaches, preferring to travel with locals. I was longing to get into the Himalaya, but the people and the journey were every inch as important as my destination. The bus headed north for Kashmir. I was lucky, I had friends who had been dreaming and trying to get into Kashmir for years, but it had remained closed to foreigners for decades, disputed territories, a tense state of secret war as Pakistan and India waged guerrilla warfare against each other. Now India felt more confident and had opened the state of Kashmir up again and for a short, sweet window in its troubled history we were allowed in. No terrorism, no bombings, no kidnappings or secret war. A fragile uneasy peace prevailed.

The bus wheezed ever upward towards Srinagar, and the mountains finally came into full view. The sheer size, force and power of the Himalaya fell like a spell upon me. The sun reflected off the snowy majestic, towering distant peaks, a never-ending rolling range of mountains stretching into eternity. I was mesmerised by their beauty, like nothing I'd ever seen or known before, I sat in silent awe of paradise.

Watching from the windows as the bus headed higher and further north into the mountain valleys, I saw the first signs of another people, another race. Shepherds and nomads were herding vast flocks of cattle, sheep and goats from valley to valley, higher into the mountains, in search of free pasture. We passed huge caravans, camels carrying homes, merchandise, Hazara tribesmen, Pashtuns, Pathans, Mongols, Afghans, all mountain men, surrounded by their herds and flocks. The women were wild beauties who stirred my heart with a longing and desire. Their eyes shone out proud and clear, fierce, independent – no hiding behind head scarves and shawls or burkas here. They looked like the race from whom all true Romanies had been born.

☆

Climbing down from the bus into the ancient mountain town of Srinagar I was pulled and tugged at by a dozen hotel boys eager for commission.

'You come my hotel, Sahib.'

'My hotel very best hotel.'

'Hotel very cheap and friendly, you come meester.'

'You want hotel, hashish, taxi, food, hotel?'

'Mister, Mister, come please, I am showing you very best, most pleasant hotel.'

Jeff had told me to travel light and always carry my pack on the bus, otherwise your baggage was held ransom by the hotel boys.

'You go Dal Lake?'

'My father is having a very special house on the lake. You want come and see?'

'Okay, fella, lead the way.'

I placed my hand on his tousled black hair and pointed forward.

'Challo, challo.'

We walked through a maze of rickety streets with overhanging balconies and close packed walls. Timber framed, Tudor-like, it could have been a medieval town. The houses had white-washed and coloured walls, they were old, worn and decaying. Kites circled and mewed overhead.

The people were mainly Kashmiri, Hazara and Afghans, men with long beards, dyed red with henna. White Muslim caps and Afghan caps everywhere, and the flowing shalwar kameez. At every turn there were packs of dogs, big mangy, skeletal street dogs, mean and threatening. Every now and then my guide would pick up a stone, and hurl it at the dogs, with a shout, and shoo them away. The narrow streets opened out onto a quayside where wooden boats were plying their trade.

My guide led me to the water's edge and jumped down

into one of the empty shikaras tied to the quay. He motioned for me to get in. I stepped nervously onto the swaying boat and looked at the water swilling in its floor.

He deftly untied the boat and kicked hard, pushing away from the quayside. He jumped round me and settled in the other end of the boat. Unhurriedly and lazily he paddled his way through the mass of shikaras barring our way and pulled out into the middle of the waterway. The old houses of the town soon gave way to greenery, willows and bushes that hung down into the water, lush and green. A large snake slithered in the water close to the bank. The waterway opened out ahead and I had my first view of Dal Lake. Tranquil, calm, still.

The mountains towered over us on every horizon, the sky deep blue with not a cloud in sight, the water was still and stretched for miles. We paddled out towards the middle of the vast lake, then he headed north towards lines of moored houseboats. Past the rows of house boats, moored like a Surrey suburban avenue, was a straggle of small, interconnected islands. To one side stood a few smart chalets, raised on stilts above the water line. They were new, and freshly painted with a veranda and railings all around. The boy slid the shikara with ease up to a small landing. He leapt out, flicked the rope around a mooring post and ran across the veranda and out of sight.

'Baba ji, baba ji.' I heard him calling, excitedly.

A tall man appeared, unhurried, relaxed. Clothed in a clean grey shalwar kameez, a white Muslim cap upon his head, and a small white beard. He walked across the veranda as I stepped up from the shikara. Firmly and gently he gripped my arm and steadied me as I balanced on dry ground.

'Welcome.' His face was strong, peaceful, gracious and lined. He looked like a man who had survived a war, or torture, or both.

'A saint?' I thought to myself.

He exuded a warmth and kindness, a fatherly wise man, yet he kept a formal distance in his exchanges throughout my stay; I was an infidel.

That evening I ate simply, content to sit and gaze at the lake and the mountains that climbed up like vertical walls in the distance all around. The sun fell and turned the sky orange and pink, the mountains reflected and bounced colour all around. They changed from silvers and whites to every shade of pink, yellow and ochre in an unearthly display, all reflected perfectly in the calm water of the lake. The smell of a thousand wood fires filled the air. I soaked in the tranquillity, thirsty for more, it was not a peace like the absence of noise or busyness, it was a peace, powerful, pregnant with promise, it had a power, a presence, an energy I could feel. I was beginning to taste the magic, the purity of the Himalaya undefiled. Beyond the mountain range to the east, even further into the heart of the Himalaya was Ladakh. Ladakh, one of the most secluded unexplored countries in the world.

Lights began to twinkle and flicker across the lake and a still hush fell as dogs and children slept and adults withdrew indoors. Alone for the first time since sitting in my emptied-out room in Earl's Court, it felt like months ago, in another world, but it had been only weeks. I pulled out the opium and skinned up a small joint. I sat in the darkness, watching the embers of burning tobacco and ash glow bright in the night, as I inhaled and drew in the smoke.

Everything was still, even the world within me. India had absorbed me, fully, totally, demanding my all, I hadn't had time to think about myself. It had exhausted me and left me drained. I would rest a while, but in the darkness the mountains glowed, calling me.

Summer 1981
Hidden Kingdom

The days on the lake merged into one. I lunched on fresh fruit and vegetables bought from the shikaras that came trading each day. For the first time in my life I was learning to be still. I did not leave the house on stilts for the whole of my stay. The years of my violent self-destruction and the exhaustion were falling away, replaced with a calm. Each day the same; a few press ups, some squats and lots of stretching before settling into the lotus position to practise yoga and meditation. Usually I would roll a joint when I'd finished stretching, and sit in 'my' chair, gazing out at the lake and its unhurried pace of life. Once the opium had made its way through my blood, I would ease my way into the lotus position and drift away. Not asleep, but active, as I sifted thoughts and threw them away.

'Om mani padme hum.'

It was when I sat, stock still like a statue, occasionally just moving my eyes, that the kingfisher would drop by, perching on the veranda railings, just an arm's-length from where I sat. Sometimes it settled, I saw it often flashing by, a blur of metallic colours, in a blink from the corner of my eye. Somewhere he had a partner and a nest, for his visits grew more frequent and always with a tiny fish clamped in his long beak.

I had been studying Kundalini yoga for a couple of years. Now I had time to practise the benefits seemed to be beginning to flow. The centring of my 'being' and finding a oneness with the natural world, was taking me back to something of my childhood innocence and peace. Awakening the seven chakras and releasing the inner energy, peace and power was something I was only just becoming aware of. Yoga, though rooted in Hindu traditions, seemed well suited to my pursuit of the jewel in the Lotus – Siddhartha's Nirvana. It enabled me to be still, to search myself, look deep within, and sift and sort through the rubble and ruin of my life, discarding ugly and negative thoughts and feelings and wait for the calm, peace, quiet. It was a discipline I longed to master, but I had no master to teach me.

All these weeks alone on the lake, I spent looking, seeking, searching for the place of calm 'knowing' – far from the madding crowd, that 'place within', and something did quieten in me. Something was changing from within as I emptied away the covetousness with which it seemed I had been born, even the inner torment of my feminine identity and the insatiable craving for love seemed to abate and fade away.

My heart had been set on exploring Ladakh ever since I had first read about it. It was known as 'Little Tibet', an entirely Buddhist nation, a hidden kingdom, one of the most isolated and least visited nations on earth. It sat on a plateau at 10,000 feet. Once it had been a crossroads for trading routes between Afghanistan, Persia, China, India and Tibet. It was locked behind massive mountain ranges. Only one road into the country, and that was often closed by snow for seven months of the year. There were other passes into Ladakh from Tibet and India and China, but they were only accessible on foot. I bought more opium from one of the shikara traders – it was time to go.

The bus to Leh was packed with Ladakhis, returning from their trading trips in Srinagar, the Hindu Kush and beyond. There were Nepalis, Tibetans, Kashmiris and Mongols, Afghans, Sikhs and even Indians from the south – a couple of soldiers, smart, in uniform from Rajasthan. The luggage rack on the roof bulged and groaned under the weight of sacks, chests, crates and bags that were roped to its frame. The road climbed up steeply from Srinagar.

The driver was a cheery Muslim, his face battered, bloodshot eyes, a large broken nose, unkempt grey stubble and a grin more gum than teeth. We were going to be in Allah's hands for the duration of the journey.

As the road climbed, it zig-zagged a path on rapid hairpin bends, but after only a couple of hours the smooth tarmac petered out. The bus rattled, jolted and shook over the rough stone and dirt road. We had two days of this to endure. The road soon narrowed, often to a single lane, where avalanches and rock falls had swept the original road away. The road was carved out of the side of the mountain, that sometimes fell sheer away. Lines of traffic waiting in queues to pass, God only knows who controls the right of way up or down.

Sat on the rear seat, by the window, several feet beyond the rear axle, I had the most terrifying view. As the bus turned the apex of the tightest of these corners, the rear end of the bus swung out well over the edge of the road. I was suspended in these moments, over the precipice. Sometimes the bus would stop, mid-corner, waiting for a jeep to squeeze past. They were moments of terror, my stomach was in my mouth, my heart beating crazily with panic and fear as I looked down, an almost sheer cliff face and many, many thousands of feet below I could see occasional villages, the houses mere dots, and herds of sheep and goats that appeared little more than specks of dust.

There were some passing places; other times the oncoming traffic squeezed, inch by inch, literally metal to metal, scraping by. We all breathed in and prayed. The driver sang and cursed and offered up the usual 'Insha'Allah' whenever we had a close shave. Further up the road we came across a crowd of people stood around a line of vehicles. Lorries, jeeps and a bus had stopped, passengers spilling out, a crowd at the edge of the precipice, looking into the valley far below – a lorry had just left the road. The bus driver blared the horn and muscled the bus impatiently through the crowd.

'Insha'Allah.' He bellowed angrily.

An overnight stop in the small transit town of Cargill. It was the coldest night I'd ever endured and even the opium did not numb the pain. In the morning, the drivers set fire to rags and paper beneath the buses to defrost the fuel and brake pipes, even as people sat, waiting on board.

'Challo, challo!'

From the heights of the Zoji mountain pass, 16,000ft high, it was one long crazy slalom run down into Leh, capital of Ladakh. Everyone was excited to be nearly there, if not a little afraid. I was not even sure if our driver was sober at nine o'clock in the morning. It was good to feel the heat of the sunshine gradually warming my bones and to know, Allah willing, if he was smiling down upon our driver, we would be arriving in the land of my dreams in time for ... tea.

We roared along to a Bollywood anthem, and the cheery singing of our driver – he clearly felt himself 'King of the Road'. He leaned on the horn lavishly and swung the bus around, overtaking at high speed as he let gravity have its way with his overloaded chariot. He cursed when cars failed to move aside and hammered the horn with a malicious glee. Anything that didn't move aside would be crushed beneath us, as we were descending out of the heavens like the four riders of the Apocalypse. He was high, high as a kite. You're either on the bus, or off the bus, there ain't no halfway! I was terrified.

Across the plains we flew. White painted stupas, the Buddhist shrines, containing the bones and ashes of Buddhists saints, dotted the landscape. From their small domed peaks, lines of brightly coloured prayer flags fluttered in the winds, like bunting at an English summer fair. Here they revered and remembered their Bodhisattvas, the ones who had devoted themselves to leading the world into the path of enlightenment. I wondered if the stupas had names?

'Stupa of the one-legged monk who never spoke.'

'Stupa of the smiling one who lived alone in a cave and lived to be a hundred and thirty-one.'

'Stupa of the one who sat naked in the snow for a month and did not freeze to death.'

Scarcely a mile would pass without another stupa. Rather than hoard and secret them away in hidden graveyards or cathedrals, they had scattered their bodhisattvas extravagantly about, they were spiritual beacons by the roadside, each with a story to tell. Every religion has its myths and legends, a reminder to us all, life is short and death is long. India was closer to death than anything I'd ever known.

I was a self-taught student of Kerouac, and hungry to learn. I thought him a romantic, even if his romantics smelled of drugs, sex and booze. Funny that he, champion of the Beat generation, should have fallen for the teachings of the Buddha, who taught detachment from this world of temporal illusions and earthly vanities? Be-bop-alleluia, the beat goes on. What drew me to Kerouac? His searing honesty and realism, the honesty of the existentialist with no point to prove, save say it as it is and be damned.

What drew me to Buddha was the simplicity of his words and life. So free from ego, materialism and spite, he lived charity, compassion and truth – a simple enough pursuit. Perhaps I was more inclined to the Buddhists' Tantric school of life?

'Nothing that exists is not divine', the fundamental belief undergirding all Tantric practice, like; even sex is holy! Rather than teaching that all the world is illusion, it removed that separation between 'spiritual' and earthly. That appealed to me.

Coming to the realisation that nothing exists that is not divine, you hoped to find freedom from ignorance and the cycle of sufferings, or *samsara*.

'Whoa, boy! Where was I going?'

I was just a little white 'boy', an anarchistic hedonist! Here I am goofing off about some spiritual holiness. I'm growing old too soon. I was though, a Dharma bum, I was hungry, starving, desperate to find some meaning in this life. Some meaning that made sense of all the pain.

Kerouac had wrestled to reconcile the world of his Catholic flesh, with the spirit and soul of his Buddhist instincts. He was ever-seeking, searching for truth, perfect love – Nirvana. Kerouac was a sinner and a saint to whom I could relate. He accompanied me, along with Kim, wherever I went. They had joined me the moment I alighted from the plane in Delhi. I smiled whenever I heard their voices. Sometimes they disappeared into the crowds, no doubt they had their own stuff to do. Other times we sat around and shot the breeze, chatting, like you do.

We rolled across the plain nearing the city of Leh, I could see the Gompa, clung to the mountainside, like a swallow's nest to the side of a barn. It sat on a cliff-faced peak, a massive, white, multi-storey palace towering over the surrounding villages and the town, or city as it was known. It was an incredible feat of engineering, hundreds of years old, one of the ancient wonders of the world.

The bus pulled into the bus station, a dusty polo ground, with a final, wheel spinning flourish of dust and came to a metal grinding, shuddering halt. We spilled out into the arid dry heat, I shouldered my bedroll and looked around. A bunch of ragged young boys played football with a scrunched-up ball of rags, wrapped around with a length of twine. I raced into the midst of them and gave a childish shout. They kicked the ball away from me and I launched after it in pursuit. My legs buckled underneath me, my lungs searing and my eyes seeing stars, I face planted to the ground.

The boys gathered round and stood over me, staring down at this tall, bearded stranger who had just landed in their midst. They laughed at me and fell about in fits of giggles. I lay on my back, winded and looked up at the gang of gangly-legged and mop-haired kids. Not a pair of shoes between them. Two days of sitting on a bus, my legs felt like lead, but it was the lack of oxygen that knocked me off my feet; my lungs simply could not cope with exercise at 10,000ft.

The boys carried on laughing and pointed and joked at me. I sat myself upright and held out my hand. They grabbed my arms and helped me upright. I was dizzy and lightheaded as I limped to the side and found a store to buy a couple of bottles of fizz. I poured one down my parched throat, and handed the other one to the 'gang', who took long swigs and excitedly passed it round.

I left Leh United to their game, Jeff's advice at the forefront of my mind.

'Walk straight through town and head up into the mountains. You will find the water supply cleaner and less likely to poison your system, essential if you are going 'native'. By the time you are out of town, local people will be begging you to stay in their homes. You'll get to know India far better and you help the poor survive.'

Walking through the small town – the capital city, it felt like the set in a spaghetti western. Restaurants, and bars, Nepali, Balti, Punjab and Tibetan cuisine. Traders, monks, soldiers and shoppers, shepherds, sheep and goats, wandered to and fro. An occasional backpacker, and mountaineers, mainly Europeans, with their Sherpas, passed by. They carried the entire world upon their backs, tents, stoves, sleeping bags, full winter clothing for the mountains, heavy boots, thick socks, ice axes and crampons strapped to their bags. I was happy in my flip flops, thin cotton clothes and nothing but a blanket.

As the shops thinned out on the edge of town the road climbed steeply up. My breathing was hard, laboured and I was finding it heavy going. I had walked less than a mile into open countryside. Leh Gompa towered almost directly above me. People were busy, working in the fields. Crops were growing. As I was musing on the impoverished farming, I heard a horse trotting up behind me. I turned to see a small boy, perched precariously on the back of a scraggy, tiny mule. As he drew level he slowed. He was a Tibetan, or Ladakhi, I didn't know enough to tell. He pointed up the hill at some buildings, then at me, and then back at the buildings. All the while not taking his eyes off of me. His nose ran with thick green snot that he wiped on the sleeve of his thick greatcoat.

He slid off the little nag and led it by its rope reins. I followed him up the hill. When we reached the buildings, he tied the mule up outside and opened up the front door. He beckoned me in. Inside it was a hovel that stank of poverty, a primitive agricultural existence. There was one small window with glass that was barely opaque. An ancient old lady sat stoking an open fire of dried out dung.

He gabbled excitedly at the old lady and pointed at me. She waved at a door to one side. He opened it up and led me through, the next room was a barn, where they kept their animals. Outside was a rickety ladder that looked a hundred years old, we climbed onto the roof, on the corner of which stood a small square room. It was about ten feet square with a window that looked out over the town and straight across the valley to the Himalaya that rose, majestic and dominating. Behind me mountains, all around mountains. The secret, hidden Kingdom of Ladakh. To such an outpost of the Empire, Kim had once come. Out the other window I could see the fields and the gompa on the top of the cliff. There was no glass in the windows. It would be cold! I liked it. No creature comforts, but a view unrivalled in all the world.

Behind a low parapet wall on the far side of the roof

to my bedroom was a hole in the flat roof – the toilet. The smell of animal and human excrement rose and assailed me. Below was where they stored it all. To be spread out the following year on the land. Maybe not so grand. It was the most primitive place I had ever seen ... or stayed in.

Downstairs we entered into negotiations. Neither of them knew any Hindi or English, and I knew no Ladakhi. We mimed our way through a good-humoured game of charades. The little boy mimed sleeping, pointed upstairs and then counting out some coins. He took a total of six rupees from my outstretched hand – the princely sum of thirty-six pence. That wouldn't even buy a packet of cigarettes back home, more like half a pint. Thirty-six pence for a room to sleep and breakfast and supper!

Grabbing my bedroll, he darted up the rickety ladder and threw it in the corner of my new digs. The boy thumbed his chest and spoke out his name.

'Gunz-ant-ing-lay.'

'Gunz-ant-ing-lay.'

'OK, Gunz-ant-ing-lay, I'm going to have a kip.'

With my back against the wall, I looked out the window at the mountains, it was time for a celebratory joint. After two days of travel and snacking I was hungry, ravenous. There was one last bread roll left in my pack. I peeled a couple of cloves of garlic with my pocketknife and thumbed them into the bread. It would quiet my stomach till the evening meal. I must have drifted off after finishing the smoke. Gunzantinglay was knocking on the door. I opened it up and he waddled in with his arms locked around a huge bundle of bedding which he piled on the charpoy in the corner of the room.

Moments later he was back with dinner. A pile of rice sat in a plate of thin liquid 'gravy' and on it sat a meagre scattering of what looked like chives, it could have been grass. He gave me an old metal fork and sat down to watch me eat. I looked at his filthy snot covered face, I was living on the edge. The rice was gritty, bits of stone or husk that nearly broke my teeth. The greens were sharp, and the gravy had a whiff, a hint of meat.

That first night alone on the roof of the world, I sat outside wrapped in the bundle of bedding. The sky above was the clearest I had ever seen, the stars so bright and close, there was nothing between me and them, I could reach out and touch them. I picked out the few constellations that I knew. The lights twinkled down below in the town. Dogs barked and the last lorries rumbled into town. I was more peaceful than I had ever been. The night was bitterly cold, I went to bed fully clothed. If I kept my head under the bedding and created a cocoon of body warmth it was just about warm enough to sleep without shivering.

I was woken by the house shaking beneath me, tremors rolled through the floor and walls and into my body. At first, I thought it might be an earthquake. Then as I came to from my slumber, I realised the shaking was steady, rhythmic and coming directly from below. It was barely light yet. Intrigued, I got out of bed, still fully clothed, I wrapped my blanket around me, and stumbled down the stairs. In the kitchen gloom sat the old lady. She sat on a low stool and was working a thick woven belt which passed round the main wooden post that supported the entire roof, the belt was wrapped at her end round a tall narrow wooden barrel, hooped with iron, which she steadied between her knees. As she pulled the belt back and forth the barrel span. She was churning milk to make curd and butter, and it caused the whole house to shake.

Each day I woke to the earth shaking. The weeks rolled by. I felt at home, like one of the family, I joined in their routines. I worked the fields, churned curd and butter with grandma. Gramps was an alcoholic. He had got me blind drunk one day whilst harvesting their crops. I had spent a week bedridden, not knowing if I had alcohol poisoning, food poisoning, altitude sickness, or some kind of disease. I survived chewing opium and drinking bottled water that Gunzantinglay bought me from town.

There was a restaurant in town with a bar that spilled out onto the street. It was a favourite haunt of westerners in need of alcohol. Walking past, I found myself hungry for company, someone to talk to after weeks of isolation. I bought myself the luxury of a bottle of cold beer. A small bunch of guys was locked in an animated debate, good humoured heckling and posturing, they moved over and made room for me on the end of the bench. Hippies, travellers and a couple of climbers, tanned and lean, with all the quality boots and top end gear, everyone glad for company. The banter ebbed and flowed.

The focus of the conversation revolved around a young, attractive Swiss couple. They were talking about their God, the Christian God of the Bible. I listened to their sincere defence for a God who created the earth, the universe and had then left it to unwind. A German guy was taking it very seriously. A young Irish lad, sat back a bit, chimed in.

'All Jesus did was leave us saddled with a religion that has torn my city in two?'

His gentle, lilting Irish brogue hung in the air with a calm authority.

'Can we really blame him for that?' the Swiss woman countered.

'That's not Jesus' fault, it's our failure to live according to what he taught, "love your neighbour, as yourself".'

The Swiss girl was unfazed by the heckling or the barrage of questions and the fierce debate. She stood her ground and looked us all straight in the eyes. I could feel my blood beginning to boil, and my hatred for Christianity rising in my chest.

'Didn't Gandhi say something like, "I like your Christ, but I don't like your Christians, they are so unlike your Christ"? Until I see the church take its head out its own backside and genuinely love the poor, your religion is the most morally bankrupt and hypocritical I've ever encountered, all the Christians I see are just western materialists, capitalists, chasing the latest this and that!'

She looked at me, warm, unhurried, unperturbed by my hatred.

'Have you ever studied the words of Jesus?'

'No, your church has put me off doing that!'

'Have you ever read the Bible?'

'Yes – enough to know that Bob Marley was right. The Christian west, colonialism, capitalism, church and state, have recreated a "Babylon system" and it's all going to collapse, like a house of cards.'

Downing the last of my beer, livid, I walked away, too angry to stop and listen or argue about a religion I saw as spiritually bankrupt. *'Sweet girl'*, I thought to myself. I never forgot the beer-fuelled debate, or the radiant enthusiasm and love she had for Jesus – it always seemed to come back to Jesus – it stuck with me over the weeks and months.

Days later, preparing to move on, I bought provisions for my travels. Returning from town, coming down the hill towards me was the young Irish lad. Neither of us in any rush, we sat down at the side of the track.

Diarmuid was only nineteen, and already extensively travelled. Fit and healthy looking, with a wild straw coloured hair, he was a chilled character. He wanted to travel and write books and make a home in the country some day. Pulling out a tobacco pouch he rolled a cigarette. We chatted and laughed and discussed each other's plans. He was about to leave, back down to Kashmir. I asked him if he knew where I could buy some blow. He pulled out another pouch and unwrapped a large lump of opium.

'How much d'you want? I can afford to sell you half of this, as once I'm back in Srinagar I can easy buy some more.'

I bought half an ounce and stashed it in my shirt. We talked about Dal Lake and I told him about where I had stayed and the 'herbs and spices' shikara. We laughed about my rant at the bar the other day.

'Seems to me that all religion is crooked.' He smoked his cigarette through his fist, taking a long draw, like a sadhu smoking a chillum, he let the statement hang out there in the smoke.

'Well, you look at Jesus, he was undeniably cool. You look at Buddha, and he was nobody's fool, they both taught charity and kindness, loved the poor and laughed at worldly wealth.'

His voice had a musical lilt to it, a gentleness. He paused again and took another long draw. Puffing the smoke out in perfect rings.

'That girl was right you know. People who love religion, they don't care about the poor. Look at religion here in Ladakh, it is secret and dark, rituals and gurus, esoteric and unavailable to the likes of you and me. I mean, the monks, on the whole, are about as unfriendly as you can get, and they are supposed to be devotees of The Man, The One and Only, Original Bodhisattva?'

He was warming to his subject. I liked him and let him roll on. We skinned a joint, lay back and looked out over the mountains.

'People who love, who "do religion", they don't do relationships very well, they replace people with things, bigotry and dogma, it's safer for them like that.'

'In my hometown, they are killing each other for religion. That's why I had to get away, come to India.'

He looked up at the mountains, sat musing for a while.

'Have you noticed, that in every religion, they pay a Priest to tell them what to believe?! Seems kinda dumb to me. And the Priests, they end up climbing the ladders of power, speaking judgements from their positions on the people "below" them, claiming they hold "The Truth". Man, it just seems kind of hateful to me. Only folks I see Jesus judging are the religious leaders?'

I didn't want to talk, I wanted to hear him out, he was offloading his burdens, his frustrations and anger at religion, all religions. He was a lot like me.

'The Mullahs they are no better. The Sikhs – now the Sikhs are cool, just don't get them mad with you.'

He looked at me hard.

'Be careful when you come off the mountains, when you're coming "back down". It's a massive shock to the system, a really heavy vibe. You feel the change in your body, it's so pure up there, you look down and see all the pathetic efforts of man, for what they really are. The mountains are holy man! I mean it, they really are. They get inside of you and mess with your head. You stay up the mountains on your own and you see visions, you see the world for the whore that she is. You know she's going to lay you, rob you and leave you pissing razor blades.'

Jeff had always stressed the same thing: 'Be careful when you come back down'.

With the sun starting to dip in the sky we shook hands and promised to meet up again some-day, and I sat and watched him stroll on down the hill. Every ounce the Dharma Bum.

I said goodbye to Gunzantinglay and his mother, before they left for school and whatever it was that she did in town. The Grump had gone to the fields, or off with his cronies, to get hammered, like any other day, on the dense, heavy chang. I sat with Grandma. She had cleared away the curd bowls and finished her morning's chores, she sat by the ever-burning fire with her back against the wall. Her face was that chiselled deep brown of the Tibetans who have spent their whole lives burnt by the sun, the weather, the wind. It was creased and wrinkled in a thousand lines, making it impossible to tell her age.

She looked at me and started to talk. I had no idea what she was saying, absolutely none at all. Her voice rose and fell in the strange Tibetan tongue. She spoke without fear, I listened intently to her stories and her questions. She was pouring out her heart. I was astounded and enchanted.

We had no common language. She had been reading me, all these weeks. Maybe she saw her angry, embittered husband in me. She knew I smoked the dreaming drug. When she had finished, I waited a few moments and wondered what to say, I didn't know what to say, sat in the silence. Then my lonely heart broke open; I started to tell her about my travels, I told her about Lizzy and how I missed her so much, how losing her had broken my heart. I forgot the awkwardness of language and my heart opened up like a fountain. This old woman and I had connected across the divide of language, culture, religion, class, and age. Tears began to flow. We laughed and we cried. We just sat and looked into each other's eyes. Mother and child. The silence was full, sweet, complete.

Eventually I stood up to go, and bowing before her, I placed my hands together and said a solemn, heartfelt, 'Namaste'. She came across and hugged me. The smell of her body odour no longer rankled me, I smelled just the same.

I was heading east, up the valley and out over the mountains through the Bara Lacha Pass, and down into Manali. I was thinking of buying a large amount of blow there. Not so much for myself, but so that I could sell it on and make some money and prolong my stay in India. Maybe if all went well, I could stay in India indefinitely.

The Bara Lacha Pass was one of the few ways out of Ladakh, one of the old trade routes, not a road, just a trail, and only passable in summer months, it was high, one of the highest of all the Himalaya passes. It would be an epic walk. But first I wanted to visit some of the remote monasteries and see them for myself. Make my own decisions about the religion, even though I thought Diarmuid was probably right. I wanted to be on my own, totally alone and wander in the mountains. I caught a bus up the valley to Tiksi, where there was a large gompa. My plan was to walk from there up to Chimray, then onto Upshi, each with its own significant Gompa. From there I hoped to be able to cross the beginnings of the mighty River Indus and head south for the Bara Lacha.

I left the Gompas, religion and the last remote dwellings behind me. I'd found the vibe in the Gompas dark, heavy, oppressive, like the cathedrals back home. None of the monks took the slightest notice of me, ignoring me, the stranger and pilgrim, squatting in the shade. I had sat there for hours, reflecting, meditating. Religion, it seemed, was only for those on the inside.

I crossed the Indus northwards and headed into the mountains, following narrow tracks, and climbed up and up, till they petered out. It was a remote and desolate place. Only the stupas, like lonely ships at sea, lay in the barren valley below, prayer flags trailing out in the wind behind them. After several hours climbing I found a sheltered ledge and stopped to bed down in my solitary lair.

I rolled two huge spliffs of opium and settled into the rocky craggy platform. I sat and smoked one and kept the other for the night. How long had I been in India? I was losing count of the weeks and months, I didn't know what day it was, let alone a date. I had no watch, only the sun to determine my time.

I sat in the lotus position and drifted off in contemplation.

As the sun dropped behind the mountains on the far side the valley, I felt the chill of evening bite. I had been mindful of collecting any timber to burn, even twigs to use as kindling but the land was arid and barren and I had not found anything at all. My meagre supply of dried fruit and nuts felt like the choicest meal as I savoured each chew, and rolled the fruit beneath my tongue. The day darkened and the stars began to burn their holes in an incandescent sky. Fully dressed I snuggled into my two blankets, lay back and stared into space. Cold seared deep into my flesh and penetrated the core of my being, the marrow of my bones. All my reserves of fat had been stripped away.

The permanent state of suicidal despair I had lived with in London seemed to have gone. My money was going quicker than I liked, and I was unsure of how much the opium was colouring my life. In India I had been immersed in the culture and the crowds, now I was in every sense, far removed, from anyone, and everyone. Alone in a way few ever experience. Just me, and the universe.

The heavens stretched infinite above me. I shivered and rattled with cold. Painful throbbing bit at my toes. Eternity stretched out all about me and I felt its magic, something awesome, something terrible yet clothed in rapturous beauty. The tranquillity of the mountains bathed in ethereal light masked their hideous power that could just as easily destroy me. Alone in the mountains I was touching a different reality, a different world, touching upon something outside of me, but I could also feel it growing within me. My ego was shrinking beneath such majesty. The sheer enormity of everything, a sense of power pulsated around me, a life force, an energy. Too cold to fall asleep, I lit the other spliff. Cupping the match in my hands I watched the flame burn down till it fizzled and spat as it reached my finger-tips, my fingers so cold I did not feel the burn.

I drifted in and out of dreams. My past life seemed aeons

away, not even a part of me anymore. The orange glow of the sun rising up behind the far mountains was the most unearthly display of nature's power. It held me in its thrall. Small wonder we had worshipped it. The golden orb, the ball of fire, rose quickly, its warmth yet to come, but its appearance spelled hope. I was begging for its rays to kiss me. I stood before it and stretched and twisted and pummelled the air in an effort to keep warm. I was ravenously hungry, drained by fatigue and fighting the cold, but now as the sun rose, I felt more confident.

Retracing my steps, I climbed down to the valley floor and followed the long walls that ran between the stupas. Many of the stones in the 'wall' were carved, hundreds of stones, inscribed with prayers and placed by a pilgrim, miles from anywhere, in the middle of nowhere! My mind boggled at the incredibleness of it.

My own prayers were not so concrete, just a vague longing for something, Did I even know what it was that I was searching for? If I didn't know what the question was, how would I ever recognise the answer? I knew the emptiness, the hopelessness and the despair and something in me was crying out for a lucky break, a sign, a moment, an understanding that would sustain me for the rest of my life.

I spent days exploring the remote valleys that ran as deep ravines back into the feet of the mountains, I climbed as high as I safely could, and holed up at night. I managed to find enough firewood to stave off the cold. I refilled my water bottle from the ice-cold streams that cascaded down exploding in rock pools. Water, crystal clear, it felt almost magical as I washed beneath its tumbling, singing surging flow. Alone at last, I felt cleansed, purified, released into a different state of being by these days and nights alone in the mountains.

The hunger and loneliness forced me down; yes, I felt bitterly lonely, starving for human love, affection, intimacy.

Was it a needy part of me that would not die? What is love? Is love some cruel joke? Was Siddartha right, was I just frightened of the void?

I retraced my route back down to Kashmir. I spent a couple of nights back on Dal Lake, but was restless and flighty as the kingfisher that came by. It was the Muslim festival of Eid. I watched a man perform a ritual slaughter and cut the throat of a large goat for my Muslim host. It kicked and thrashed beyond the slash of his knife. Terror in its eyes as it smelt its own blood and death. Blood gushed forth and the creature struggled, then quivered and lay quiet, unmoving on the ground. A sacrifice for sins?

Did God really ask Abraham to sacrifice his own son? It seemed a bleak, ugly, primitive and truly extortionate price to pay – appeasement for some god who needed to see blood spilt to satiate its need for control of the human race? A primitive religion indeed, but then most religions were rooted in the notions of sacrifice to appease the wrath of their gods. The greater the cost of a sacrifice, the greater its efficacy – the sacrifice of a human, preferably a child or a virgin, the ultimate pay off for peace? My dislike of religion was growing by the day.

Jeff and Diarmuid had been right, coming off, down from the mountains and back into humanity was a mind blowing, shattering, distressing shock. Good and evil, kindness and hate, religion and love, all had become so starkly exposed, contrasting and conflicting. I had become hypersensitive, to people, atmospheres, and the presence of good and evil. It was as if a veil of blindness had been wiped from my eyes. I was reeling with the shock. I knew too, that my body was beginning to break down, and my mind was feeling fragile. I was malnourished and possibly diseased. Opium was taking its toll.

Autumn 1981
On the Street

The bus rolled into Dharamshala. It nestled in the foothills of the Himalaya, home to the Dalai Lama and the majority of the Tibetans who fled when China invaded their homeland in 1950. I'd come, in part, to study in the Buddhist library.

Climbing down from the bus, glad to feel the dirt once more beneath my feet, I slung my roll over my shoulder and walked straight through the town. I headed uphill, winding my way through the pretty streets, mostly built in the colonial style of the Raj. Eventually the road petered out into a path. I looked down over the town, sprawled out below. It was a busy, teeming place; I kept going, keen to leave it behind and find the rural community that I knew would be eking out a living on the stepped hills stretching out above me. Clean water, somewhere cheap to stay, a local family, away from the hotels, the shops the crowds and the noise.

I was rewarded by the sight of beautiful, terraced fields and small farmsteads dotted around. Sheep, goats and cattle grazed amidst a mass of huge, giant pine trees and everywhere the profusion of richly coloured rhododendron bushes, their flowers swaying in the gentle mountain breeze. A young man waved at me and shouted a friendly 'hello'. I waved, and stepped off the main path and started across the field towards him.

'Do you have a room?'

He smiled, turned and walked away, motioning for me to follow. His home was a tangle of white-washed rambling buildings, all thatched and clean and leaning in together like sheep in a storm. It was a small farm of sorts. A young woman was sweeping the bare, worn earth outside her door, the veranda casting shade from the heat of the mid-day sun. He shouted some words in a language I did not recognise or understand as we walked past, heading for a small building at the end of the yard.

It was a small room, empty and swept clean. A charpoy, a small table and a window looking over the land that curved around to form a small, sheltered valley. We negotiated a month's rent, and I threw my roll on the bed. This was home from home, with glass in the windows. The smell of wood smoke clung to the valley. I squatted against the wall outside and rolled the last of my opium, sat and smoked and watched the family go about their daily routine. This was my favourite part of the day, the sun fell, the sky coloured and the snow and ice on the mountains glowed in a magical evening, otherworldly, ethereal display. Kingfishers, peacocks, lotus flowers, Himalaya in the reddening night sky, visions that no one could ever adequately describe.

A curl of smoke licked up from the hole in the roof and wafted the smell of baking into the air. My stomach rolled and churned in hungry anticipation of a meal ahead. Somewhere along the way I had lost interest in food and mealtimes and a regular diet. I sat there for an hour or two, glad to be done with travelling, happy to be alone again, and hungry again for the solitude and serenity of the mountains above.

The evening meal was ready. Washing my hands at a tap above a trough I wiped my face of dust, enjoying the chill clear spring water on my skin. I kicked off my flip flops and left them at the door with the row of sandals, flip flops and battered old shoes that lay against the wall. Stooping through the doorway, my eyes adjusting to the dim light, the family sat in a circle on the floor, food spread out before them, on a brightly coloured rug. I bowed slightly and joined my hands.

'Namaste.'

The father showed me a gap in the family circle. Sitting cross legged, I tucked my feet away, careful not to point them at anyone. A large, extended family, children and parents, grandparents all stared at me, reading me. I heard Kim, telling me to relax. In the wall was a Shivite shrine and a small idol. The blue Shiva danced with his bloody swords. Another shrine held Ganpati the elephant god. This small family clan was devoutly Hindu with their family gods scattered around the home, watching, protecting, demanding and brooding. That night, I sat and enjoyed their abundant generosity, kindness and hospitality to the stranger, the traveller and the pilgrim. They performed their daily puja and settled to enjoy their meal and family time. I was a guest and I felt their kindness washing over me. Tears fell quietly down my face. I was broken.

Wrapping chapatti around the rice and meat, I ate my fill, and my plate was refilled till I could eat no more. The food was good. It was honest, warm and spicy. Hospitality and kindness to a stranger, good karma flowed. The children whispered and giggled. The father and I conversed in a halting, stilted English. They seemed an open, friendly family, not hung up on caste or fear of outsiders like me.

My days were quiet and I avoided the town as much as I could. I was spending longer hours in my yoga, still feeling my way into the practice. Some days I wandered higher up the slopes of these foothills that stretched out into the mountains above. The paths wound their way across the foothills, a maze that only locals knew. I found quiet, secluded glades and rolled large joints, smoked and sat and meditated.

One day, way above the house I found a Shivite shrine in a small, secluded clearing. I spent the afternoon there, lost in the lotus position and the warmth of the sun, meditating until I felt still. The scent of pine needles and rhododendrons filled the air.

The air suddenly went cold, a storm blowing in. I scrabbled to my feet and ran for shelter beneath a colossal pine. In the mountains you don't hear the distant rumble of thunder, here it hit with no warning. Almighty cracks and deafening explosions as the forked lightning started crashing into the ground all around me. I was stood in the centre of an electric storm of immeasurable power, reverberating with deafening noise. I was terrified of a strike hitting me. I watched a forked bolt, like a serpent's tongue, strike the Shivite trident embedded in the shrine, just yards from me. The explosive flash of thousands of volts. The terror I once tasted as a child gripped my heart, I felt a flood of fear, like an evil, hit me, like nothing I had ever known. Stood there, petrified and watching death hit yards from my frozen butt, fear flooded through me in huge surges. Lightening-bolts were hitting all around me with the noise and force of exploding bombs. The physical energy was colossal, and I was small, about to be fried. Adrenaline had frozen my body. I was rooted to the spot.

As suddenly as it started, the storm rolled over and the rain crashed down. I leaned into the trunk of the massive tree, the bark warm against my bare back. Frozen and shivering, rain battered the rhododendron bushes and I watched the fragile flowers getting torn. Wired, frazzled, by the power of the storm, it seemed more than merely physical, it felt like a melting, a shaking, a ripping in my secret, inner world, a knowledge I couldn't unknow, like death was stalking me, staring me down, a cold primeval call.

The rain was sheeting, slashing down, falling like bullets, hail starting to form. They bruised as they ricocheted off my flesh. In panic, already shivering and hurting from the cold I snatched up my wet clothes and scrambled back down to the path and ran. The nearest place was the Hindu temple at the end of the main track. The cold was hideous.

Entering into the temple gate, I bumped, half-naked, into an old hag, one of the temple prostitutes? She was crazy-eyed and agitated. She screamed something at me – I didn't understand the words, but I could feel her intent, she was cursing me with a rage. I was repulsed backwards out the gate by the torrent of her madness and hate. She stooped to pick up a stone, and hurled it at my head. I turned back down the path and ran. Stones rained behind me. Sheltering under a rock outcrop far from the temple, out of the worst of the driving, lashing rain and hail, I watched it bouncing off the ground. Shaking uncontrollably, I knew I was close to hypothermia. I could taste and see evil and my own death, for the first time in my life.

The sky cleared, the rain passed and the sun blasted down again. Steam rose off the rocks. I walked shakily and briskly back down to the little farm. The wife was standing beneath the veranda and saw me coming in. She walked across the yard and stopped to look at me, quizzically, she flashed a warm smile, took my sodden clothes and pulled me inside.

Standing, still half naked, shaking, teeth chattering, I tried to thank her, but the words wouldn't come out. She shouted urgently for her husband. They wrapped me in blankets and sat me in front of the kitchen fire. She was a beautiful woman, with dark flashing eyes and long black hair. They had the contented air of lovers, those two humble hosts. Minutes later and my hands were cupped around a mug of steaming, spicy chai. It was warm and sweet, milky and strong. They stood over me, with concerned looks until they saw me smile, and then they laughed. My clothes were hung on a line in the yard. They told me to stay and eat with them. I was too weak to move.

That evening, as I sat in the twilight world of fading light, the children came out to play. They carried jam jars and cloths and sat with me awaiting the night. They chattered along with the myriad cicadas, invisible but never silent. As the darkness wrapped itself around, the children leapt off with excited shouts. I watched them as they hunted the fireflies down, catching them, cupping them, collecting them in their gentle hands, careful not to crush or bruise. The jam jars each filled, came alive with a small town of flickering light. Nature, so infinite and cruel, yet so tender and kind. Something like happiness flickered through my heart, just for a moment and then was gone. Would the Buddha approve of my enjoyment or fear? Or should I be detached, beyond it all, for all was nothingness, the eternal void? They left me a glowing jam jar, full of fire-flies and I pondered it all, the cicadas continued all around me, their never-ending song.

Days and weeks rolled into one. The money dwindled away on lodgings and food, I survived on bread rolls, garlic and fruit. Occasionally I was invited to eat with the family. Most of my money was spent on opium. I was ready to hit the road again. One last Travellers Cheque sat, lonely in my pouch, along with a passport, and a return air ticket, the vast extent of all my worldly wealth.

I was attached to this place. I had withdrawn from any regular contact with anyone. The family left me alone. Weeks passed and I spoke to no one. The small farm was a quiet reminder of a childhood, a home, a time I had almost forgotten.

One morning I woke up and heard the bells clinking on the cows' necks as they were herded back onto the hills after the morning's milking, and I knew it was time to move on.

I didn't even know where I was headed or why. Was it the opium, taking its toll, was it the malnutrition? Was it the result of diseases I had picked up along the way? I could feel myself sliding, slipping uncontrollably into mental illness or worse, a madness.

For several days I stumbled through the foothills.

Everyone was hostile to me. Was it their rural isolation, suspicion and fear, or was it me, maybe they could smell the death that was stalking me? The usual warm hospitality had dried up, maybe I had run out of good karma?

Late one afternoon I stumbled into a town. I was feverish and sick, sweat was pouring off me, I was badly dehydrated. I headed for the bus station and bought the cheapest ride to Delhi I could find. It was the roughest bus I had ever seen. Windows were missing and the usual garish paintings that adorned these chariots was a faded memory of its glory days, as if the owner had given up, or hit upon hard times. Around it squatted an assembly of villagers, farmers, and a troop of the orange clad Shivite Sadhus holding their begging bowls and trident spears, they sat apart and beneath the usual cloud of hashish.

I bought a big hashish cookie in town and downed several bottles of pop. I had a few rupees left. I would need to cash in my last Travellers Cheque as soon as I hit Delhi. As I headed back towards the bus, I passed through a small street of shops, an old silver-haired man, selling shoes from his small shop stall, was watching me intently as I approached. Our eyes met and locked, he looked deep into my soul with an unwavering gaze, reading me. As I drew close, he spoke to me,

'You're lost.' His face was gentle, kind.

'Pardon?'

'You are lost, my son.'

There was the same calm authority in his voice as the peace that filled his eyes. Something about his calm assertion unsettled me. I was neither a child, nor lost. I stopped right in front of him.

'I'm sorry Baba-ji, I'm not lost, I'm just headed for my bus.'

He just sat there, calm, composed, no hint of fear or anger.

'Son, you are lost.'

I could feel my anger rising. Anger, an emotion I had hardly noticed in months. I was too angry to speak. *'Who does he think he is!'* I cursed to myself, and glowered back at him, raging, stumped for words.

On the bus, after days of walking with little food and hardly any water, some kind of sickness, I was almost delirious. Sinking into sleep, dreams came in waves as I drifted in and out of consciousness. They were turbulent and disturbing. Fights and thieves, knives, a brooding evil and a menacing fear. This was a heavy trip, a high gone wrong. It was a relief to find myself jolted awake. I watched the lights shining out of the night as we passed by remote villages and tiny towns. The bus rumbled, rattled and rolled down through the dense lush jungle of Himachal Pradesh, at a sedentary pace, for sure the slowest ride of all my time in India.

My body ached all over, but I could find no comfort, sat upright and wedged in by a sleeping farmer slumped against me. Warm night air blasted in through the broken windows. I used my blanket, rolled as a pillow against the vibrating glass. I was suffering all over. I tried to meditate and empty my mind of the violent thoughts my dreams had left, but I was too tired, too weak and my mind wandered. My body was shivering and racked with pain. I chewed on a lump of opium and hoped it would numb my senses. What did he mean? *'I was lost?'* What had he seen?

My nerves jangled; I had come down from the mountains, something had happened to me; I could do more than read people, I could sense both the good and the evil in those around me! All my fleshly senses had been stripped away; I was living in the 'spirit' world. It seemed as if I had become sensitised to atmospheres, even the good and evil vying for the uppermost place in human hearts. I was now immersed, submerged in the surging, roaring tide of India. Was I becoming conscious of the djinns, the spirits, the ghosts who were an ever-present reality to all of India? India lived in the spirit realm, a world of spirits, gods and demons, it was only us in the west, the 'enlightened' ones, who could not see.

We stopped at a wayside shanty of food stalls and chai shops. I rolled a spliff, cupping the joint in my fists and made a large chamber to fill with the smoke and then I drank it down, thirstily, greedily – body and mind hungry for more. The tip of the joint glowed like a furnace being fed by bellows as I milked the joint to the dregs. The fire burnt, my lungs filled and the waves rolled through me as I craved its relief, the soothing numbness of its black magic. The truth? I was a junkie, a slave to opium.

This Dharma bum had run out of money and was running for 'home', even though I had no idea where home was. The fresh page, a clean slate, a new chapter? My life was unravelling. Had I been running away, running from myself and the mess of my life? Or was I facing and searching myself? Perhaps some creature comforts would not ruin me any further. I dreamed of a warm bed, a bath, warm food and sleep for many days. Crippled with stomach pains I hobbled back to the bus and found my place by the window. People were quiet, mellowed out with food and chai and smoke. We rolled on, down into the dawn, the flat lands and onto the Grand Trunk Road.

We had been nearly forty-eight hours on the bus. Now we crossed the dry, dusty plains. Stopping and starting, spilling out our human cargo. Places filled with poor villagers heading for the city. This was one bus that never travelled empty. It heaved and lurched and wheezed along, I fully expected it to break down forever, to spew us out and leave us stranded in the dusty plains that spread out on every side. Fields, dykes, ditches and telegraph poles, stretched out to the horizon line.

The city, Delhi, loomed into sight, a pall of smog hanging in the heat haze over the skyline. Relief swept through me. A hotel, the airport, home. The ancient bus ground to a halt, grateful we disembarked into the blazing heat. Stiff limbed and sore I stretched out and sat myself down to take stock and make a plan. I had maybe enough money for a few nights in the cheapest hotel, taxi fares for the airline office and airport and a few meals at the most, then I would be well and truly bust.

My money lasted for a few meals, but then, like Lady Luck, was gone. I begged from food stalls, they were kinder than the restaurants, whose staff would turf me out as soon as they saw I had no cash. There was a stall near the Jain Temple that sold sugar cane juice and the vendor gave me a glass of juice once a day. One of those first nights, after wandering the streets into the early hours and watching the shops and stalls close down, I waited for the streets to quiet before finding somewhere to hide. A burnt-out car in a quieter road provided hope of shelter, waiting till I thought no one was watching, I climbed in and curled up to sleep on what was left of the rear seat.

Living on the street, my mind 'caved in'. All common sense and reason gone, I could no longer think clearly or logically, I was terrified, knowing that my mind was giving up on me. I went crazy, throwing away my passport, my return ticket home and my last Travellers Cheque. I had hit the bottom, I knew I was just another forgotten body left on the refuse heap of humanity to die, and I knew my own death was not far off. I was resigned to my fate, I had given up the will to stay alive, to fight.

I dropped the pouch with the last of my earthly belongings behind a low wall. I took out my stone chillum and smashed it angrily against the wall, but it would not break, frustrated I threw it into the grass. Drugs had killed me, drugs were evil; they had robbed me of my life – it was an epiphany too late. I was done, with everything. Inside I made my peace with the world.

'Okay, I'm done. Whatever is out there, luck, fate, karma, God or gods, come and get me, I'm ready to die.'

There was no obvious agency in India to pick up the broken dregs of the western world like me. There was no door to knock on. If there was, my broken mind could not think of it.

I jumped trains to try and get out the city. In my wanderings I found quieter stations and sidings in the slums and industrial areas where one could jump a train, grabbing a tailgate as the wagons rolled slowly by. One day it seemed as if I was suffering a minor stroke, lying motionless for what seemed several hours on the platform of some quiet railway sidings in the Old City, gripped by crippling chest pains and unable to move. Eventually I stumbled off the platform, only to be overwhelmed and nauseated by the site of rows of body bags, lying stiff in the sweltering heat, the white but grubby canvases barely concealing the corpses they wrapped. Not just one or two body bags, but whole piles. Victims of some disaster or disease?

In the busy streets and shopping quarters near prosperous hotels and restaurants I sat in the dirt, held out my hands and begged for food,

'Bagsheesh, bagsheesh.'

Middle-class Indians give me a wide berth as they passed me by, a few spat on me and cursed me,

'White trash.'

I gravitated towards Old Delhi, and the ramshackle crammed maze of streets heaving with the multitudes of poor and poorer still, I felt safer with them. I slept in doorways, and one cold night could find nowhere warm or quiet and ended curled up with the holy cows sleeping in the centre of Connaught Circus. I pulled my blanket over my body and lay in the dirt. The heat from the cows helped me survive the night. Sleep was a long sequence of nightmares, fever and hallucinations as my body shuddered and shook. I was in the midst of total breakdown, a mental, emotional and physical collapse.

Somewhere in Old Delhi begging in the street I was picked up by a police crew, who dragged me to the cells. I had no visa, no ID, nothing. They beat me with their 'lathis' and kicked me mercilessly with their heavy, black booted feet. Physically I don't think I felt a thing, but inside it was just another session on the whipping stool of life, another humiliation and degradation. They had no real reason to hold me, and they threw me out as soon as they got bored, knowing they could get no response, reaction or bribe from this washed out junkie; they weren't to know I was already dead inside. I was just making up the ebbing tide of human flotsam and jetsam that flowed forever and relentless through the city, in the never-ending cycle of life and death.

I fell into the company of a gang of street kids whose 'home' was the pavement under the colonnade outside the front of the Jain Temple at the end of Chandni Chowk, opposite the Jama Masjid. They 'looked after me' and fed me, they made a space for me in their line of cardboard box beds. They begged and stole, cajoled and pick-pocketed, grazing on crumbs and leftovers, throw-aways and refuse.

Here I was in an underworld of gangs, and thugs, of child slavery, exploitation and perverse abuse, of organised crime and the laundering of money, passports and all manner of stolen wealth. A world where both children and bodies went missing.

Each night we would squat on our haunches to keep our butts out of the dirt, we passed around beedis and drank down their acrid smoke, they shared what food they had. Then we would all lay down on sheets of cardboard, shivering, huddled together and try and find some sleep, but I could not even begin to fall asleep. Was it paranoia or was it a genuine fear? I dreaded being murdered and robbed. Even as homeless white trash, I might be carrying a passport, or hidden cash.

Every night as they whispered or tossed and turned, or wandered off to relieve themselves, I lay awake, terrified, waiting for the cutting of a razor, of having my throat cut from ear to ear. I could imagine them 'turning me over' and finding ... nothing. Perhaps they could sell my corpse, for body parts, perhaps they would just dump it in the garbage piles under some underpass for the street dogs and kites to tear at and feast upon. It was a mental torture, a sleep deprivation that tipped me over the edge into mental breakdown. Opium withdrawals held my mind and body in its vice like grip and tortured me night and day. This was no monkey on my back, this felt like every demon from hell was feeding on my body and soul.

One night, in the early hours, I found myself lying in the gutter of Chandni Chowk outside the Jain temple. I knew I was dying; I was pathetically weak, throwing up, and choking on a hideous bile, the result of a poisoned body and soul and months of malnourishment and disease. It was not so much a gutter, more of an open sewer, fortunately for me the monsoon rains had been and gone. I lay in the filth and refuse of rotting food, dirt and dust, and the excrement of dogs and cows, powerless to move.

Feeling my life slip away, I raged inside. I began to curse – the bile and the bitterness pouring out, I cursed my family, my friends, my country, my whole life. Then as a good pagan does, I began to curse God, I cursed God as an impotent deity who was useless. I raged at some God who had never done anything to help me. I raged at this God I did not know, and then all my hate turned upon Jesus Christ. I realised in my heart and mind with a total clarity, that this Jesus I was cursing to hell, was good, that he was pure, that he was innocent and that he had been crucified.

People will so often say, in those moments when they have faced imminent death, that all your life flashes before you. For someone in such a powerless, feeble and wretched state, I experienced my life in its entirety, a vivid encompassing awareness of all I had ever done or been. In a moment, a millisecond, I knew that if anyone deserved to be crucified, it was me; I was ugly, I had become entirely selfish and self -absorbed, I hated and I stole, I abused, I had used violence and hatred to get my way. I saw all the evil I had done, all that I had destroyed, it was me who was evil. I knew I was the one who should have been hung to die. I didn't deserve this life. I lost consciousness.

In the morning light, it could have been heaven, it could have been hell, there was a cycle rickshaw almost parked on top of me. A young man, little more than a boy, pulled it away, helped me sit on the gutter's edge and motioned for me to stay. It was a done-deal, I could not move. He disappeared. Minutes later reappearing with a simple bowl of rice and dal, which he placed in my lap, it was the first food on a plate I had seen or eaten in many days, perhaps weeks. Then he gave me a beedi which he lit for me. The food and smoke began to warm me and soothe the pain.

He was watching me intently, concerned, I broke down and wept as I felt washed and bathed in a love I had never felt before. It seemed as if someone was looking down over me, watching over me. It broke open my feeble cold heart, it seemed all I had experienced in years was hatred, failure and breakdown in all my relationships, and here was this total stranger offering me the most ordinary help and love I could accept. In being handed this bowl of food, and a beedi, the cheapest cigarette you could buy anywhere in the world –

I encountered God, God as love. If I have ever heard God speak, then it was in those moments of initial clarity.

'Go home and love your family and your friends and everyone who I put in your path, because you have never loved anyone – not even yourself.'

My mind had given out. The realisation of my true state was finally sinking in, I could grasp the reality of my situation and its utter futility. I was lost without hope in a foreign land. Sooner or later I was going to die on these streets. Time was not on my side.

One day, I wandered across Delhi's maze of tangled streets and across the vast green manicured lawns that were laid out in the days of the 'Raj', vast and sprawling greens, a legacy of an opulent empire. In the furnace heat of midday, confused, frightened and broken, the only thing I had left, the only thing I owned in the world was the thin cotton longhi wrapped around my waist. A troop of loud and noisy women passed by. Two of them carried tablas and were drumming. One of them noticed me stretch out my hand and mumble a feeble,

'Baksheesh.'

She came back, with a few of her friends, and stooped down to look at me. They gathered around me, squatting in the dirt, their beautiful saris and choli, shawls and shalwar kameez a blaze of colour. Arms of bangles, nose and ear piercings, gold and silver and cheap metals, sparkling in the sun. These were no ordinary women, they were Hijra. I'd seen them before in my travels, from afar. The Hijra, a community of eunuchs. For four thousand years India has celebrated and feared those who were born intersex, or chose to live as eunuch. My soul ruptured as the truth hit home, here I was, face to face with women who were the embodiment of everything I had spent my life denying, running away from.

This was the reason I was dying, a junkie, an opium addict. I had been running away from myself, my feminine self, all my life.

She looked into my eyes, and all I could see were pools of light, love, flowing from her somewhere deep within. She had found and emanated a peace, a love, a joy. Rummaging in her bag, she pulled out a bag, and a small bottle of water. She smiled, stood and bowed gently, hands pressed together,

'Namaste.'

With that they turned and left me. She turned and looked back over her shoulder at me, before disappearing out of view into the teeming, heaving crowds. I opened the bag, some vegetable somoza. I opened the bottle and drank; water, the gift of life.

A couple of American Peace Corps workers found me as I was begging one day. Kindly they fed me, listened to me and heard me out. They realised my instability and explained to me how I could get 'repatriated' They placed me in a taxi and told the driver to take me to the British Embassy, and paid the man in full.

In the Embassy, that bastion of democracy and bureaucracy, before they could 'repatriate' me they had to identify me. They gave me forms with multiple pages to fill in. I sat there, frozen, mind numb. The shock of watching my own hand shaking uncontrollably, knowing I was incapable of even writing my own name, sent me into an even deeper spiral of despair and mental, emotional collapse. I had lost the most basic of motor skills; being able to write, even my own name.

I found myself outside the embassy gates shivering as the cold chill of night began to eat into my body. The Ghurkha guards who stood on the gates, and watched me from the warmth of their guard room, took pity on me. Two of them came out bringing gifts of a blanket, some cardboard boxes to sleep on, some trousers, a shirt and some flip flops. I think they gave me a meal and hot drinks too. There was a frost on the ground. Without their kindness I don't think I would have camped outside the Embassy gate. I would have wandered back into the city to die.

Next day, I went back into the Embassy and begged the Embassy staff to phone my parents. In tears I explained that I was too sick to even write my own name. I knew I was on 'borrowed time', and that the chances of me surviving any longer in the city were pretty much zero. The officials relented and gave me a verbal interview. They made a phone call to my father. They flew me home next day.

Winter 1981
An Apple, a Bible, Dog Crap, an Exorcism

Mum opened the front door, and looked at me, perplexed. I watched as the shock hit her forcibly, she gripped the door frame for a moment to steady herself. She was looking at a skeleton, a pale, hollowed out, deathly vision of her son. I was numb, half-dead, sick, exhausted and near collapse. Recovering herself, she stepped out and hugged me as I stood there, frozen to the spot, mute, stiff as a telegraph pole. My every muscle and sinew was screaming in pain. Instead of collapsing in her embrace, my body spasmed, nerve endings raw, being touched causing me to convulse in reaction. My mind was shattered unable to get any words out. Opium withdrawals had begun to rack me in a tortuous grip. I was crippled in the midst of a total mental, nervous and physical breakdown.

My bedroom had long been turned into a dumping ground for the family's rubbish. It hardly mattered, my mattress still sat on the floor, in the middle of the room. No one had ever expected me to come home again. John had left mum, was having an affair with someone else. My little brother now at Senior school. Mum had been made redundant from her work. She was struggling to hold things together and had been forced to sign on for benefits to survive.

It was winter. Days and nights rolled into one unbroken, never-ending nightmare. My body was trying to flush all the poison out. Waking frequently in the night, the sheets wet through, the mattress sodden, as I sweated out disease and toxins. My body craved relief, begging me for help, for medication. Abdominal cramps pulled me into a ball-like foetus, I whimpered and groaned. Me, who had once felt the master of pain, using my pain to make me faster on the bike, was now pleading for it to stop. Vomiting and diarrhoea hit me like a boxer's jabs and left me reeling, body slammed, crumpled on the floor.

The mental torture was no better. Nightmares rampaged, and when I was awake, I was hallucinating such terrors that they forced me to hide beneath the blankets. I was seeing sinister figures, clad in turbans and shalwar kameez, stood on the landing at the top of our stairs, as I attempted to get to the bathroom, they launched at me in a frenzied attack, slashing at me with their knives, I felt each stab, every cut, and knew I was about to die, bleed to death at their feet. I knew they were drug lords, come to collect their dues. I could not tell which were nightmares and which were hallucinations, I could not tell if I was awake or asleep, dead or alive.

When I wasn't so terrified that I was forced to vomit in a bowl by my bed, or have diarrhoea explode all over the sheets and my own body, I might actually make it to the bathroom, where slumped on the floor, clinging to the toilet bowl, my life drained away. Shivering and shaking, teeth rattling, my insides came out and I cried tears that felt like acid on my skin. This was the opium, finally exacting its toll. I knew it wanted my body and soul, it was the scythe of the grim reaper.

Gradually the fever and sweats began to abate, and my body was lulled into a false sense of hope. Then the spasms and convulsions began, they would hit me as if I were being electrocuted whilst strapped to the bed. It was like the epileptic fits I had once watched in horror, helpless, as a school friend writhed on the playground tarmac. These physical muscle contractions came in relentless waves, they were violent and bruising, leaving me washed out, wrung out, the hours of rest and peace I felt I had gained, suddenly flushed away.

My mother had initially tried to comfort me, tried to wipe the fever from my brow, but her touch and her presence only seemed to aggravate the intensity of the stabbing, ice cold pain that gripped my head. I cursed her and pushed her away angrily. It felt like someone had wrapped a crown of barbed wire around my brain, and was now pulling it, in sudden jerks and jabs, tighter and tighter. The barbs were piercing and breaking my skull, the poisoned tips biting into the soft exposed flesh of my brain. It was a physical, mental agony unlike anything I had ever known or could imagine. I was being tortured by my own addictions.

I was refusing any medication that my mother offered or suggested. Five years of drug abuse, and now I had made some kind of inner vow, and no amount of suffering could cause me to break it; I was never, ever, going to take drugs of any kind, ever again. The thought of even mild painkillers was anathema to me now. Not a rational, helpful resolve, given my current state, but I was not in any sane state of mind. I was frightened and fighting for my life and sanity, any drug, any drugs at all, seemed evil.

How many days and weeks had this been going on? Time passed too slowly, days came and went, and any sense of healing still seemed far off. Mum was running out of patience, and money. She was struggling to keep enough food on the table for the three of us, and pay the bills that John had saddled her with. She said I had to go and sign on, either that, or she would have to call in a doctor. She had been pleading with me for days, if not weeks, to see a doctor. She could see I was not just battling through withdrawals, but that my emaciated state was also due to whatever diseases I had caught or picked up in India. Both she and I, knew that I was physically and mentally ill beyond addiction and cold turkey.

Now she was insistent, she was going to call the doctor. I grabbed her by the wrists, shook her with all my feeble strength, and screamed into her face,

'You call a doctor, and I will kill you!'

She knew I meant it, or at least she knew I was unstable enough to be unsafe; neither rational, nor entirely in control of myself and what I was going through.

In my state of withdrawals and mental, nervous breakdown, hearing voices and having hallucinations, I knew that if a doctor were to see me, they would section me. It would mean the mental asylum for me. In the state I was in, the thought terrified me. I had no hope that I might ever get out. The thought of being incarcerated and drugged for the rest of my life terrified me. Beneath all my attempts to find peace and reconcile my warring soul, I still believed I was schizophrenic.

Mum's request for me to go into town, to sign on for benefits, was an impossibility. Paranoia was paralysing me. The thought of stepping out our front door, to catch a bus into town, filled me with a dread, a chaos of mental torments, that made me physically shake with fear. I was in the grip of severe agoraphobia. I did not know that the opium had broken down my nervous system, that the opium had attached itself to receptors in my brain, my limbic system and my spinal cord and guts. Neither did I know about the hepatitis and dry beriberi that was attacking my body and nervous system as well.

It was a bright winter's day; spring was trying to break through. I could feel the sun's warmth through the curtains. They had been tightly drawn each and every day since my

return. I could not bear the glaring light of day that burnt a hole straight through my retina, into the back of my brain. It felt like sunlight magnified to intensity through a magnifying glass, burning holes in the white paper of my mind, which threatened to burst, at any moment, into flame.

Today, I felt like I was well enough, brave enough, to face daylight. I pulled back the curtains, there, tucked back, in the far corner of the windowsill, was an apple. I must have left it there the spring before, on my last visit, only days before I had cleared out of my bedsit in Earls Court, and fled for India. The apple had lain there for a year, in a heat trap, between the glass and heavy curtains, drying out in a summer's heat. I picked it up, curious, intrigued at this shrivelled survivor.

Sat back down on my mattress on the floor, I leant back against the wall and soaked in the warm sunshine that flooded the room. I held the apple in the palm of my hands, it weighed nothing, dried out of all moisture and goodness. It was wrinkled, shrivelled up, like the shrunken heads made by Amazon tribes, that I'd once marvelled at as a kid in the Pitt-Rivers Museum. Eating it was out of the question, as food or nourishment it was both inedible and useless. I sat there, for the first time since the Himalaya, able to reflect and be still: the apple was speaking to me; I was looking at myself.

Five years of alcohol abuse and drug addiction had ripped my insides out. I was a waster, and wasted. I was useless, to myself, to my family, to society. Worse than that, was the realisation that I had become a destructive parasite. I'd given drugs to kids, believing I was doing them a favour. I had honestly believed that drugs were good; they helped you block out the pain and horror of life. I gave people drugs because I genuinely believed they helped. Looking back, I saw, now, with startling clarity, that all but one of the drug users I knew well, and that was many, came from broken homes, divorced parents and abusive families. They, like me, had been trying to escape and numb their pain.

What did I have to offer society? I had despised school,

and left with a poor bunch of O levels that I could count on one hand. I had never applied myself to study or work. I had skived and played truant, rebelled and been absent, even as I sat in classes. I was pretty much uneducated. What skills did I have other than an uncanny ability to avoid the police? I hadn't paid tax for a single-day's earnings, not a penny in the five years since running away. I had stolen, I had lied, I had beaten guys up, and abused every woman I thought I had loved. I was a dealer, a user, a user of drugs, a user of people.

I put the apple back in the centre of the windowsill. I couldn't, for the life of me, see a way out. The hopelessness was total, a crushing weight of guilt that pressed down heavy on me, stressing and suffocating me. I couldn't throw the apple away. Its presence on the windowsill somehow seemed to reassure me.

'I'm still here.'

My conscience was awakened.

I could always plant the apple in the garden and see what happened. Whatever happened I knew there was no quick fix, if there was a fix at all.

The first thing I had done, after sleeping for many hours, if not days, after I had fallen through the door, and onto the mattress on the floor, was to search for the Bible Paul had given me as a gift, to take on my travels. I had thrown it in disgust, somewhere into a corner of the room. I emptied out every box, their contents strewn across the floor as I searched, desperate to find the bloody book. There were piles of books everywhere. The Bible must have been thrown out. We were not, nor ever had been, a religious family. If anything we despised religion as a judgmental, outmoded, medieval way of life. Cycling was our religion as a family, it had always seemed a lot healthier, a lot more fun, and far more rewarding to body and soul.

Eventually, having cleared the contents of every box away, dripping in sweat, and exhausted I found the blasted book, buried underneath a pile of scrunched up clothes, on the floor at the back of my wardrobe. It was a small, pocket-sized Bible. A Gideons New Testament. I had no idea who Gideon was. It was light brown, tan coloured leather, soft bound and light as a feather, its words printed on paper thin as a Rizla, the print small, in long blocks of text.

From the moment I found it, I read it compulsively, through the screaming pain, fever and sweats. I read it whenever I was woken by nightmares. I read it between the hallucinations and the terror of paranoia that stalked me during the day. The stories grounded me, took me out of myself and into another time and place. I was looking for the Jesus and the God that I had seen, encountered and been touched by as I lay in the gutter on Chandni Chowk. I wanted to remake that connection with God, whoever, wherever, whatever they were. Jesus seemed to be a part, a missing piece in my jigsaw puzzle of dharma. The Bible seemed the best place to start.

I read through the gospels. I read the little book, over and over again. Especially the gospel according to John. I was mesmerised, beguiled by the beauty I saw in these stories. Jesus seemed altogether different to Siddhartha. The poignancy of these stories, the literacy, the humanity that oozed from this book touched me, impacted me and intrigued me.

I watched as Jesus placed himself between a crowd of religious bigots and a woman who had been caught in adultery. The crowd were ready to stone her to death. I couldn't relate to Jesus, but I related entirely, totally with this woman. I felt her fear, I knew her shame, I tasted her uncleanness like it was my own. She was me, and I was her.

That Jesus stood there to protect her, shield her from the stones and then turned the crowd away, revealed his heart to me. There was an earthed real humanity here that I'd never encountered in any other ancient literature or religious texts. I'd read the Bhagavad Gita, Greek myths, Buddha's teachings and the Dalai Lama's, but nothing had ever resonated quite like this.

When Jesus cast the seven evil spirits from Mary, sister of Martha and Lazarus, I understood her response, her gratitude. I knew the reality of her misery and torment. Everything was so real, so tangible, these characters felt closer to me than anyone I had ever known. Mary washed Jesus feet with her tears. I felt her relief and longed for it.

John had an insight into these women's lives that the other writers lacked, it was like they were his closest friends, like they'd told him everything. The account of Mary Magdalene at the tomb, in the garden, spoke to me. The desolation, the emptiness, the abandonment and despair. Her tears and her anguish. It seemed I knew these women, each one of them, intimately. I was them, and they were me. I was connecting, through time, with them. If I first saw Jesus, it was through their eyes.

Though I had followed Siddhartha and his teachings, I had found him a remote, detached and austere, ascetic figure. Jesus, by contrast seemed to pulsate with a compassion and humanity I could feel, that moved me, despite two thousand years and three thousand miles, between Galilee, him and me. I found myself kneeling at Jesus' feet, begging for forgiveness, hungry for his love. It struck me too, that I was caught in an utterly feminine devotion, a love, a response entirely suited to my soul.

I did not, could not, for a moment believe that Jesus was the Son of God, no matter how many times I read and reread the gospels and all the letters and tried to believe. He was, just like all the rest of us, a man. His humanity was all too easy to comprehend. He had dirt beneath his fingernails, and white rings of sweat beneath his armpits. He smelt of fresh sawn wood and the seaweed of fishing nets.

One weekend, in a spring that came early, mum took my brother away with her and her new boyfriend. The atmosphere in the house seemed to lighten and the tension, dissipate. I ventured downstairs and sat in the back garden, soaking up the sun. My agoraphobia and paranoia still paralysed me from leaving the front door, even for a short walk. I decided to cut the grass. Pushing the mower over the long grass, I felt myself slip. A stench assaulted my nose. I'd stepped in a dog turd!

Someone had left the side gate open again! I sat on the steps, and pulled off my shoe. It was caked, hideous, gross. I gagged. I pulled off my shoe, and poked and scraped at the foul congealed crap that clung tenaciously to the sole. It stank. I felt sick to the core. I grabbed an old scrubbing brush and put the shoe under the outside tap, flushing the last bits of crap away. The shoe, the only pair of shoes I had, was sodden and stank. I could not get rid of the foul smell, it clung to me.

My mission aborted, lawn mower slammed back in the garage, I sat down in the sun again, shoeless, frustrated, empty. The whole episode had drained me. I began to weep. The tears would not stop coming.

'God, I hate myself, I am a useless piece of stinking shit!

I'm no good for anything, I'm a waste of space on this planet, taking up valuable air.

I can't even leave the house, I've got nothing I can give to anyone, I can't even cut the grass for my mum!

I am that piece of dog shit stuck to your shoe, God, just let me die.

I want to go home, heaven, I'm ready, I'm done.'

☆

I must have gone back to bed, frightened and shaken, in the middle of a beautiful sunny morning. I woke up, feeling refreshed, I remembered the paint pots I'd had to move, angrily out the way, to get to the lawn mower that hung on the wall of the garage. I went to look in mum's sad bedroom. The walls were bare unpainted plaster.

I had come home last spring, upon hearing about John's adultery, I'd come home to beat his brains out with a pickaxe handle I had bought, specifically for that purpose. He had disappeared again. In frustration, I decided instead to do something more helpful, something that might cheer mum up. I'd started to redecorate her bedroom, but stripping off all the wallpaper was as far as I'd got. Probably the pub and someone needing to score had pulled me away.

Taking out the bed, removing the curtains, the cupboards and strewn clothes, rolling up the carpet, I washed, sanded and dusted everything down. I threw open the windows, for once glad of fresh air, and began to paint. Music was drifting in from somewhere, it was an awesome set of songs, all stuff I knew and loved, Johnny Cash, The Doors, Hendrix, the Stones; Sympathy for the Devil, it was freaking loud too.

I leaned out the window to try and work out where it was coming from.

It was all in my head! I tried to turn it off, but couldn't. I was freaked. It was just like all the other voices in my head, I could not turn them off. I was scared. I wanted the music, the noise, the voices to stop, but they wouldn't.

I screamed at the voices in my head, 'SHUT UP!' and banged my head in despair on the wall.

I picked myself up, fragile, shaking and sweating with fever and fear. I pushed myself through the pain barrier. Over the rest of the weekend I finished painting mum's bedroom. Carpet back down and strewn clothes in the washing machine. Freshly washed curtains rehung. It looked so nice. I was exhausted and wrung out, every fibre of my being ached and hurt from the effort, but for once, I felt good.

What I didn't know, was that mum, desperate and frightened after my threats to kill her, had gone to see our Christian neighbours across the road. She had sat on their sofa, broken down and wept, for once vulnerable, weak and helpless. They listened, loved her and prayed with her. They suggested,

'Why don't we ask the vicar to come and see Paul?'

Mum had seen me devouring the little Gideons Bible. She agreed.

Sunday evening mum and my brother are home in time for dinner. Boyfriend is with them. For the first time since coming back I venture to sit with them to eat. It's an uneasy meal, they can all see I'm still sick. He's a nice guy, gentle, kind, thoughtful, I hope it lasts. I'm too shattered to speak. I'm just waiting for mum to go to bed, to enjoy her new room. Just as I'm leaving, to climb the stairs, mum calls out,

'Oh, by the way, the vicar is coming to see you tomorrow afternoon.'

'*No way!*', I think to myself, when was the last time we ever saw a vicar?

Like, never.

The vicar was a weedy little man, an intellectual, with no real physical presence, and a timid manner. A nervous smile in a dull grey suit, pale blue shirt and the ubiquitous dog collar. With no chairs in my room, he sat down awkwardly on the end of my mattress, whilst I sat, still tucked in the sheets at the other. His presence provoked the silent seething white hot rage inside me. He was everything I detested about religion and the religious. He seemed to find it painful talking to me, but at least he didn't do small talk, and for that I was glad.

He looked over his square wire-rimmed glasses at me. We talked about my past. I was honest to a fault. We talked about India, he asked me a few questions, poking about in my experiences.

I couldn't help but notice, his hands were shaking, and the cup of tea he was delicately holding, was rattling against the bone china saucer. It could have been a parody, except neither us saw anything remotely funny. I got the clear, distinct impression he was more than nervous, not of me, but of something he was experiencing. It was a short interview. My anger had abated a little, and I had actually warmed to him a bit.

'Are you serious about following Jesus.' That was all he said.

The question hung in the air, appearing to echo around the empty room. It was a good question. The right question, in fact it was about the only question I'd been asking myself for weeks.

'If I ever get out of here alive, following Jesus is the only thing I want to do with the rest of my life!'

I heard the words come out my mouth before my brain had a chance to think things through. Here I was confessing faith to a vicar?! His next words hit me like a Viking's axe blow to my brain.

'You need an exorcism.'

He said it quietly, matter of fact, like he did one every day after first enjoying a leisurely breakfast. I was stunned, shocked. Clearly, I had underestimated the man. I'd never been into anything that I would call remotely occult. Such things held no interest to me whatsoever. I detested things like horror films. I wouldn't watch a film like *The Exorcist* if you paid me big cash in advance. I had no comprehension of anything to do with witchcraft.

He was reading my shock and incomprehension.

'You've emptied your life of everything, and it's been

filled with destruction. You are tormented and oppressed, aren't you?'

It wasn't an accusation. It was a question of compassion and authority, that much I could discern.

'If you are serious about following Jesus, come down to the vicarage on Friday, and my wife and I, and another minister from town, will pray for you. First, we need to fast and pray for three days.'

For the first time, he smiled, relieved. He'd discharged what he felt was his duty. It was up to me now, how I chose to live. Clearly, he had known beforehand what was needed and had planned it all out. He stood up to leave, I stood up and shook his hand. It was the start of a most unlikely friendship.

'I'll see you Friday,' was all I heard myself say.

I sat down, totally perplexed, but I knew too, that the next chapter of my life had just begun. Mary, out of whom Jesus had cast seven evil spirits was much on my mind for the rest of that week. I read of the man who lived in a cave and cut himself with stones, of how his rage even broke the chains the villagers tried to bind him with. The Gadarene Demoniac they called him; Legion. I could relate, only too well. Jesus had healed them both.

Friday came and went.

The walk to the vicarage was hell. Stepping out the door, I had voices in my head, screaming at me, telling me to kill myself. My body felt like it weighed two elephants, each step seemed to take every ounce of my feeble strength, like I had concrete boots and was drowning in quicksand. It was bitterly cold, and the autumn leaves still fell from skeletal trees and got blown from corners where they had settled, driven by an icy gale that swirled them around my feet. I shivered and sweated, the fevers and toxins still creeping from my skin. Paranoia jangled my nerves. The worst thing was that my mind was scrambled, like whisked eggs. I had not stepped into the world for weeks. I read car number plates and saw conspiracies to kill me. I felt like I was being watched, followed. I felt haunted, spooked. It was barely a mile to the vicarage, but it took forever.

As I approached the motorway bridge, just above the church, the voices in my head reached a deafening crescendo,

'What's the point?'

'You are a loser.'

'I am nothing but a piece of shit stuck to your shoe, God.'

'Kill yourself!'

'I'm worthless.'

'Kill yourself!'

'I'm worthless.'

'Kill yourself!'

Sweat poured from me. I was using every part of my being, all the strength I had left in me, to stay on the pavement and not throw myself into the thundering motorway traffic.

I found myself at the vicarage. We went into what looked like a study. Books and books and books. Religious icons, a cross. The three of them prayed for me. I felt not a thing, I saw nothing, heard nothing. I can't remember a thing, except there was none of the shouting I had imagined and expected, just a total blank, numb, emptiness.

Next thing I know, I'm out the door and walking home. Raging. I feel cheated, conned, sold a lie. Nothing had happened, nothing at all. I felt the despair, the loneliness – flooding in again. I cried; salty tears of despair and hopelessness streamed down my face. I wiped the snot away and the hanky was full before I'd even got up the hill. The expectations I'd had of Jesus touching me, healing me and filling me with his love, and the disappointment was too much for me. I had said not a word to mum, other than I was going for a talk with the vicar. I sneaked up the stairs and fell asleep, exhausted, feeling like a wet towel that's been wrung through a mangle.

All he had said was, 'Rest up, eat and sleep well. Pray, read your Bible and pray. Come to church on Sunday.'

1982
I Got Religion

Sunday morning, I woke with a sense of dread. I was not looking forward to church. I had no desire to become part of the Sunday parade. I did not want to become a Christian and shoulder the label, or take part in a religion that has oppressed and killed millions, either directly or by being complicit in colonialism. All I wanted was to know Jesus, follow him. His teaching was so simple, so easy to understand.

If anything, the walk to church was harder than Friday's had been, the voices in my head louder. I wanted to end it all, stop the pain, the torture and torment in my body and mind. The voices were screaming at me again. I was crushed. On a cold wintery day, I found myself walking up the path to the church doors, sweat pouring from me, I couldn't remember the walk there. I had got past the motorway, but I couldn't remember how? I was totally exhausted, physically spent and emotionally wrung out.

The door was still open and song flowed out. I was late. A man in an expensively cut suit shook my hand too firmly and ushered me in. A woman in smart clothes pointed me to a space in the pews between two elderly ladies. Everyone was standing for the hymn. I sat down shaking, empty, I had no strength left. The church was packed, heaving, old people, young people, families. The two balconies either side were equally rammed. Everyone looked smart, wealthy, together. Everyone was white, middle class. I felt conspicuous in my torn filthy jeans, ripped second world war fur bomber jacket, stubble and dirty shoes.

'Junkie at a wedding.' I thought to myself.

The hymn stopped. The two elderly ladies sat down stiffly on either side of me. The vicar was in the pulpit, six feet up. He leant on the lectern, a huge eagle, made of poor man's gold, its wings outstretched, its huge claws clasped around the globe, a symbol of the Nazi Third Reich, of the Holy Roman Empire, of Napoleon's armies.

'What on earth was that doing in a church?!'

A huge Bible sat on the back of this symbol of Empire. The vicar was dressed in a long white flowing robe over a black cassock, his dog collar shining white beneath his bobbing Adam's apple. There were notices, tea rotas, home groups and Bible studies announced. More hymns, stand up, sit down, stand up, sit down. Someone read a passage from the Bible. The vicar began to preach, he was learned, clever, passionate and compassionate.

Next thing I knew, I was crumpled on my knees, wedged on the floor between two old ladies. I was weeping, snot pouring from my nose, my eyes were pouring, torrents of warm, salty tears. I felt washed in a warm, liquid love. It was pouring, flooding into me. The vicar was in full flight now as he led the church through his text. One of the little old ladies, complete with blue rinse, gave me her handkerchief. She placed a reassuring hand on my shoulder. I had no real idea what the sermon was about.

There was more stand up, sit down, stand up. I sat through it all. I was broken, lost, in love. Love like I had never known or felt before. My whole being was washed and bathed in love. The service ended, noise erupted as people moved around and chatted excitedly with each other. I didn't want to talk to anyone, I just wanted to run. The vicar stood at the door, chatting kindly with his elderly parishioners, addressing each one by name. I shuffled behind in the queue to escape. He shook my hand warmly, smiled and looked straight into my eyes. Compassion and kindness impressed upon me.

I walked home, oblivious to the cold. I felt light as a feather, almost like I was floating. I noticed how beautiful and blue the sky was. I heard the birds, chitter chattering in the hedges. I said hello to people as we passed by. It was too early for lunch, so I walked past our road and out to the fields that looked down on the river valley below. I sat my back against a tree and thanked God I was alive. I didn't really know what had happened, but I think I had just met Jesus?! My agoraphobia was gone.

Every Sunday I experienced the same battle getting to church, but gradually it abated, it got easier. The strangeness of church remained. The alienation I felt, socially, culturally and personally remained. Each week, I would sit myself next to Audrey, who had first offered me her hanky. She was a rock, familiar, safe, kind and gentle, and always welcoming.

The vicar was leading the church through the letters to the churches; Romans, Corinthians, Galatians and Ephesians. Every week the same thing happened, as he preached, I was overcome, overwhelmed and floored by this love. Love that I can only assume was coming direct from God. Each week I found myself crumpled on the floor, wedged between Audrey and her friend, being washed by a divine love as I wept. I could feel love flowing through me. I was bringing my own supply of tissues. It appeared I was the only person in church going through this strange process, I had no control over the love that poured through my whole being, mentally, physically and emotionally, Pure love. I'd never experienced anything like it, ever. No orgasm, no high, no love relationship came close. Everyone else sat there, emotionless, ramrod straight and listened, or dozed, or daydreamed away, just as I had done at school.

It was a strange place. Sometimes when the church sang, it sounded like a dirge, like people had no heart to sing, like they were bored and dreaming of their Sunday roast. The vicar would stop the congregation, mid verse and rebuke them. He'd ask them if they were glad to be alive? If they were in fact, grateful for anything in their lives? I liked him a lot. I liked his attitude and style, despite the robes and priestly airs. I still remember, forty years on, many of his throw away lines,

'Sliding down the razor blade of life.'

'Fridge full, Jag on the drive, foreign holidays.' And I heard Marley singing, even as the vicar spoke that phrase. Well, well, well. A vicar singing from Marley's hymn sheet?!

'You can't take it with you, what do you really want to leave behind, a fat bank balance? What will your legacy to this world be?'

'Love is the only currency of the Kingdom of Heaven!'

He seemed to despise mammon and materialism almost as much as the Rastas did.

We met up over a cup of tea once a week to talk about whatever I was needing to talk about. He appeared to know more than the doctors about addiction, rehabilitation, about the brain and body and all the practical things I needed to be doing. He felt like a friend I could trust in. I asked him about the exorcism.

'These things we call demons, evil spirits, these deep "disturbances", these "shadows" in our psyche, are being gradually driven – starved out, as we heal. It is perfect love that sets us free. Nothing and no one else but God can provide such perfect love – that is what you are tasting each week – it has nothing to do with me. You have been searching, hungering and thirsting for the truth for so many years, maybe you have an advantage over us all. We are all content, well fed and satisfied?'

The voices, agoraphobia and paranoia had gently receded. I got to the doctor, who referred me to the hospital and the Ward for Tropical Diseases. I had hepatitis and beriberi. I needed to restore some strength, health, fitness into my life. I couldn't afford to buy a bike with the dole money I was forced to claim, so I bought the best pair of running shoes I could afford and two pairs of running shorts.

I was getting drunk, not with alcohol, but on sunsets, clear starry nights, birdsong, walking alone through the woods. It was as if a grey suffocating smog had cleared from my mind and vision. Colours seemed more vibrant, alive and beautiful. The clouds in the sky enthralling, the cold, the rain and the wind didn't seem to bother me anymore, they just made me feel more alive. I could see the miraculous nature of our existence, clinging to this spinning globe floating through space – everything was wonderful, bursting with life. The vision of innocence I had enjoyed as a child had been restored, but it was deeper than my childhood experience, there was a soaring, exhilarating freedom within me. You watch a child run, for the sheer joy that they can, for no reason, no purpose, other than to feel their heart beating, lungs pumping and that childish sense when you almost feel like you are flying. That kid was me.

By the summer I was running every day but Sunday. I had several regular road circuits, just short of eight miles, which I ran most days. The weather made no difference, cold rainy days I would savour, not in a punishing way as I once had with my cycling, but with the simple joy and gratitude of being alive. I'd feel the rain on my skin and forehead, I'd stick my tongue out and drink it in. I was alive again, reconnecting with the world of nature around me.

I had bad days, bleak days, difficult days. I felt an alien and a stranger in church. I still longed to die, 'to go home', to be in heaven and have this mess of a life over and done with. I could not see the point in me living, I had nothing to offer anyone and felt weary, broken and cynical of the world, beyond any mere words. It was a weariness of soul that church could not shift, no matter how hard they sang, or how many Sunday lunches I was invited to. If anything, the Sunday lunches and normalness of it all only served to emphasise my hopelessness and otherness all the more – that I did not belong.

Some missionaries from the Bible translation school nearby asked me to their home group at Audrey's house. Audrey was wonderful, she was sixty, widowed, and still dressed beautifully. She cared, in a good way about her appearance. Always sassy, her make-up impeccable. Her honesty and attitude were like, 'Cut the crap!', though she would never dream of saying that, not publicly at least. I loved her. She was elegant, yet she clearly had a working class rooted sensibility that I identified with. I loved this group of missionaries who rooted their faith in social justice, health programmes and fighting for the rights of indigenous and oppressed peoples. They introduced me to liberation theology. From my experience and perspective, it made perfect sense. It seemed a lot like the Jesus I knew.

Mum divorced. The house was sold; it had never felt like home for me. She moved with my brother, to be closer to her partner. I had no reason to move with them. Our relationship had healed a lot as I tried to put things right from my side. I apologised for the years of hell I had put her through, but our relationship still seemed fragile and strained. Sorry – so often an empty word. I did not know how I could ever recompense her for the suffering I had caused her in all my years of rebellion and hate.

Audrey was renting out a room, board and lodgings. Immediately I moved in, all my femininity was stirred. Living with a woman, brought everything in me to the surface, my own feminine nature was too real, too undeniable, and it hurt. It had been the least of my worries through my breakdown and withdrawals, but now the reality of who I was, tormented me with a vengeance. Now it hit me forcibly, how split, divided and broken my personality was. I had come to see it was just that, not schizophrenia, as I had feared since my teens. The self-hatred intensified again. This feminine self would not die.

We would sit and chat for hours in the evenings. She was totally relaxed with me and poured out her heart, her thoughts and feelings, fears and hopes, with not a shred of vulnerability. I had never known such transparent honesty. She spoke about female problems as if I was her closest female friend. It was as if she knew exactly who I was, yet I never shared a word of the war within my soul. I felt so at home in this dialogue of feminine vulnerabilities, my male mask dropped as we shared and prayed for one another. No barrier of age or gender. I'd never had a friend like this before.

My experience with male friends, was one were we lived and spoke about only our external world, our 'doing', our 'things', our lives, but only in a surface manner, as if sharing our inner world, our thoughts and feelings, our weaknesses and vulnerabilities was a taboo. I came to realise that most men did not have a vocabulary to share their innermost lives. Male identity was predicated upon strength – weakness, sensitivity and vulnerability seemed to be despised, unknown.

Living with Audrey opened my eyes to my own feminine traits; tenderness, gentleness, sensitivities and desires. I could swear Audrey and I were relating more as sisters, than as an older woman and a young man. All of which left me feeling wretched again. This feminine soul wanted to breathe, to express itself, to live, as I did with Audrey, relaxed, myself, no mask or pretence. I didn't know that this was the intimacy that Jesus desired for us all to enjoy; no masks, no fears, no pretence.

☆

David phoned me one day. He thought he might have found me a job. Intrigued I walked down to the vicarage to see him. I was troubled and he knew it. I poured out my heart, my lifelong struggles with dressing and presenting as female. He opened his Bible and read:

'If any man wears a woman's clothes, or any woman wears a man's clothes, they are detestable to God.'

Deuteronomy 22:5.

No qualification, no explanation. It confirmed my worst fears. I was unworthy of love, I was sick, I was worthless to God, I was detestable to Him. It wasn't that I wanted to wear women's clothes, that I knew, was only an outward expression of who I was. Beneath this ugly macho mask, I was intrinsically, inherently feminine, in nature and outlook, feelings and thoughts, I was a feminine soul. Life had brutalised me into adopting this empty aggressive male shell, this charade, a suit of armour, a defence against a world of hate. The Bible left me with no choice than to kneel down and beg God to heal me, to make me whole, to make me a man.

He explained it was a deviant behaviour, a pagan practice which was all part of worshipping the pagan gods of Ashtaroth and Baal. He explained the centrality of the lingam, the phallus and sacrificing to these gods. It was at source, demonic, he told me. I needed to repent, and seek God – it was a form of sexual idolatry from which I could be freed. There were only two sexes, and to mess with sexual identity was to break the created order of God. It was a rebellion, just like Satan had rebelled against God in heaven – and been thrown out, cut off from the presence of God forever.

I knelt and prayed, asked God for forgiveness, and begged God again to heal me. Once again David prayed evil spirits out of my life, I didn't know what they were. He spoke forgiveness over me, prayed for me and gave me a warm hug. I left feeling utterly undone, broken and helpless.

I was in recovery and withdrawals, still recovering from the total breakdown, my mental health was fragile. I was a very vulnerable young adult. I left, feeling sick to the core. I had even less cause to want to live, I was detestable to God.

David had given me a Bible, and now as I struggled through the Old Testament, I found a very different God: capricious, angry, vengeful, vindictive. A God who sent plagues, struck people down, a God who commanded genocide and demanded child sacrifice, so different from the God that Jesus claimed to be in my Gideon's New Testament, the gospels I had come to love and had almost memorised. Was it the same God? I was in love with Jesus. I had determined to follow Jesus, as best I could, and the Bible was my guide to getting to know him. Jesus, I got, and fully understood, but the God of the Old Testament was a tyrant.

I was still battling suicidal thoughts, feelings of worthlessness, and the crippling nature of my gender conflict. Only months into church life, I experienced a total existential crisis of faith. It was triggered by one verse:

'I have been crucified with Christ, and I no longer live. The life I now live, I live by faith in Jesus, who loves me and gave himself for me, and Christ lives in me.'

Galatians 2:20

I knew my old life was over, my old ways, my old self, yes, I was more than happy to say goodbye to my sin and ugliness, I could accept that in some strange metaphysical, mystical and real way, that it had died with Jesus, on the cross. My despair was that I had no evidence that Christ was living in me. I was totally overwhelmed by this lack. It was a daily battle to put the old me to death, in the hope of experiencing a resurrection life. My hunger and thirst, my desire to know this risen Christ, living in me, was insatiable.

Nowhere did I try harder, than in the area of my

sexuality, my gender, my core identity, to crucify myself. My feelings never changed, but I came to see that I was a junkie through and through, dependent totally upon my senses, my feelings and my moods.

I took a leap of faith, and chose to accept the truth that Christ did indeed live in me, whether I felt it or not, and I would let him, and the Holy Spirit transform my life by their grace. It felt like a sudden growing up, a being set free from the tyranny of both my unstable emotions and the pain of my body and identity.

That one verse became the bedrock of my faith. My one desire was to know Christ, living in me. There was nothing in myself that I felt I could trust. I was a totally broken person with the emotional maturity of a child. I entrusted Jesus with my whole life, picked up my cross, and set after him. All I had to do was put this feminine part of me to death, crucify it.

David gave me an advert for the post of a graphic designer in a Christian publishers. He thought it would be a good environment for me to grow and heal in. I started work there a month later. Life in the office was boring as hell. I never really enjoyed the job, but I was trapped by my debts. I owed thousands in the unpaid taxes I had confessed, and two huge bank overdrafts hung over me from before my running away to India. I so wanted to repay my debts to society that I even declared the income of my dealing to the taxman, listed as income from 'other sources'.

1983
The Kingdom of Heaven

The coach station was a grim, grey, diesel polluted basement of the shopping precinct and multi-storey car park. Dossers slept there at night; alcoholics, the homeless and beggars scrounged all day. The place depressed me. It was a subterranean suffocating stinking hole of a station. One morning, having overslept, I had missed my connecting bus. I stepped out into the sunlight, I was angry, fed up and discouraged, I would be late for work yet again, maybe by hours, I'd have to hitch hike, I was totally stressed and wound up.

A body landed on the pavement in front of me, it was a sickening thud that went right through me. A young girl. She had jumped or fallen from the multi-storey directly above me. I watched in horror as her body twitched, blood pouring from the skull and broken face. The place was crowded, rush hour. People came running, others backed away and watched from a distance. A couple of people pushed through the gathering crowd.

'I'm a doctor.' I heard someone say.

I turned and walked away. Kneeling on the grass, I threw up, and began to sob. I remember little else of that day, or days, or weeks. It took a long time to find any composure, any peace. I was alive, but numbed, going through the motions.

Memories of a girl I had unsuccessfully tried to date in London came flooding back; we used to ride the same bus to work together. She had attempted suicide. Whilst I had been in India, she had set fire to herself, and had lain for weeks in hospital. On release, she did it again and succeeded in ending her life. Her death had shaken me deeply, she had been someone I loved, if only from a distance. All this needless death.

One day I was reading my Bible, praying for answers, praying for some hope.

> *'Offer your body and soul as a living sacrifice, this is your pleasing and acceptable worship to God. Be transformed by the renewing of your mind, that you might know the mind of Christ.'*

> Romans 12:1

The words hit me with a force, I determined every time I thought about suicide, I was now going to offer myself to God, as a *living* sacrifice. I wanted to follow Jesus, I wanted with all my heart to be one of Jesus disciples, to reflect him to the world. I didn't want to be yet another tragic statistic, I wanted to live. Nor did I want to be one of the fickle crowd of believers, who cried 'Hallelujah' one moment, and 'Crucify', the next, nor did I want to live my life as pew fodder.

For the first time in my life I had found a purpose and a reason to live; an unselfish purpose, something good, something healthy and life-giving. The young girl who had died at my feet had turned my heart inside out; my heart cry changed from a longing for death, to a desire to live, a longing to save life and not take it. She had ripped my heart wide open, with an ache, with a longing to save such lives.

> *'Come follow me and I will make you a fisherman of souls.'*

> Matthew 4:19

A young woman came and went at church, she breezed in, a wild, irreverent and fun-loving girl. Sarah and I got on like a house on fire and started dating. She was Ruth's sister, the previous vicar's daughter. My friend Paul had gone out with Ruth and been adopted into their family. Dennis had the most incredible white hair, not grey, not even silver, but pure white?!

At that Christmas Midnight service only a year or so ago, in that brief encounter he had seen the fullness of my hate and despair, he had seen a very lost young soul. Dennis had prayed me safely through a very real hell. He had never even met me, or spoken to me, yet I discovered he had prayed for me throughout my whole time in India, as if I were one of his own children. He had prayed for me when others had said I was beyond hope. His love was the faithful, long suffering kind. He was a warrior, a man's man, a soul winner. I had not dragged him down with me, but he had loved me into heaven. It was a no contest really.

Going out with Sarah, I got to see Dennis nearly every weekend. He was one of life's giants, a character who shone, burnt bright and demonstrated so clearly how to love, in a world full of small men and haters like me. Dennis, more than anyone, set my feet upon the path of discipleship. He gave me a tangible example of how to live my life, how to love and treat people. Being around Dennis had enabled me to see Jesus, in the flesh, but he was no religious vicar, he was one of the funniest, best humoured men I have ever met. He had that magical ability of being able to lift everyone up. Dennis was my spiritual father, he oozed positive energy, life – the Holy Spirit.

The phone rang, it was an old cycling friend, he told me that one of my racing buddies and long-time rival, Tony, lay in Stoke Mandeville hospital, paralysed from the waist down. Someone had flicked him whilst racing on the oval track at Reading. Tony was a natural and prodigious talent, we had been good friends, and I loved his warm, easy going, fun loving character.

I used my first wages to buy an old car. It made getting to work easy. It meant I could see friends. I felt less trapped. More importantly I could visit Tony in hospital, and Sarah after work and at weekends. Visiting Tony in hospital was heart breaking. It was quickly obvious that there was little chance of any recovery for him. His back had been broken, snapped by the force of his landing, his spinal cord damaged too severely. It meant spending the rest of his life in a wheelchair, with all the consequences and restrictions of disability. I have never felt so useless in my life as I did, sitting with Tony those evenings he was in hospital, struggling, wrestling, coming to terms with what lay before him. He was locked in a total despair. I would drive home in the dark, weeping. I prayed and prayed and prayed, but all I ever felt was his devasting loss of freedom and choice. I tried my best to cheer him, but I felt beyond out of my depth, I couldn't find the words to say, I just sat and listened.

One night as I was climbing into the car after another evening with Tony, I heard a voice call over – it was a guy sat in a motorised wheelchair. I walked over to say hello and see what he wanted. I reached out to shake his hand.

His hands were claw-like, withered and useless, his fingers bent and twisted. We couldn't shake hands. I felt ashamed, I hadn't noticed how disabled he was.

'My name's John, come on in.'

He flicked at the knobs on the arms of the chair, span it round and retired through his bedroom doors. John was another hippie. He still wore his hair long, over his shoulders. He had gotten high one summer's day, and dived off Folly Bridge in Oxford, into the river. His back had broken in several places, only the quick actions of friends saved him from drowning. In the darkest days of his recovery, he had an encounter with Jesus, not unlike mine in the gutter in Delhi.

We quickly hit it off and became close friends. I shared my feelings of despair about Tony with him. He suggested that I come and pray with him, before and after going to see Tony. It meant less time with Tony, but I figured prayer could do no harm. I did not understand prayer, or pretend to, but I enjoyed prayer, I had got used to 'talking to God', even if it felt like God wasn't always listening. John and I began to pray for Tony, to feel a little of his pain and hopelessness, his anger and frustration. Both John and I were in lament, we petitioned God to lift Tony's spirits, to brighten his days, to give him something to live for, to bring him hope. Tears would roll down our faces. Love does strange things to you.

My times with Tony seemed much easier, and he seemed a little brighter, his humour began to flicker again. We even joked about old times. We chatted about my time in India. He grew less bitter and more philosophical about his future. Maybe, one day they would find a way to make the paralysed walk again. My faith felt puny in Tony's presence, but my self-centred, hard heart was being softened.

John was paraplegic, paralysed in all four limbs, he had no use in his lower body or legs and only partial use of his arms. He was fully and wholly dependent upon nurses, carers and friends. I marvelled that he even had a faith in God. That he could laugh about himself, his accident and his disabilities, was beyond me. John radiated love and peace. Sure, he too had his bad days, and they were bad, but generally and consistently he exuded love and encouragement. I could see Jesus in him, in his character and in his longsuffering, he always tried to put the needs of others before his own. He was one of those precious souls like Dennis who always lifted others up. He encouraged, loved and prayed for me.

Many evenings, after sitting with Tony till visiting time was over, I spent with John and we would pray for hours. He would pray for me in wave after wave of petition and prayer. I have never felt so challenged, in my character and feebleness of spirit, as I did in those times with John. He led me into a much deeper, more intimate relationship with God. It would often be gone midnight before I got home.

John frequently got sick, with stomach troubles, diarrhoea and the like, and I would clean him up. At first, I squirmed inside, at cleaning up the mess, on his wheelchair, or bed sheets, his legs and backside, and John felt my struggle, and he felt bad too. I began to realise, we were in it together, this was what life was all about, about loving one another, not a feeling, but practical, servant hearted love. Jesus was speaking to me, loud and clear,

'I am the servant of all, if you follow me, this is the path I will always take, to serve the least, the last, the weak and the sick, the poor and hungry.'

It was a downward mobility I understood. Love is the only valid currency of heaven.

Then the penny dropped, Heaven wasn't any pie in the sky. Heaven wasn't for 'then' – when we die. Heaven was something God wanted us, me, to live in, in the here and now. God wanted me to taste and know Heaven now, to feel it inside and to share it with everyone ... I was dumbfounded, gobsmacked, bowled over ... Heaven is for now! That's what Jesus had been demonstrating and saying to me all along:

'I LOVE YOU! The Kingdom of Heaven is within you – now go out and share it – Just love people, that's all you have to do.'

What John had been trying to show me, explain to me, pray into my heart and life for months, something I just couldn't see or grasp, had become a reality within me. I saw now how it was the source of John's love, strength, joy and hope.

Sarah and I split up. I clearly wasn't ready for a relationship. I moved to the town where I was working. It was a huge relief to leave the Anglican church behind, with its rigid religion, ruled more by tradition than Jesus' teaching, as far as I could see.

Someone from work invited me to their church. The church met in a school on a council estate, and that in itself was refreshing to me. It was actively seeking to be an integral part of the community, not set apart, holy-like – behind four walls. All my life I felt working-class, uneducated, inferior, looked down on, and my experience of Christianity and Christians just compounded those feelings. In this church I felt at home, accepted, loved.

Church became my family. We shared a rich communal life, our worship times pulsated with energy and love. It was freeing and liberating to be able to get lost in wonder with God in the worship, and not have to endure the desperate control of the stand-up, sit down, stand-up routine. I babysat for families, helped out with people's homes and chores. We helped each other, and those in the community, particularly the poor on the council estates, with food parcels, furniture, carpets and decorating homes, practical caring everyday kindnesses set it apart. They gave me a hope and a vision of what church can be. I loved the people who made up this rag-tag church.

The church grew rapidly, not just with the well booted and suited, but working-class families from the local council estates. We were multi-racial, which in this small rural town was rare; deep friendships transcended the class divide, both were a big win for me, the church felt earthed, rooted in healthy, if at times painful, relationships of honesty. There was no religious veneer, it was refreshing and inspiring.

For two years I was absorbed in a rich community life that felt like my home, I had a sense of belonging and fulfilment, even happiness. We had grown so fast that the Pastor felt it wise to affiliate with a large American denomination who were overseeing several local churches. That summer we dug deep and paid for the Pastor and his entire family to go to the parent church in America for the summer holidays – a sabbatical.

1983

On the Pastor's return, one of the elders accused my closest friends, Bruce and Jo, of trying to take over the church in his absence. It could not have been further from the truth, but the Pastor swallowed the bait, and within days the church was plunged into bitter acrimonious accusations. I stood up and called out the lie in a church meeting. The entire church was instructed to have nothing to do with either my friends, or myself. We were put out in the cold, like heretics or the unclean – excommunicated, I think they call it. The entire church, bar one, turned their backs on me and never spoke to me again. This was my welcome to Christianity.

It was a crushing blow that sent me spinning into despair and depression. I had, to the best of my knowledge and integrity, stood up for love, truth and honesty. For that, church had cast me aside. My faith imploded. Life lost all direction and meaning. I sank back into drink, smoking and the battle to control my feminine self was lost. I went out and bought clothes and make-up, and began secretly to dress and go out as female again. The feminine self I had tried to crucify was still more a part of me than I had ever comprehended, I gave up fighting it, I went to the doctor to ask if I could be considered for a 'sex change', but I was in no fit state to even begin the process. She considered my mental health to be too vulnerable, I was offered pills for depression instead.

My faith would not let go entirely. Through all this I studied and read voraciously. Church history, ancient and modern, theology and mission. I kept up to date with contemporary Christian news across a wide spectrum of the church. I was desperately searching for evidence of Jesus in the weird religion I'd landed in.

Pik Botha, the devout Christian President of South Africa, hit the headlines. He had just thrown the black Archbishop Desmond Tutu into jail. Nelson Mandela had been languishing in jail for two decades. The church in the west was largely politically silent as the townships erupted into riot and Christian policemen killed black Christian youths. An Anglican minister, Trevor Huddleston was one of the most outspoken and active critics of apartheid. Huddleston's book lay by my bed, as Peter Gabriel sang his protest song, 'Biko' through my headphones. I wept, I had no words, only tears to offer God.

The white Christians in South African were now exposed in a global spotlight, they either supported the injustice of apartheid, or they denounced and fought against it. Silence was not an option, it meant complicity. As Martin Luther King had said: 'It's not the words of our enemies we will remember, but the silence of our friends.'

Botha's church, the Dutch Reformed Church actually taught and preached apartheid, they had created a 'biblical' theology to justify it, just as the Southern Baptists had taught and preached a theology to defend slavery and uphold segregation. Christianity was one sick and perverse religion.

AIDS was now claiming thousands upon thousands of lives. I listened in disbelief as American TV evangelists proclaimed AIDS to be the wrath of God against gays. These same millionaire evangelists who preached, 'Come to Christ and all will be well' were getting caught in adultery, or with rent boys, as they criss-crossed the world in their private jets. Prosperity gospel had seeped into almost every church. 'Live righteous and God will bless you with wealth.' I was sickened to the core of my being by Christianity.

Thatcher was waging war on the mining communities at this time, closing mines and offering nothing in their place. The miners protested. Thatcher's oppressive policies had triggered more race riots, whilst she posed for photo opportunities outside her local church. The poverty of the mining communities and their destruction cut deep.

I had come into the church as someone who identified with black, rather than white, with working class rather than middle. I knew deep down I was 'other', a kind of other that the church feared, hated and oppressed, and it seemed pretty clear, church did not want me. I wanted to belong to a church that was healthy, wholesome, attractive, that lived the life of simplicity and compassion, a life that reflected Jesus. I wanted to belong to a church that gave it all away. Instead what I saw was Christians, clinging to power and their right to judge, clinging to wealth. Christians often seemed more pre-occupied with material wealth and living standards than their humanist neighbours, and far less radical, they reflected their culture as much as they ever reflected Jesus to me.

'Love justice, be merciful, walk humbly before your God.'

It seemed to me as if the Church was involved in a continual never-ending expensive 'make over' to hide its hideous past. No one in church ever spoke of its evil history, of its blood-stained past, even in whispers. It lived with a blind, blinkered revisionist history. The history of a white victorious Jesus; The Conquering King, the white saviour syndrome was all too real, tangible. It felt to me like they were trying to deny vital truths, sweep them under a carpet of collective amnesia, when these very issues were the keys and roots of their integrity and standing in the world. The politics and power play of the world was so obvious in everything about church, from its hierarchies and denial, to its posturing, preaching and judgements. Judgements over blacks, women, gays, and me. Where was the suffering servant, the outspoken prophet, the one who stood and identified with the oppressed and marginalised?

'Christian' was a label which from the beginning, I was ashamed of, and deeply uncomfortable with, as un-natural to me as wearing a suit and tie. Christianity was synonymous with oppression in my eyes.

So, who was I, if I was not a Christian?

In my cycling, my yoga and my Buddhism, I had always recognised my need for a coach, a teacher, but had never found anyone I could trust, but now, in Jesus, I knew I had found the one who could command the allegiance of my heart. I knew too, that I was likely to fail in following him; I understood all too well the ugliness within my own heart, my own innate propensity to selfishness, but I longed with all my heart, to be someone of whom Jesus would be proud. The only name I could find, that seemed to fit my passionate desire to follow, to be like Jesus, was 'Disciple'.

I trusted Jesus that he could and would transform my shattered life; make me a 'fisher of men', a saver of souls. You think souls don't need saving? You haven't lived a life like mine, Jesus had saved me from a living hell.

Church had kicked me out and shut the door in my face. If I had, or believed in a church, it was the friends in whom I could see Jesus; Dennis, John, Sarah, Audrey, Bruce and Jo. Christianity, this castle in the sand, this thread on which I had hung my life, seemed washed away forever, I was done with it. I had tasted the Kingdom of Heaven. Jesus remained, we watched each other, me from afar, wounded, outcast and unclean. I was back on the road, a pilgrim, searching for better answers, for a more substantial truth.

1987 – 1991
Mission, Marriage

Our paths crossed in a serendipitous way.

In the wake and aftermath of being thrown out of church, and the resurfacing of my gender identity crisis, God met with me in a beautiful way. At rock bottom, I was locked in suicidal ideation again, unable to pursue the 'sex change' I longed for. My mental and emotional state was precarious. I was chain smoking, I'd even bought the occasional lump of dope, I was drinking heavily and had started writing the beginnings of my story, hoping for some kind of cathartic healing, to make sense of this screwed up life, to find some understanding about who I was and why.

One night, poring over the typewriter, a bottle of wine on one side, a bottle of Tippex on the other, I was listening to Tracy Chapman on my deck. As she sang, she was asking, making a plea, a cry for peace; who would go, who would go across the lines, under the bridge and over the tracks, that separate whites from blacks?

It was a haunting song; two black boys are killed, a white boy blinded, my attention was arrested, a quiet, calm, loving voice:

'Who would dare to go... would I? '

I knew the Holy Spirit was talking to my spirit. Even after only four years following Jesus, I had learnt to recognise the beauty of the Holy Spirit, the loving, gentle, conviction. I'll paraphrase the conversation as best I can:

'You are frightened of surrendering to my call. You are

frightened to go across the lines, under the bridge, over the tracks,
even between the whites and the blacks.'

In a millisecond, I could see how my promise to follow
Jesus was empty words. I was frightened of going to America,
or Africa, or Afghanistan, to stand between the whites and the
blacks, unwilling to risk my life and work for social justice, as
a peace-maker, a reconciler.

'Come, follow me, and I will make you, a fisher of souls.'

The words hit me with the devastating force of love, a
power of love that sent me to my knees. I literally hit the
floor and started to cry, in the knowledge of Jesus' love. All
through this time, after being thrown out of church, I had
come to believe that I must be some kind of Judas. Why
else had they thrown me out? In that moment I saw Jesus
embracing Judas, forgiving him everything. Even if I was like
Judas, it didn't matter, Jesus loved me, embraced me, and
forgave me, all that I had ever done. More than all of that, I
heard Jesus calling me again,

'Come, follow me.'

Not dead words on the page of a dusty book, but alive
and compelling, so compelling and alive in me, that I could
not resist them.

I sold my car, all my belongings, gave up my flat, bought
a motorbike, and began a season of sofa-surfing with friends.
All with the aim of paying off my debts, saving money and
joining a missionary organisation.

'I'll follow wherever you lead, even war-torn Afghanistan, if
that's where you are headed, Jesus.'

This time I meant it. My despair and depression lifted
almost overnight. The suicidal thoughts disappeared and I
forgot all interest in drink or cigarettes. I buried my gender
crisis again, as deep and far down as I could.

'Repress, suppress, deny, and crucify.'

I found a mission organisation that excited me, Youth
With A Mission; they had a Discipleship Training School in
Glasgow. I recommitted myself to being single. I was at peace

again, it was becoming obvious, even to me, that every time I set my heart, will, mind and feet to following Jesus, I found peace. My experience confirmed my faith, abundantly so.

Monday morning, nine o'clock, I handed in my letter of resignation. It was time to move on. Monday morning, coffee time, looking up from my desk, I watched a stunningly attractive woman walk through the open plan offices. I had never seen her before. I was struck by her beauty and her spirit. There was something in her that shone, a fire, a strength, a love? I did not know what it was, but I knew in that moment that I wanted, needed to talk to her, to find out what it was. Whatever she had, I wanted to be part of it.

Pam joined the company. We clicked. We began to date, meals out, drinks at the pub. Most weekends and evenings when we were free, we would walk for miles in the countryside around town. All the while we talked and talked and talked. Both of us had come to that place and time in our lives where you realise the only way you can build any kind of safe relationship is by being totally open, honest, transparent. We spent a great deal of time acknowledging the pain, wounds and baggage we were carrying from childhood, broken homes, our parents' divorced, dysfunctional marriages, and our own relational failures. It felt like we were in therapy. With a similar childhood experience, we understood each other, we knew we were in need of a great deal of healing if we wanted marriage to work.

We enjoyed dating, and courting, and physical love, we enjoyed romance and fun, but we wanted far more from life than to live a picture postcard marriage – the illusion of living happily ever after. Both of us had tasted enough tragedy, to know life can turn, all too suddenly, into a perfect storm. We wanted a marriage based on something more than dreams, something far greater than our own fickle desires and wants. Both of us were agreed that our first call, was to follow Christ. If we put him first, through everything, then maybe our marriage could work and last where we had seen our own parents fail. We did not want to hurt each other yet again. Broken marriages had scarred and scared us both deeply. We wanted our marriage to be the place of healing and safety for each other.

I told Pam, from the very beginning that I struggled with issues of my identity, and with what I still believed was a 'transvestite thing'; I didn't really know what the problem was, I just knew God was going to heal me, so I had no fear in being honest, open and transparent with Pam.

Pam:
'The first two things that I first noticed in Paul – a deep abiding sadness, and an unusually attractive bum. Previous relationships had centred around intrigue, shared humour, lust ... this one was different from the outset. It felt serious, intense, weighty, scary ... but "right".

That said, I wasn't excited by the prospect of marriage. I had had a series of relationships with varying degrees of success – each ending bringing an additional layer of cynicism and self-reliance. Marriage wasn't for everyone – I had never really seen one at close quarters that I liked! I was reasonably content, had a good social circle and only felt the pangs of loneliness when attending friends' weddings, and there were a lot of those. If marriage was going to happen, my own rather flighty priorities were changing – I wanted a man who reflected Jesus' love, who would commit their life to seeking God's best. That rather radically narrowed the field!'

Youth With a Mission, or as it is more affectionately known on the inside, Youth Without Any Money, or Young Women

After Men. Everyone, new student, to seasoned leaders with decades of experience, served as self-funding volunteers. That was part of the radical, sacrificial spirit that drew me to the organisation. No salaries, freeloaders or professionals here. We did what we did because we loved Jesus and wanted to share that love freely. None of us had come from supporting wealthy mega churches. We had given up careers, homes and security, many had even sold homes, cars and more to pay their way. Some had grafted for a few years, to save enough to come and serve on the base. This sacrifice was enough to break open the hardest heart, it created a fire and a culture of genuine and sacrificial service.

YWAM Scotland, as a voluntary organisation, had a hierarchy that was by its very nature, loose, flexible, fluid and creative, constantly evolving to meet the needs at hand. Each base had a real autonomy and freedom to pursue its own vision and work out its purpose in the community and world. I landed in YWAM Scotland to find a leadership of servant-hearted, selfless givers. Yes, there were one or two big egos, but they were obvious and everyone took them with a pinch of salt. From the word go, the stated aim of the base and leadership staff was to raise others up, to do their jobs, and they moved out the way to enable and empower us to serve and lead.

'Our ceiling is your floor' was their motto; they meant it, they lived it.

For me it was a model of church I had believed in and been searching for. My experience of denominational churches, the community church experience and the rejection by Christians had left me distrustful of church hierarchy and authority. YWAM healed me of a lot of the wounds that church authority had inflicted on me.

Many of us had been badly burnt by 'heavy shepherding', not just in charismatic churches, but in the traditional ones too. Authoritarianism, hierarchy and patriarchy were gods that some church leaders found it hard to let go of; it suited their style and characters. Too many pastors and priests, acted like 'over-Lords'; trying to dictate and control the lives of those they led, rather than love and serve them. Control all too often equalled abuse. I couldn't even find a sound biblical basis for the traditions of pastors and priests ruling over the church, it seemed an absurd hypocrisy for those whose idol was 'Sola Scriptura.'

My favourite teacher on the school was a guy called Rodney. He was unremarkable in so many ways, ordinary, humble, plain spoken, down to earth. His CV said it all – he had been a bus driver, a factory worker and a dustbin man for years. He knew Jesus in a way that challenged me to my core. His working-class honesty, the authenticity about his own poor upbringing, about his own warped, broken nature and tendencies, penetrated deep into my heart. For a week he spoke on families, and the love of God. He spoke about all the dysfunctional ways that families learn to relate; anger, sulking, coldness, freezing others out, bullying, lying, violence and much more. I was guilty of them all. He exposed us by making us laugh, laugh till we cried, until we too realised, we were guilty, guilty of all the sins he had just described. He exposed the cruelties of language and behaviours that leave us as children so damaged.

Five short years of total self-destruction had ingrained all the worst aspects of my character into a congealed and frozen mess, and this is where Rodney's ministry was uncanny. Seems like he had my number, had read my mail. He told me things about myself that only God knew. Every dysfunction he illustrated, either from his own past life or from Bible stories, I found manifest in me. I had put on a Christian mask, but still these behaviours and belief patterns lay hidden, rooted in my character. I was devastated by his teaching, it took me apart. Yet, through it all, his love for each one of us was exemplary and far reaching. He opened wounds that church had walked all over. He listened to us, prayed with us and wept with us. Jesus washed our filthy feet and wounds, and many of us found a healing. Healing from our bitterness, and from the unforgiveness that chained our hearts.

Rodney the dustman's week of teaching about family, right relationships and the love of God, changed the entire course of my life. I spent the bulk of that week weeping, prostrate, face down on the floor, 'carpet time' as we called it. I was crying out all the pain of my childhood, I was burdened with guilt for the damage I had caused others, all flowing from my own unresolved pain. My bullying of others, the violence I had indulged, my vicious and uncontrollable temper, I had manipulated and controlled others with my rage. I had been blind to it all. It was a horrendous week, the burden of my guilt nearly crushed me.

I found forgiveness at the foot of the cross. A love and grace so sweet.

'Father, forgive them, they do not know what they are doing.'
Luke 23:34

I was so challenged and transformed by that first Discipleship school, but I also knew the depth of my own brokenness. I knew I needed to go through it all again. I finished the school, and went back to work for a year to earn and save so I could return and help serve and lead on the next schools. Selling my motorbike and being careful with my savings, I paid my own way for the next two years.

I came back to Scotland and helped lead on two more schools as a member of staff and mentor, just so that I could go through the cleansing and healing process all over again. God knows I needed it. I was more damaged than most. There was so much love poured into our lives in those schools, it was the closest I'd ever felt to heaven. For three years I lived my life in Glasgow and Portugal, serving local churches and communities, happy and stretched to my limits. We learnt how to serve people, not by reducing them to 'victims of charity' status, but how to empower and equip them, through discipleship, to rebuild their own lives. Discipleship was all about empowering others, releasing others, working your way out of a job. It was the exact opposite of the clinging to positions, privilege and power I so often saw modelled in the church.

My infectious enthusiasm for YWAM and the Discipleship Training Schools led Pam to pack her bags and move to St Helens to start training with YWAM there. Our long-distance relationship was flourishing, we were moving closer to marriage. I felt more confident now, with what I had learnt in the schools, that I was both ready for marriage, and was equipped with the life skills and understanding I needed, to love and honour Pam, and make marriage work. Up until then, I had only felt like damaged goods.

On the last term of my last school, my gender identity resurfaced with a violent vengeance. It was as if I had been in denial, throughout the school, of my deepest, most painful secret. I had been so busy, occupied, fulfilled and absorbed it had created the perfect smokescreen behind which to hide my struggles. Ian, former Glasgow rent boy, one of the students I was mentoring, read me like an open book. He saw right through me, sensing the conflict and pain in my soul that no one else could see. He cornered me, and in his usual blazing love told me to get real and spill the beans, but I could not. Shame and fear paralysed me.

Nothing in me was able to bring this secret into the light. I was terrified of rejection from the church, from the people around me. If I was detestable to God, at the core of my being, then I knew Christians weren't going to be able to cope with my secret self. The torment and suicidal ideation, were back with a vengeance. I told no one, limped to the end of school and tried to bury it all over again. It's amazing how we can compartmentalise our lives so effectively and block off parts of our own personality, burying them – locking them in some secret dungeon of our soul. My only resort was to return again to an even more rigorous attempt to repress, suppress, deny, crucify and bury this part of myself.

Despite this crisis, I emerged from YWAM inspired and on fire, with a practical vision of what healthy church looked like. I'd never had that before. Serving the poor, the weak, the needy and the vulnerable had earthed my faith, made it seem more whole, complete. I understood mission, not as a missionary endeavour to some far-flung place or people, but as a way of life, not as conversion, but as healing love. Not a ruling over, but a serving under; Jesus washed our filthy crap-stained feet.

The Discipleship Schools had laid deep foundations, built upon equality in community, an egalitarian leadership that stepped down, rather than up. It had deepened my relationship with Jesus into a richer intimacy, I trusted God as a loving parent and was becoming more attuned to the guidance of the Holy Spirit. Without my experience of YWAM I would never have been able to survive the abuses of the wider church. YWAM gave me hope, and a vision of what church can be when it is surrendered to Christ.

Pam and I moved to Oxford; we wanted to belong to a church that was a 'sending church', a church that believed in mission, on a global scale. We didn't want to be trapped in a church with only a parochial vision. We joined a large, thriving city centre church. We spent time with the new vicar, he was going to be marrying us within the year. We shared with him our plans and hopes of returning to serve with YWAM. We truly believed that YWAM was the launchpad for us to a lifetime of serving others, discipling and loving, serving and empowering the poor, and we told him so.

The homeless and street community in Oxford numbered hundreds. At night it seemed almost every other shop doorway was home to someone sleeping on cardboard boxes in a pile of torn and worn old sleeping bags and blankets. For the year in Oxford before we got married, I immersed myself in the homeless community. Something very powerful happens when you sit on the pavement and share your lunch with the homeless. I'd been there, I was able to build deep friendships and trust with those on the street.

Frank had poured out his heart, he wanted out, he wanted to die, he wanted to end the stinking mess his life had become, he was on the brink, and it was obvious his life hung in the balance. We talked about Jesus, about eternal life. Frank started knocking on the door of No 9, our community house. Frank was different, he didn't want our money, he wanted out. He wanted to leave this life of alcoholism behind, he wanted heaven. Like me he was faced with the stark choice of death or 'salvation'. Like me he had read his little Gideons New Testament and the love and truth of it had exploded in his soul.

I adopted Frank. It wasn't hard, I loved the guy, he was one of the sweetest, most gentle, thoughtful men I'd ever met. I was living on the top floor of the church community house. For me, it was a no brainer, I had escaped death, people's kindness had saved my life, now it was the time for me to start pay back. Frank was chronic, last stages alcoholic. I moved him into my bedroom to detox. Like me he wanted to do it the hard way, no meds, he hated the medications they detoxed him on. He slept in my bed, I moved into the tiny spare room. I held his hand through the nights and through the bad times and together we prayed. For several days and nights, he sweated, rattled, shook and shivered as all the toxins poured out.

Frank detoxed, he scrubbed up well. He was a true, working class gentleman, a beautiful soul. He came to work with me in the church's busy restaurant. We worked in the steaming, sweltering kitchen together. I did all the cooking, meal prep and baking. Frank washed up like a legend, keeping on top of all my stuff, and the entire restaurant as well. I loved his company, and I could keep an eye on him when he was the fragile eggshell. I'd put my arm around him, we'd sit in the graveyard and pray, whilst he rolled a fag, and breathed in the 'fresh air'.

It might sound like I was doing the loving and the giving, but Frank was actually one of the best friends I've ever had. In Frank, I saw and met Jesus. Frank discipled me, showed me a beauty and gentleness of character, as much as I could ever do anything to help him along the road. Of the two of us, I thought him profoundly more like Jesus; good, kind, gentle, where I was still prone to anger, sullenness and resentments.

Marriage

Pam and I had spent our life savings serving in YWAM, so we planned a small wedding on a shoestring budget for family and close friends. Pam's father intervened with an incredible generosity. Our wedding day was a wonderful day, we were lucky enough to be able to invite everyone who had been a significant part of our lives so far. It was a lavish celebration of family and friends. We invited our friends in the homeless community along, they were as integral and valuable a part of our lives as anyone, watching them feast with us was a gift. It was symbolic of our desire to serve the poor as Jesus has served the poor, not with charity handouts, but with an invitation to share in friendship, intimacy and healing with us. We knew we were as broken as they were deemed to be.

Dennis came and gave our wedding address. I had briefed him on what we wanted, we wanted him to share all about the love we had found in Christ. Dennis had his own ideas, he read the love song from The Song of Songs,

'How beautiful you are my darling! Your breasts are like two fawns, like twin fawns that browse amongst the lilies.'

Pam and I sat before a few hundred people, blushing, bright red. It was pure Dennis. Dennis at his mischievous, irreligious, irreverent best. I looked over to my step-mum, she was grinning ear to ear, she could barely stop herself from laughing. His humour and love were just what we needed.

Marriage was immediately painful for us both, we loved each other dearly, but it felt like walking in shoes too small. We realised pretty quickly, despite all the healing and teaching we had received in YWAM, that we were still carrying a lot of wounding from our childhoods. Both of us were bringing a huge amount of 'baggage' – emotional and spiritual brokenness into marriage. Somehow we had to learn how to unpack it all and leave it behind us. We learnt to be patient with each other, we tried to never go to bed with unresolved anger toward each other. We learnt to ask for 'time out'.

Pam:
'There was nowhere to hide. An extrovert by nature, I nonetheless had always enjoyed the luxury of retreating into solitude when things got messy or I wanted to avoid the demands of people and the world's gaze. I would re-emerge when I was ready, facing my inner struggles, by choice, alone. Marriage in a tiny flat didn't just interfere with that option, it annihilated it!'

We both felt a calling, a sense of belonging and purpose to return to YWAM. They had invited us come and help lead

the Discipleship Training Schools, in St Helens, where Pam had been. It was exciting and daunting to be asked into such a role, but we knew it was right for us, the next step. We worked hard and saved. We hadn't really unpacked our rucksacks from our last stint with YWAM, we were ready to go.

The vicar opposed our return to YWAM, he did not believe in or want to support para-church organisations like YWAM. We were shocked and devastated; he had said not a word about this when we had sat together discussing marriage and our future hopes. We were living in a church culture of 'obedience to authority'. You couldn't lift a finger without a 'blessing' (approval), from leadership. It was a huge blow that left a deep residue of bitterness. Our dream and vision had been swept aside by his prejudices. I felt a deep sense of betrayal that he hadn't said anything at all about his beliefs at our initial interview with him.

Judith was a tiny grey-haired bundle of high-octane energy. Her eyes twinkled and shone, and her enthusiasm for life was infectious. We had met her walking in Christ Church meadows. She already knew that we were involved in the life of church. A church she sometimes snuck into to enjoy the preaching and challenge their Zionist views. We parted company, but not before she had taken our phone number, promising to invite us to her home.

A week later, Judith called us and we went for tea in her one bedroomed flat on the infamous Blackbird Leys Estate. One of Oxford's social housing estates, home to drug and gang culture, and at the time, the racing of stolen cars through its labyrinthine streets. Judith loved it there, 'in the thick of it', she said. She was no shrinking violet. We shared our stories. She was long divorced, and happier for it. She was passionate about so much; social injustice made her mad. She campaigned for the Labour Party in local elections. She had been a formative member of the very first CND march from Aldermaston Nuclear Storage Facility to London: fifty-two miles and four days, a year before I had even been born. She had made a tent against the barbed wire of Aldermaston her home for several years. She was close friends with Laurie Lee and his wife. She was in every way a remarkable, learned and courageous woman. She oozed Jesus, a radical, fiery love and compassion, and gave herself to issues of social justice, not least the standing before Israeli bulldozers and bullets on the Gaza Strip.

When she heard our story, of our hopes to return to YWAM crushed, and our thoughts to settle in the city, and the exorbitant cost of rent, she sat back a moment,

'I have money sat in the bank. I fly to Israel once a year to join in the vigil over Palestine, but apart from that I spend very little. I'm never going to buy another house, I'm happy here, right where I am. All I really need is enough to live on and to cover the costs of my funeral.'

Pam and I looked at each other, both gobsmacked and amused, if anyone was about to die, it certainly wasn't Judith.

'Why don't you borrow whatever you need to buy a house, it would cover the deposit. You can pay me back whenever you want, interest free. There is no rush. It's the least I can do for you.'

I fought back the tears, and bit my lip.

'That's really kind, but we couldn't possibly do that, you don't even know us, we're little more than strangers.'

'Don't be silly, you're my friends, it's what Jesus would do! And anyway, we are church.'

That was that. In the middle of a recession we were able to buy a house, our first home. Feeling very grown up, we moved into our new home. It was time to settle down, put down roots and build our marriage.

1991 – 2005
Home and Family

Paddy was the craziest guy I'd ever met on the street. When drunk he was an uncontainable riot of belligerence and attitude. He hated the police with a vengeance, and violence was his trademark in the town, his reputation went before him. He had the same, emotional instability and hair-trigger temper as I had once had. I sensed that, like me, it was his means of defence, but unlike me, his violence had landed him in prison, more than once. His crazy was more out of control than mine had ever been. I saw through his machismo and bravado. Beneath it all was a deeply sensitive and hurting man.

David the church verger and I had gotten lost in prayer one morning before work. Sometimes we prayed in his basement flat, other times he unlocked the ancient old church, and we would wander up and down the aisles, praying as we went. When the Holy Spirit alights on your heart, you don't always know where she will lead. Today we were led into praying for the gang leaders and dealers on the street. I found myself on my knees weeping, calling heaven down. Weeping for a gang leader I had never met or seen before. It was such a vivid encounter 'in the spirit'. I knew I had touched heaven and heaven had touched me.

Paddy turned up in church one evening service, drunk out of his mind. A few of the students had met and befriended him, and they attempted to settle him down. The vicar's sermon was broken with Paddy's loud expletives, his singing was raucous, out of tune, out of synch – drunken Hallelujahs. In the time of prayer, I found myself drawn to Paddy, I'd never met him, or seen him before. As we prayed together I realised Paddy was the man, the gang leader, I'd been weeping for.

This pattern went on for weeks. Paddy would turn up, wrecked, wasted, high on drink and drugs. I would sit with him, calm him, and pray with him before, during and after the service. Both he and I knew that he was meeting Jesus for the first time. He'd weep in the worship as the love and songs broke over him. Each week he left church, pretty much sobered, and washed in the love of God. I was watching God doing to Paddy, what he had done to me, my first time in church, ten years ago.

Paddy had been banned, because of his continual violence, from every shelter in town. No one would take him in. It was a bitter, cold, harsh winter, the death rate for the alcoholics in the town was high. They were found, frozen where they had fallen, or they fell in the river and drowned as they staggered back to their tents, hidden under bridges and in the bushes all along the riverbank.

Pam and I had been asked to come and teach on the Discipleship Training School in St Helens, the one we had just been prevented from joining. That Friday as I was preparing to lock up the restaurant, David came in, looking worried and stressed.

'Paddy's outside. I've never seen him so bad. I've asked church if he can sleep in the Parish Centre, they've said no.'

We went outside to find Paddy rattling and shaking, empty and exhausted. He was coughing like his lungs were bleeding. He was in a poor state. We were stood next to the old boiler room of the church. It was currently used as a bike shed.

'Perhaps he could sleep here?'

He unlocked the stone outhouse, six-foot high, six-foot long, it was dank, the walls and floor sodden. We looked at each other. Even if Paddy were healthy, we couldn't put him in there.

All I could think about was Jesus saying, *'If you give someone a cup of water, if you give someone your coat, then you are doing so unto me.'*

There was only one thing I could do, I called Pam at her work.

Pam:
'I couldn't help but like Paddy. It was easiest when I made the conscious decision to "forget" what I knew of him. What I knew he was capable of. How his violent temper could flip in an instant. The physical violence that was his first response to aggravation. I just liked the guy!

But having him in our home …? Madness didn't even cover it. I felt angry that Paul had even asked … if I said "no", I get to be the "mean" one. If I said "yes" then the chance of our home being either stripped bare or filled with the city's users and alcoholics was staggeringly high. I didn't want him here. Certainly not when I wasn't around to check up on him. I wrestled for what seemed ages. The irony that I was going away for the weekend to talk to a bunch of people about giving up everything for the God who owned everything anyway, was not lost on me. I was resentful. I was scared. I said "yes".

I took Paddy home on the bus. Jesus came too. We sat him in the living room, gave him a big mug of hot sweet tea, and read him the riot act. I gave him my front door key. I was giving Jesus our house keys. Jesus lived in Paddy, I wasn't going to let Jesus sleep in a cold, dank, wet outhouse of the church, he was coming home to sleep under our roof.

'There is only one set of rules; you can have as many

baths as you want. Help yourself to some clean clothes from my wardrobe. You can eat whatever food is in the house. Drink as much tea and coffee as you like. You can lie in bed all weekend with the heating on full. The only thing we ask of you is that you do not drink, and no one – strictly no one else is allowed in.'

Paddy was in tears, broken.

'Paddy, look, we are really sorry, but we have to go, we are away for the weekend, we'll be back late Sunday night.'

Pam:
'It was a good job the weekend was full. The busyness was a very welcome distraction. It was the late evenings when the realisation of what could be waiting at home hit. It was hard not to conjure up images of carnage. An exhausting and fulfilling weekend of sharing done, the journey home was pretty silent as we wondered what we were driving back to. My fear rose with every mile ... what damage? What if we couldn't get Paddy to leave? What if our home, now known by the drinking community, became marked ...?'

We got home late on Sunday evening. Paddy was sat where we had left him in the front room, looking out the window, waiting for us.

'How are you feeling?'

'After you left, I sat here and cried, I bawled my eyes out. I haven't cried in years. I haven't been able to. I can't believe anyone who knows me, would trust me with their home, I can't believe anyone can love me that much? As I sat here bawling my eyes out, I felt washed in God's love, like I was drowning in it, which made me cry even more. It felt like I'd died and gone to heaven.

'I must have sat here for ages. Eventually I made myself

some dinner, in between crying. I had a hot bath, I don't think I've had a proper wash in weeks! Then I went to bed and collapsed and woke up on Saturday afternoon.

'I got myself some breakfast – at three in the afternoon. I sat in the garden and had a fag, but really, all I've been doing all weekend, is crying. I'm wrecked! I feel happy, peaceful, clean.'

Paddy moved in to live with us. Sober, he was an angel, an absolute joy to have around. I watched his love and respect for Pam, and I could see her growing by the day. He doted on her like a mother. It was not the usual manipulative love of a user, but a deep down, genuine reverence on his part.

Pam:
'Paddy taught me so much. I don't think he had any idea. I judged him at every turn but he won me over. I would love to say that I found a joy and fulfilment in reaching out to the poor and marginalised. I wanted to – and I did it anyway, hoping the feelings would catch up with the decision – but there was an inner conflict; I couldn't understand how people could get themselves in such a mess. After all, I'd gone through some pretty tough times and still retained some self-respect. It took many years to see the many unmerited privileges I had that kept me cushioned. As I say, Paddy was the teacher in all of this, he was discipling me!'

Paddy would give us all his benefits, not for rent, but so that he wouldn't be tempted. We kept it for him, so that he would have money for a flat deposit, when the time came. He kept enough for tobacco and small treats. So often, come next benefits cheque day, he'd be gone, disappeared, his cravings too severe to overcome. It was an emotionally exhausting helter-skelter ride that left us spent. We loved Paddy like he was our brother or child, we weren't sure which. One day he disappeared for good. We heard nothing; we were distraught. We could give him a home and love, but we could not find or access the therapy he needed to come through to a life of sobriety.

Frank had fallen, again. He was a fragile soul. The alcohol was destroying him. We didn't think he had long to live. We brought him home to live with us. We detoxed him. It was the same story, he was such a wonderful presence in our home. Kind, thoughtful, gracious and sensitive. He carried the pain of the world in his heart, one of the most caring men I'd ever met. As with Paddy, he'd last a few weeks, and then be gone, back on the drink. We kept bringing him home, loving him, knowing God was on his case.

It was a powerful spiritual battle raging over their lives, they like me, were living as I once had, on the brink. Death only a step away for both of them. One drink too many, it was as easy as that. It had been the death that I had longed for, but the suicide I was never brave enough to carry through. Sometimes life leaves you, hanging by a thread. We experienced and suffered all their highs and lows with them. The cost on us as a couple was enormous, but we would do it all over again. We were only doing what we saw Jesus doing. It was a no brainer really.

'He places the lonely in families.'

I was on church staff, managing the church restaurant and café. We thought our home group pastors would look out for us, make sure we were ok. I thought church leadership would keep an eye on us, check in with us pastorally, they knew full well what we were attempting to do, rehabilitating addicts and alcoholics in our home. Despite serving them their lunches every day, over the months and years, the clergy said nothing. They never once asked how we were doing. It was an obvious neglect and a cold shouldering, that cut us both deeply. The contrast I saw between the love and affirmation that Paddy and Frank gave Pam, they really did treat her like a precious sister or mother, compared to the cold shouldering of the priests, who hugged us and told us they loved us on Sundays, was just too stark.

Jackie Pullinger came to speak to the church. Jackie had a well-established ministry to opium addicts in Hong Kong. She had started with nothing, a nineteen-year-old woman on her own. She had moved into the slums, and rehabilitated these men, one by one on her own. Now she oversaw the rehabilitation of hundreds of addicts and had people from all over the world coming to help her. I have never heard anyone preach with the passion, fire and conviction that Jackie did that day. It was a blistering message of rebuke.

'You walk to church on a Sunday morning and you do not even see the poor! You walk through the city to your religious meetings and you step over the poor as if they are not there! You are blind and your hearts calloused – hardened.'

She was clearly feeling God's grief about the attitude of our church towards the addicts, alcoholics and homeless. Yet she could not possibly have known the truth, she was only visiting for a day. Her message was a great comfort to us, we knew through it that God was watching over us and caring for us, even if the clergy weren't. We really did feel very isolated in serving the poor, even in our own church. It confirmed it was time to move on and find a more supportive church.

The church had many home groups, but the ones we tried, whilst loving and kind, invariably ended up as intellectual, dry and almost argumentative Bible studies, all the pride of Oxford intellectualism came seeping out. People seemed too desperate to show off their biblical knowledge. Pam and I were tired and weary, we didn't need more Bible knowledge, we craved the presence of God. To be refreshed, renewed and replenished by the Holy Spirit.

In frustration we opened our home up to anyone else who was spiritually hungry and thirsty. A whole gang of young folks descended on us each week. I cooked soup and baked bread. We sat and shared our lives and stories, we prayed for each other, and deep friendships ensued, but more than anything we worshipped. Worship that was free and uncontrolled, it was the most incredible time. God ministered to us all deeply. We shared the bread and wine, communion. We did this because we needed to receive as well as give, we needed love, as well as pouring it out. At times it felt like leadership were actively opposed to us, because we were not 'toeing the party line', that we were running our own home group, not under their authority and 'blessing'. Nothing could have been further from our hearts – it was about finding spiritual health and nourishment.

The vicar had arrived in the church not long before us. He led a large staff of associate vicars and curates, administrators and pastoral staff. It was a large, successful church. One Sunday, it was announced that all groups and ministries in the church were to be stopped – 'laid down'. Everyone was asked to give up their positions, from worship leaders, home group leaders, youth group leaders, support staff, everyone. We watched the members of church, who had been faithfully, selflessly giving of their money, time and energy, some for many years, reeling in shock.

It was a harsh dictatorial command, the sort of draconian authority I expected to be exercised in the army, or by a school headmaster. It lacked any resemblance to a mentoring, discipling approach, it was authority devoid of either relationship, love or friendship. If the leadership had problems with a ministry, then they needed to counsel and mentor those concerned. Instead they took an axe to the tree, and cut it down. Many in the church left, hurt, discouraged, wounded and feeling abused.

It was a re-emergence of the heavy-handed controlling leadership I had seen so many times before. I was shocked to hear that even friends running successful and growing charities outside of the church's jurisdiction, charities that ministered across the globe, were asked to close them down. It was very much the same spirit we had already seen in the 'heavy shepherding' churches.

We did not feel the impact of the edict because we were not running any church ministries and what we did in our home was beyond leadership control. It was something we felt God wanted, and until God asked us to stop we would carry on.

This experience of authoritarian, harsh and distant church leadership damaged both of us. For me it raised again the trauma I had experienced in being expelled from the first and only church where I had ever really felt I belonged, but I didn't know then what trauma was, or how it worked. I just felt overwhelmed with a bitterness of soul. It wiped me out spiritually for months.

It was years later, before my intuition was confirmed; the vicar did not want the church or services messed up and disrupted by the homeless, the addicts and alcoholics. The cold shouldering had been intentional. They did not want us bringing more broken people into church, the only reason being – the only excuse I ever heard – was that the church's ministry was to the students. 'If we could win students, we could change the world.' I heard this from more than one member of church staff.

Church is reluctant to admit spiritual abuse happens, but there are many of us who bear the scars and carry the wounds. In the controlled and controlling atmosphere of this church, I felt like a round peg being forced – smashed – into a square hole. The stand up, sit down, stand-up routine, was killing me spiritually. Instead of embracing and nurturing our gifts and vision for their church, they crushed them.

Why do I talk so openly about Christian leadership and its glaring failings? Is it because I am still bitter? I hope not. I write about church leadership because I believe we have got it so wrong. Often, I think we learn more from the things we suffer, the things that are wrong, than we do from small encouragements that come our way, nice as they are. No one ever writes about the dirty back side of church, so church leaders live their lives accountable to no one but a token oversight.

God was working into my heart, writing into my heart, a vision, a model for church leadership that was more reflective of the teachings of Christ. A vision for an emerging, progressive and contemporary church with a culturally relevant model and practice of leadership. That is why I write about the painful things, the bitternesses, the abuse, because they teach us how not to do church, they lead us, hopefully, to a conclusion; to a better, healthier place and church.

To be fair to the vicar, we watched the church transformed before we moved on. If the church had once been subject to spirits of pride, perfectionism and performance, those things were totally broken from it, as the Holy Spirit fell. I had never seen a whole church go through what I can only describe as a deliverance. It was a sovereign move of God. I don't think it was because of what leadership did, I think it was in spite of what they did; their controlling spirit was exposed and broken from them. Looking back, I think Jackie's words had been both truly prophetic, and a catalyst for hearts and proud spirits to be humbled.

What they then did do, and did so well, was to allow the Holy Spirit access to their own lives, the life of the church, its services and corporate life. In that, their leadership was exemplary. They really humbled themselves, got out of the way, relinquished control and often lay face down on the floor before God. They allowed God to reorder their traditional ways of doing things, to have a greater influence on their personal lives, their hearts and attitudes. In that they modelled a gracious and inspiring leadership. The stand up, sit down routine opened up into the real freedom of Holy Spirit led worship. You could taste it! All the pride, performance and perfectionism that feeds control, so much the spirit of Oxford in the church, gave way to real humility, spontaneity and a freedom of the Holy Spirit in the church's life.

It was a humbled leadership. It was an inspiring time to be in a church. It gave me renewed hope that church, when surrendered to God could be an exciting, truly transformative community to be part of. We watched hard hearts melted, we watched controlling people undone by love, we watched them learning to let go. A church of nearly a thousand people was moving in the freedom of the Spirit I had tasted in YWAM, it was an incredible season to have been part of. What it all proved to me, beyond a shadow of doubt, was that even the best leaders make horrific mistakes.

I think of Peter in his relationship with Jesus; one minute he has a revelation of Jesus as the Christ, and Jesus promises him the keys of the Kingdom, the next minute Peter is opposing Jesus, and Jesus has to rebuke the devil in him! We put church leaders on a pedestal and fail to hold them accountable. We hold to a badly flawed concept of church.

Moving church meant leaving the church restaurant too. I took a job as a Chef-Manager at a successful delicatessen/ sandwich bar at the end of the high street. One day a distraught Judith turned up in the shop, and asked if we could chat. I downed tools, grabbed us both a drink.

'Oh, Paul, I am really, really, very stupid, I don't know what I've done.'

She was teary and visibly shaken. I waited patiently and let her tell her story.

'You know the Catholic refuge house where I live, they've thrown me out – they had to.'

She looked at me like a lost child.

'What on earth have you done?'

'I hit one of my co-workers!'

I couldn't help laughing. Judith, sweet little pacifist Judith had broken her eleventh commandment; she was mortified and utterly disappointed with herself. When she told me why, I laughed all the more. She had been sorely provoked.

Tears were now welling up in her eyes. When I heard the story, all I could think to say was, 'Well done!'

We sat together for a while, chatted and prayed. She began to see the funny side of it all. I made her a sandwich and snuck out the back to call Pam.

Pam:
'Every girl needs a mother figure – particularly when about to become one themselves. All women have anxieties about impending motherhood, but I was terrified! I really had no idea how I was going to nurture this new life that I already loved with a passion. I felt ill-equipped and very alone in a pregnancy, marked by severe "morning" sickness which subsided only minutes before delivery! Judith seemed to radiate a peace and order in our home and I relished her presence. She was a Godsend.'

Both Pam and I felt a little estranged from our own mums, so Judith's love and presence in the home was a tangible evidence to us of God's love. It was a daunting time for us – neither of us had enjoyed a healthy childhood, we had no real role model in parenting. Judith brought us calm. She cooked and cleaned for us, loved our little garden and busied herself there too. They were precious days.

Frank, Paddy and Judith were part of our home, they were our family, our 'loved ones', before we ever had a family of our own. They brought us so much joy.

In marrying me, Pam had married into the homeless community, the addicts, the broken and the poor. It was not an easy marriage for her, but in it, all the beauty, strength and love that I had seen on that first day, grew and shone with a radiance and power, from within her. She has been a true spiritual mother to many.

Lauren was born by caesarean operation. Before Pam was anaesthetised, she lay on the stretcher bed, shivering and shaking, uncontrollably, with fear, like a rabbit caught in the headlights. The fear of the operation, and the fear of motherhood, was a journey into the unknown. As Lauren emerged bloody from the womb, Pam and I were hit by a tidal wave of love. A small miracle in our eyes, a wonder, a beauty and a love.

Wave after wave of love washed through us. Pam and Lauren stayed in hospital. I returned home, alone, exhausted and emotionally drained from the day, the waiting and the worry, and the whole experience through the surgery and delivery. I lay down on my bed, and again was overwhelmed by the love flooding through me. Tears flooded from my eyes and soaked the pillow. The tears did not stop. How could a newborn baby do this?

Maybe this is the love God has for all of us?

We found a new church. The moment we walked through the door; we knew we had 'come home'. It was the family, the 'tribe' we had been longing, praying, searching for. It was a new church, bursting with life and energy. Relationships were easy, open, strong and healthy. Worship was perhaps the most incredible part of church life. We were able to worship God as we wanted, without either interruption or control. In the worship we experienced a peace, a freedom and an unburdening of our cares and worries. We had two young student worship leaders whose musical skills were sublime. Their song writing echoed the cries of our own hearts. They bared their hearts and souls before us each week in worship, it was a costly demanding role they took on, with joy and humility.

Worship through song and music had always been the primary way in which I connected with God. It enabled me to get lost in love and wonder, devotion to Jesus. In that place I found resolution to so much of the pain and frustrations of my life, it was a safe and sacred place in which I poured out my soul to God. Many, many times I felt God, not just answer me, but meet me there; Spirit to spirit communion.

With such a profound sense of the presence of God over the church in worship, and through the strength of our relationships, the church grew rapidly. Vicky and Brenton's worship and songs were being published on CD. They were becoming global bestsellers. People were checking out the new worship flowing from our community and coming to see for themselves. Worship was a gift that rested on our church movement in such a way that it had begun to influence the global church and help lead it into a new freedom in worship, which led to real church renewal. It was incredible to be caught on the crest of this wave, riding it each week.

Charlotte was born two years after Lauren, again by caesarean. Once again Pam and I were hit by wave after wave of pure, divine love as we saw her emerge from the womb. These two little girls were the best thing that had ever happened to either of us, maybe even more significant than our own marriage. Charlotte's impact on us was immediate, she had a presence and an energy, an attitude and character that both lifted us and made us laugh. She was a small bundle of joy and laughter, with a mischievous humour, from as soon as she could talk.

The girls, together and individually introduced into our lives a whole new realm of wonder, mystery, love and joy. With them we explored the world afresh and found healing from much of the misery of our own childhoods. Both Lauren and Charlotte carried a healing presence about them, a calm, a peace, an innocence. They were truly the champagne years of our lives. Our marriage was cemented and sealed by the love they gave us. Never ever could we repay them, or God, for what they gave us, not by their doing, it just flowed from who they were. The girls had opened new windows into our souls through which the healing love of God flooded.

Sunday mornings, holding Lauren and Charlotte in our arms, Vicky sang over us with her songs soaring up to the heavens. Vicky was such a precious, beautiful young woman. She had a voice like Joni Mitchell only it was cleaner, purer and more like sparkling, flowing clear water, it ministered to us and refreshed our souls. Vicky was an inspiration to me, she made me want to pursue Jesus like never before. Pam and I had found a home, a family.

Our pastor was a quiet, shy, introverted man. It was he and his wife who really birthed this new church, nurtured it, nourished it and shaped its destiny. He, more than anyone encouraged and released people like Brenton and Vicky to lead. He'd have been crazy not to!

We felt the richest, most privileged parents alive. We had two beautiful daughters who were adopted and loved by the entire church. Wherever they went, love was showered upon them. It was church as it should be, and the church grew around them, creating a wonderful safe space and family in which they could grow. We were so grateful to everyone around us for the family they created for us and our children. They were for a few short years, the happiest days of our lives.

I was still running, big miles every week. I devoured half-marathons, and moved on to bigger challenges, long distance sponsored runs. I organised a Three Peaks run, Snowdon, Ben Nevis and Scafell Pike in twenty-four hours, including the drive in-between. After ten years of distance running my knees were starting to grind and click. I had the money, for the first time in twenty-five years, to buy a bike. Riding again was such a relief. It gave me headspace, to de-stress from the enormous pressures at work, from the pressure of providing for my family, and the pressure I was feeling within. Once again cycling gave me an escape and a release for all the energy and conflict pent up inside me.

Since returning from YWAM I had buried my identity issues as deep as I could. It was both a means of trying to find peace and relief from the pain of having a divided personality, and a belief that all I had to do was 'stop it!' – repent. *'Repress, suppress, deny and crucify.'* I was literally trying to put this feminine side of me to death, to crucify it as part of my 'sinful' nature. If I were serious enough about 'stopping it' – repenting, I genuinely trusted God would do the rest.

Pam and I avoided anything that talked about the issue of sexuality and transsexual transition, as it was coming to be known. If there was a television programme, a newspaper article or a Sunday supplement story about anything or anyone who was transsexual, we looked the other way. We turned off the television, we binned the newspaper and we threw away the supplements. We both knew God was healing me.

The subconscious reality was far more painful. For months I could go without any thought of my feminine self. Having Frank and Paddy live with us had meant I was preoccupied to the full. I threw myself into my work and allowed my desire to be the very best 'witness' I could be, pull me into a state that verged on workaholic. In church I committed myself to every prayer and worship event I could manage.

Becoming a parent totally absorbed me. I was so in love with my two daughters, I almost worshipped the ground they walked on! I adored them. The energy I had left I poured out on Pam, building a home and family, or I went out and destroyed myself on the bike.

I had become a very complete and happy human when I was 'doing', but whenever I had any length of time to rest or reflect, the pain of my suppressed soul bled into my consciousness. I went through silent weeks of total despair. At nights I lay awake, hour after hour, fighting thoughts of suicide. I knew I could not, would not carry it out. I could do nothing that would harm Pam or the girls, but it did not stop the battle raging. These nights would leave me drained, wrung out and feeling hopeless.

The old thoughts and feelings resurfaced, of hating and loathing the body I found myself in. The longing to walk free in the body that could clothe my soul in a more appropriate form. It was not so much my body that felt wrong, it was my whole being. For decades, the only way I could describe the sum total and force, the strength and torment of these thoughts and feelings, was in longing for a change of sex. Yet even as I thought these things, I condemned myself as sick.

In the morning I pulled on the mask and went back to work. Every winter I was knocked out with chronic pneumonia or bronchitis. Each winter I would be laid up in bed, often for a month or more. I was drinking coffee all day at work to keep myself going, living on adrenaline and caffeine, my immune system was shot. My body was feeling the strain of being so driven. I had no idea of the state I was in; workaholic, I had no idea that I was a driven person, I was just damn good at my job, a devoted husband and father. I was sold out 'serving God'. I was the very best person I could be.

When these weeks of despair hit me, sometimes frequently, sometimes months between, I became outwardly withdrawn, sullen, moody, irritable and volatile. I snapped at the girls, and hated myself for it. Pam tiptoed around me, frightened of me and my temper, never knowing when I might explode. Yet my secret, my truth, my reality was buried so deeply within me, that I could not acknowledge its existence, even to myself. I had no idea what I was dealing with. I just put it down to work pressure, or the politics of church, or the pressure of having to provide for the family for all their needs. My denial was total.

Pam:
'It was tough. Living with a ticking, unexploded bomb generally is. My priority was to ensure the girls grew up in a home that was peaceful and safe and so I did everything in my power to ensure that was their experience. Did I resent the amount of time Paul was out cycling and competing when the girls were young? Yes, at times, but it seemed to diffuse something and so it was preferable for the sake of an overall peace. I just accepted that this had to be the way things were and got on with it.'

Beneath my casual, everyday mask, I felt I was a useless husband, a lousy father and a fake Christian. I never ever referred to myself as a Christian, I still loathed the term, and all the negative baggage it carried with it, but it didn't make my load any lighter.

Placed in context these weeks of inner emotional, mental

and spiritual violence seemed rare and few and far between. Generally, life was very kind and good to us, we had no cause to complain. Overall, the majority of the time, we enjoyed a very happy, wholesome family life. These storms always passed, as I knew they would, and I would return to the endless rounds of trying to be the perfect 'Christian'. These inner battles were the rumblings of the spiritual earthquake that was yet to come.

2005 – 2017
Easter Sunday

C ancer did not just kill Noreen, it harrowed her body, and hollowed out her soul, the disease decimated her in every way, Noreen died tortured by pain, afraid, and feeling cut off from God. Her ordeal changed my life forever. My vision of the world, my faith in God, my hope for humanity was shaken to the core. I had seen too many people die already, but Noreen was my aunt, my flesh and blood, my family.

My sister moved in to live with Noreen, in the home we had grown up in during so many school holidays. Sylvia nursed Noreen, she cooked, cleaned, and tended the garden. She sat with her hour after hour, and day after day, holding her hand, trying to comfort her in her pain. The morphine did not touch the pain that ripped through Noreen's body.

Watching the agony she went through and seeing the toll it took upon my sister, I felt utterly useless. Noreen had helped bring us up as kids whenever we had stayed with Grandma and Grandad. She came to stay with us for weeks in the school holidays, to look after us while dad worked. Her life had been spent as a ward sister, training nurses and setting the highest standards of compassionate care. She was a devout Christian, and a fun-loving woman. In the pain of her death, she felt that God had forsaken her. Her funeral was packed with nurses and patients who praised her life-long kindness.

My faith, for so long unshakeable, began to come apart at the seams, unravelling in a long rant of questions, directed in anger at God. It was the beginnings of our long Easter Saturday. Easter Saturday, that day the church skips so lightly over; Easter Saturday; the absence of God, it's not good marketing for the church, yet it is more a part of most of our lives than crucifixions and miracles. The church does not like to linger there. I understand why now.

Dennis died. He was my spiritual father and mentor. I was totally unprepared for the grief that hit me, I sobbed from the loss and the heartache; a light had gone out in my world.

Frank died of cancer, quietly in one of the town's hospices. He'd weathered the storms, found sobriety and passed his days quietly, fishing, and gardening for the church. He was in every sense of the word, a saint, he had fought hard to come clean. Losing Frank, I lost a best friend and inspiration, an older brother.

We lost another precious friend. Judith died soon after, again from cancer. We missed her fire, her love, her twinkling eyes and mischievous spirit. She had given us so much, helped us buy our first home, watched and prayed over us in parenthood and prayed for our girls as they grew up. She had been our adopted mum. The loss of people who had shaped my life and faith impacted me deeply, the grief lingered; it was these people, not the institution, that felt like my real, or true church. They had reflected Christ to me in both extraordinary and ordinary, everyday ways.

The Assistant Pastor and his wife were moving on from our church. Whilst the Pastor ran the church, in his giftings as a manager, a strategist and a visionary, James and Jenny were very much the pastoral strength of the church, managing home groups and ministry teams, and care for the poor and vulnerable. They would be a huge loss to the church. James came to me one day and asked me to consider taking on his role as Pastor. I had just moved into a managing role with a new building company.

'I think you would be great for the church; you are a natural-born pastor.'

'Get lost!' I swore at him. I was only half joking.

Pam and I had been pastoring home groups from our home for fifteen years, and they always thrived and multiplied. We loved what we did, but being part of a church hierarchy was just not my scene. Maybe God has a way of calling us; I'm not sure I heard the call. I just looked at the church, the huge hole that James and Jenny would leave, and realised someone had to step in to fill the gap. Assistant Pastor was not a role I wanted, but an over-riding urgency, the practicality of common sense moved me to apply, I knew Pam and I had the gifts and skills for the job.

For my interview, in front of the Pastor and trustees, I was asked what my favourite job would be.

'Forestry, being outside, being surrounded by natural beauty, and not having to deal with people.'

They laughed, thinking it was my introductory joke. I am by nature a loner, a hermit, an introvert, I really would love to work alone in the woods. I wasn't joking, it had always been my dream job.

I was asked what my weaknesses were.

'Well, I've battled all my life with feeling feminine, with dressing as female, you know – the transvestite thing.'

I wanted to 'walk in the light', hold no dark secrets, be humble and accountable. I gave each of the trustees a letter regarding my life-long battle with my femininity. Not one of them ever spoke to me of it again, it was swept under their macho carpets.

There was a stunned silence, embarrassed responses. I walked out of the interview, confident I had destroyed any chance of getting the job. A month later I had my feet underneath the desk, staring at a computer screen, wondering how it worked. I was responsible for pastoring, mentoring and training home group leaders, heading up ministry teams, looking over the prayer life of the church, the homeless and poor, the foodbank, evangelism and mission.

My initial response was to get before God and give my life over, lock, stock and barrel. In Christianese I think they call it consecration – 'being set apart for God's work'. I didn't see my work for the church as any different to my work in the sandwich bars and coffee shops, or my role on the building site, but I had a deep concern; I was expected to teach and preach to the church on a regular basis. What I wanted to model was holiness, I wanted to be holy, to set an example that was easy for others to follow. People have all kinds of religious notions about holiness, like the wearing of robes and religious vocations, or not smoking, drinking or swearing?!

For me it was a simple matter,

'What does holiness look like?'

Holiness looks just like Jesus. Honesty, integrity, compassion.

Nothing more, nothing less. Jesus, who hung out with prostitutes, drunkards, tax collectors and sinners. That bit was easy for me, it had always been my natural environment. What I was wrestling with was this shadow of what I considered to be my 'transvestite' sin, which I had buried deep down within. God, after twenty-five years of my sincere prayer and rigorous self-control, still hadn't healed me.

I started a three-week fast. The bulk of it was to be a total fast, water only, but I would ease my way in with a partial fast of fruit and soup, and end the fast the same way. It was something I knew the Holy Spirit was leading me into. The experience of fasting in my community church days and then being thrown out of the church had left me scarred – the thought of fasting made me feel sick. I hated Lent and being told to fast. I could not fast out of any religious duty. If I did not feel God's love leading me, I could not fast at all, even for an afternoon! I hadn't fasted for twenty years, I knew it was the Holy Spirit leading, drawing, loving me into a deeper intimacy.

Fasting for me, had never been a means of 'twisting God's arm', of asking God for things, or to do things. For me, the sole purpose of fasting was to enjoy God for God's sake. For me fasting is the fruit of a love affair with God, not a religious duty. It meant time alone with God, worship with God. It might sound crazy, but that's just how I feel. I fast very rarely, but I know if I don't respond to the Spirit's call, I'm saying no to a deeper love.

I laid my life before God, and for the first time instead of burying my secret and shame, I laid my soul bare to God. I told God everything. That first year on staff, I was led into another three-week fast, and then one two-week fast. I laid my entire life before God and told God he could have it all, do whatever he wanted with me. I prayed for the church, I prayed for whatever God put on my heart. All I wanted was to be able to stand before the church and know that my heart was clean and pure. I didn't want to be led by ego, or ambition, by insecurity or guilt, all I wanted to do was serve. Serve God and serve people with a pure heart, an undivided heart. More than anything I wanted to be free of even the shadow of this 'transvestite sin', but I knew that was something only God could do.

Through all the fasting, nothing seemed to change within. The intensity of my gender identity crisis remained, as much a part of me as my arms or feet. I found the words of St Paul echoing through my soul,

'Three times I pleaded with God, to take away this anguish, this pain, and all God said by way of reply was, "My grace is sufficient for you; my power and glory are revealed in your weakness."'

I accepted that as God's final word on the matter. God

was not going to heal me, or take my torment away. Somehow I had to learn to live with it, by sharing it with him. I came out of the desert, limping, leaning on God.

'*Repress, suppress, deny and crucify*', I continued to tell myself.

My cycling and racing were going well, I was beginning to feel really comfortable on the bike, winning races and loving the long solo training rides. During this season of fasting, I laid it all before God, ready to give it all up, it would be a huge sacrifice. I knew that sacrifices did not impress God. Surrendering my right to ride and race to God, I realised my cycling was one of my main connections with God. My saddle had become my prayer seat, my solo rides had become rich prayer times that nourished and sustained me. In my racing I was worshipping God, every bit as much as I had in mopping floors at work, or singing songs, Sunday mornings in church.

I kept training and racing. My racing was my way of showing the world that following Christ, did not mean being religious. Winning, and a big part of my motive for winning was to shut the mouths of those who saw faith as a human weakness, a crutch. My faith was an integral part of my whole life, as was my cycling. For me, the religious division between sacred and secular was a lie; racing my bike was as much a sacred act as wearing flowing robes, or a dog collar, or cleaning toilets – it was intimacy and honesty with us that God desired, whatever we might be doing.

That summer Pam's dad had a massive stroke. Pam shouldered the burden of getting him into a nursing home and care. It was huge stress and weighed heavily on her. We watched him over the next ten years deteriorating; he had zero quality of life, and every time we visited him, it felt like we were staring death in the face. The misery of his life cast a long shadow over us as a family, we were his lifeline and only outside contact with the world. That he hung onto life by a thread for ten years was an agony for him, and a crushing sorrow over us all. His death was painful beyond words, for four weeks he fought for his every last breath, it was a torture for us all.

Pam:
'How is it that however long and lingering an illness, however inevitable its conclusion, nothing quite prepares you for the final moment. I had been at Dad's bedside for the final days, sleeping in the room opposite his. I talked, played his favourite music and watched each heaving laboured breath wondering if it was the last. He slipped away when I had nipped out to the shop. I felt I had abandoned him in his final moments and felt utterly winded by the news.'

A year or so later Pam's mum died, unexpectedly. It was partly a relief as she had been ill and suffering for so many years, but it was still a huge blow. Dragging the girls to a cold grey funeral in a solemn grey church was not a pleasant ordeal. It was a tough call and so hard on our daughters. We did not know how to prepare them for facing death. We did our best, but I think we did a poor job. Grief was starting to wrap itself around us as a family.

Becoming a Pastor to the church meant working in harmony as a team. For me, in both my work and racing, I loved teamwork, being part of a team was one of my strengths, teams are where I thrive. For me there was no room for 'I' in team, no room for heroes or egos. In every job I did, I tried really hard to lay aside my manager's role to create a level team where everyone could influence and lead. I loved stepping down so that others could step up. I'm honest enough to admit my huge ego, my pride and my insecurities, I hate flying solo. I want, with an instinctive desire for safety, to be part of a healthy team and people I can submit to and learn from, people who will pull me up when I screw up. That way, I am protected, and others are protected from my potential to abuse. I've always been wary of the strong individualist, who thinks they can fly solo, who thinks they alone know best. I'd seen too often the carnage caused by insecure and dominating leaders.

No church leader holds the correct, or perfect theology. If they do, they are most likely leading a cult. Our pastor had always caused me deep concern; he would not allow women to lead, teach or preach in the adult church. In these beliefs, he was flying solo. No one else in church supported him in these views. For me, it was not just the beliefs that were so offensive, it was the authoritarian, dictatorial, out of touch relationship with his church that worried and to a degree angered me. It had taken us a year or two to find these beliefs out, and by that time our girls were so happy in church, we could not bear to pull them out. We needed a positive church experience, the church we had got married in had been seven bitter years in which we had felt isolated and shunned. The relationships in this church were rich, real and rewarding, it was our family, and we needed and missed family.

We submitted ourselves to the pastor's religious misogyny and sex discrimination, even though Pam was one of the most compelling teachers and preachers I knew. It meant from the beginning that my trust in his theology or leadership was not really there, but when you are bonded to a loving church family, sometimes you make allowances for errors of judgement, so we compromised our faith and beliefs for the sake of loving relationships, being part of a family. The fact that his theology dominated and controlled the whole church, should have been a warning sign to us. We missed it in our longing to belong to part of a loving thriving community.

Moving onto staff it came as a shock to learn the pastor's vision of leadership. He believed like many in the movement:

'Being Senior Pastor is like being a benevolent dictator – a kind and altruistic but dominant leader.'

It was an ideology that John Wimber, the main founder of the movement had used to explain his leadership beliefs, so it had become the mantra for many of the young and ambitious new leaders. It was a taint and a hangover from the authoritarian and heavy shepherding era of contemporary church that I thought we had grown out of. Our church planting movement was the fastest growing church in the UK, and its explosive success bred pride and reinforced leadership's beliefs that they had got things just right, particularly views about their own leadership and its righteousness. The concept was anathema to me, but I could say nothing. I was on staff, it was too late, we were in too deep; you cannot challenge a benevolent dictator, they dictate.

Nearly every church encourages the practice of 'accountability', submitting our lives to each other, 'walking in the light'. Rightly, the Pastor wanted me to bare my soul to him, to share all my struggles with him; to be fully accountable, but then, he told me bluntly, he did not need to do that with me. I was stunned. Apparently, his accountability was a friend in America. Immediately I had alarm bells and felt uncomfortable. Here, plain to see, the belief in hierarchy and rank; we were not equals, as brothers, transparent before

Christ. Where was the trust, where was accountability? I knew there and then; this was not a team; it was a boss and his employees. It was a recipe for disaster.

My serious concern was that this attitude was indicative of a much deeper issue; the pastor had no real accountability 'on the ground', within the church itself, it was a token accountability, a sham. I'd seen it a hundred times before, in churches in Glasgow, Portugal and elsewhere, pastors running roughshod over those who paid for their livelihoods, dictating theology, controlling their churches. Alarm bells were sounding in my spirit. I should have pulled out right then and resigned, but I was lacking in both maturity and wisdom, I just shut my mouth and stayed put. I said not a word to anyone, except Pam. I got on with my work for the church. I set services up, I set them down, every week in the school. We pastored people, loved people, prayed with people and prayed that church would grow, both in strength of relationships and in service to the community, and in holiness. I really wasn't concerned about church growth. Healthy things grow.

After only two years on staff, the church hit an insurmountable crisis. The pastor wanted to go one way, the church membership, in the main, wanted to take a different path. The church imploded. We went almost overnight, from a healthy church of well over two hundred and forty, to being an embittered church of sixty. I tried to bridge the gap between church and pastor, but it was a losing battle. I tried to hold the pastor to account and failed. He pulled rank and rode roughshod over the church. We watched as a family, as so many of our closest friends left, disillusioned and burnt. Pam and I pastored so many people through an acrimonious leaving. It was ugly. We spent ourselves encouraging people to 'leave well', to leave without bitterness. People felt betrayed, people felt abused, people felt badly let down. I felt like I'd failed everybody, I was both heartbroken and furious at the deep wounds inflicted on some of the most faithful church members and the injustice done to so many good, kind and humble people.

To everyone in the church who recognises themselves in this story, I am truly sorry, I failed you and it broke my heart. I hope you've been able to forgive us and move on with your lives. A book has been written about this church's self-destruction, a destruction I contributed to, and of which I am deeply ashamed. The book was applauded by some. This is my side of the story. I hope it helps redress, in some small way, the imbalance of truth; the myth that 'God pruned his church'. To the best of my understanding, it was no such thing, it was spiritual abuse caused by the sins of us, the leadership. The damage done to many people's spiritual and family lives was colossal. I have reflected on and prayed over this for fifteen years, so I say these things after deep deliberation.

We had just sold our house, and were mid-house move, looking for somewhere close to a good school for the girls. The church had lost a huge proportion of its income. I knew staff cuts were coming, so I told the pastor and trustees:

'Do whatever you need to do.'

I didn't want them saddled with guilt, they had tough decisions to make; I was fully expecting it to be a process of prayer, dialogue and discussion within the church's large staff and leadership team. There were lots of paid staff as well as me. I thought we were going to share the hit of the church's suddenly depleted finances between us, to share the burden.

Within the week a letter was left in my pigeonhole by the Trustees. They wanted me out, quick. I was the sacrificial goat. It was the same heavy-handed, authoritarian, dictatorial style of leadership, no teamwork, no team, no chance of dialogue or discussion, just the axe again. With a wife and two children to provide for, it was more than a slap in the face. It was an appallingly executed and ruthless management decision, with no pastoral concern shown at all. The trustees hid from us. I felt totally betrayed. They knew we were in the middle of buying and selling a home and that we would be unable to secure a mortgage. I could have been offered a gradual exit or even part pay.

Devastated by the financial bomb dropped on us, we downsized and squeezed into a tiny, cramped house. Pam and I were burnt out. We left the church. It was as bitter a blow as any divorce, our family had been blown apart. Our girls were devastated at the loss of their loving, supportive, wider family. Worse still they picked up on our disillusionment and bitterness. We tried to shield them from it, tried to be honest, but for them, it pretty much killed their faith. That was the hardest blow of all to us. I had failed them too.

My dad was due into hospital for a knee replacement. He had been battling Parkinson's disease for a number of years, but was in reasonable health. He caught the MRSA virus in hospital, contracted pneumonia and died a few weeks later. We were devastated. All of us had loved my father more than almost anyone else we knew. He had always been a gentle, kind, generous and affectionate, big hearted father and grandfather to us all. The sudden loss, the shock and grief was too much for us.

We were all still reeling from the spiritual aftermath of our church disintegrating and scattering, it was as bleak as any of the deaths we had experienced as a family, in some ways it was even harder to cope with and bear; church was where we turned in times of crisis and need, but it had been torn from us. It contributed in a major way to this sense of being locked in a long Easter Saturday, a place where all our hopes and dreams had been destroyed. Pam and I clung to our faith, we trusted God, but felt his absence dearly. The girls could not continue in their faith; if this was church, and this was God, they really did not want to be part of it any longer. I did not blame them.

We bought a dog for the girls; in the hope it might bring comfort in their grief. It was an adorable crossbred lurcher who ran like the wind. She spent her days curled up on us for hours, purring like a cat. We all grew so attached to our new family member and loved her dearly. She was a real comfort after losing dad. Less than a month after we had buried my father, our puppy dog died, shivering in our arms, she had five thousand times the normal amount of copper in her liver; copper toxicosis. Depression was hovering over us as a family. Each of us felt its numbing, cloying, sapping presence.

After the church redundancy I launched out on my own as a builder. The recession hit less than a year later. It felt like we had entered some weird world where everything was being blown apart. Life was one body blow after another with no respite in between. All of us were feeling it, the girls tried to keep on a brave face, but inside they were both struggling badly. They had started a new school. Both of them found school incredibly hard for very different reasons. Lauren was dyslexic and suffered with dyscalculia like me. Charlotte was a natural student, who loved learning but found the continual warring in classes between disruptive pupils and teachers ground her down till she found study at school almost impossible.

We tried a local church in town, it was religious and devout, but held no attraction for the girls; they hated the stuffy atmosphere of stand up, sit down. People were amazing with Pam, and gathered round her in prayer. They prayed for the girls, and for us as a family. I felt like the round peg in a square hole again. I was grappling with an onslaught from hell as my feminine nature overwhelmed me, night after night, week after week. I was suicidal again, feelings of being a freak and a failure tormented and tortured me. People were nice, they told me they loved me in church on Sundays, but I never heard from them outside of services, which left me wondering, just who were they kidding? I challenged leadership as gently as I could over its pastoral care for us as a family. All I got was another 'slap down' from the vicar for my troubles, apparently it was me who was the problem. A great pastoral response! I was sick of serving (and paying for) the hierarchy. I turned my back on the church and walked out.

'Okay, Jesus, I'm back to following you, lead me where you will.'

The only bright spot that gave me some solace and comfort was that I was regularly winning races. After five years back on the bike I had finally overcome my back pain, by using inserts and shims in my shoes I had found a position on the bike that worked and was tolerable; I was able to put the power down once more. I worked out all the pain and grief we were going through as a family, and the bitter struggles of trying to turn a profit through the recession – by kicking the hell out of my pedals. If I exhausted myself on the bike, the suicidal ideation and voices were not so loud.

The town had a thriving indie bike scene, just rock up and ride, ride hard or go home. No clubs, no traditions, no rules. Except crash helmets, and don't be an idiot. My cycling fraternity became my church. At first there was a lot of harsh mickey-taking, the guys knew I was 'church' and fair prey. The banter was funny, very funny, they ripped each other relentlessly, sometimes till we were laughing so hard it was difficult to ride in a straight line. I've always felt stupid, a bit thick, inferior, when people use humour to jostle for position in a crowd. My wit is slow, I accept that. My response was to let my legs do the talking and put the hurt on people by pressing on the pedals harder and watch them trying to hold the wheels. It was my defence mechanism against the machismo.

Three guys joined the Saturday morning rides about the same time as I did. They were based at the RAF base in Brize Norton. Mick, Toby and Mick, each of them had enough character to fill a pub on their own. Parachute instructors, they had done time at Hereford, they were archetypal, 'Grade One Alpha Males'. On the bike they loved to test themselves, they loved the cut and thrust, the aggression that was becoming a hallmark of our Saturday rides.

The first half of any ride was always hard, a couple of hours out to some café in the countryside, but the second half, the ride home was brutal. It was a full on, flat-out race, with everybody riding at the limit. It was perfect race training. I used the last ten miles to simulate a ten-mile time trial. I rode full gas. I figured if I could ride ten miles, race pace, after a fifty, sixty-mile training ride, then racing ten miles fresh and rested would be easy. Tall Mick – Spud – loved this style of riding. We would smash it up on the front together and grin. We left bodies behind, broken, all over Oxfordshire, Gloucestershire and beyond.

For the first time in my life I felt naturally at home in a macho world. I think I had finally earned male respect. In the process, my toxic male mask was building around my fragile soul once more. I was behaving like a bastard on the bike. Feeling 'the hurt' was my drug of choice, but I was beginning to realise, I also got a kick from dishing it out.

I belonged to a small race team we had formed, mostly builders and trades, and the same went there. Hard riding, no compromise. 'Let's do this thing.' Suffering, pain? 'Bring it on.' We worked as a team, totally integrated and no one pulled rank. If one of us was being an idiot, we quickly got put back in our place. We raced and performed as a team without any hierarchy, under huge intensity and stress, riding at 30 mph, only a finger's width from the tyre in front, changing positions in winds and traffic meant the potential for catastrophic, if not lethal carnage. We had seen an inexperienced rider from another team, going much slower than us, killed right in front of us.

The speed and danger was half the appeal. We worked instinctively and intuitively and bonded closer, our trust and commitment to each other was total. We won a lot of races; our teamwork was skilled and our bonds were close. Locally, we were the best. We trained together, we laughed together, we celebrated together, we watched each other bury our own parents, we weathered the recession, together.

The guys were a lot more honest, forthright and open about themselves than many of the men I'd known in church. It was refreshing. In sport we talked every bit as much about the very deepest motivations, and the issues dividing our hearts, as we did in church. Three, four hours together, suffering on the bike, means we often do it better than church. I have found fewer jerks amongst my cycling friends, than I've found in church. There is something very wholesome that goes on in the friendships formed on a bike. It is a good religion to practise. I had better, stronger, deeper relationships with guys on the bike than I did with men in the church, certainly more honest.

My experience of church was that my relationships with guys did not come near to generating such deep trust. Most of the guys in church lived behind masks of respectability. I knew from my time as pastor that half of them were hooked on porn at some stage or other in their lives. Which meant, like me, they hid from sharing the real truths buried in their hearts. At least my cycling buddies were honest about porn.

My cycling friends were there for me all through these difficult times we went through as a family. When someone

232

called to see if I wanted to 'go for a ride', they were giving me the chance to offload my burdens. There was incredible love shown to me in this long Easter Saturday, and it came not from the church, but from my cycling friends. They checked up on me regularly, where church folks had abandoned me as a 'backslider'. Riding with these friends helped keep me sane in very hard times. It was a pastoral caring community every bit as valuable and effective, if not more so, than church had been.

Thank you all.

Our tiny house felt a claustrophobic place to be, there was no space and no privacy. Having been forced by the church redundancy into a home too small and unsuited to us, the house itself was a bitter reminder of our church destroyed. Unless we locked ourselves in our bedroom, our own headspace and inner world, there was nowhere else to go. It was a house, but it never became our home, it chaffed on us all. Our emotions were raw, we all felt a vulnerability as the girls moved through puberty and into adolescence. We all felt trapped.

As a husband and father, I should have led, in weakness, vulnerability, grace and humility, but I was sinking into despair and depression. I was becoming withdrawn, I was at home, but emotionally and mentally often absent. I didn't know that all of us were dealing with so much trauma. I didn't know then, what trauma was, or what it can do to a soul. Each of us was dealing with the trauma of sudden deaths and grief.

One bitterly cold wet afternoon, Danny called. Did I want to ride? It was the weather I relished and loved to train in, knowing my opponents would most likely be stuck inside, staring out the windows at the rain. Forty years on and I had rediscovered the fire and mojo of my youth.

Glad of the company, crazy as each other, we rode out into the Cotswold hills, along lanes that were rapidly turning into streams as the torrents flushed debris beneath our wheels. Shivering and shaking over steaming coffees we huddled against the radiator in a farm shop in the middle of nowhere. Danny asked me the million-dollar question, the question no one in church had ever dared to ask me,

'Do you think you're addicted? Addicted to your cycling? Would you say you have an addictive personality?'

I fired some rapid response about being dedicated, obsessive, perfectionist and highly motivated.

Riding home in the driving rain, we were soaked to the skin, our bodies on the limit, we had maybe an hour before hyperthermia would kick in. Our fingers numb with cold and pain, we fumbled for gear changes and hitting the brakes, our core temperatures plummeting as we raced to get home before our bodies broke down. We quipped and made feeble jokes – truth was, we had overextended our limits; just another day on the bike, nothing new in that.

I was mad at Danny as we split and headed for our homes, yet I knew he was right, he had seen right through me, I was cut wide open. Now, I'm more than grateful, Danny you are an absolute legend, on and off the bike, but then I was in a world of pain. What hurt most was that I knew it was a question the Holy Spirit had been gently asking me for years, but I hadn't wanted to listen or hear. Trouble is, when you ignore that gentle conviction of the Holy Spirit, someone will come along and speak it out loud and clear; the very truth you are running and hiding from. Danny had hit me right between the eyes.

If what all the experts said was true, that all addiction is rooted in rejection and disconnection, why was I still an addict? My drugs days were decades gone, I knew God loved me, like God loves everyone. I had a loving, faithful wife, I had two beautiful daughters and lacked for nothing.

Deep down, I knew the answer, and I knew that is why I had refused to listen to the Holy Spirit. I could not bear to face the pain of the truth. Now, I knew, I had to begin the process of dealing with the shadow I had spent a lifetime trying to deny, repress, suppress, crucify and bury in my subconscious. Suppressing the truth had been an abject failure, it was the cause of my addiction to the bike, it was what I was running from and trying to hide from all the world. All I felt at the prospect was dread, fear and hopelessness, in the knowledge that I was detestable to God. I had thought life could not get any worse, but I knew it was about to.

Charlotte and Lauren had seen too many painful deaths in their short lives. They were carrying a burden of grief that neither Pam nor I had the skills to lead them through. Bereft of church and a loving family around them, they were very isolated. We were heart broken, as a family and as individuals. We were each living in our own Easter Saturday. We had buried those we loved; it had been a bleak experience. We were stuck in Easter Saturday, longing for Sunday to come.

2014 – 2019
Coming Out

Laverne Cox appeared on the front cover of *Time* magazine, under the headline, 'Transgender Tipping Point'. Laverne was one of the stars in the new TV series, *Orange is the New Black*. It had a cult following, my daughters loved it. I'd never seen it. I never watched television.

In the UK media, Frank Malone, the famous boxing promoter who managed Lennox Lewis – had transitioned, and was now she – Kelly Malone. These news stories were like stab wounds. 'Transgender' was the trending word in the media. As soon as I heard the word transgender, I instinctively knew it was me, even if I did not know what it meant.

I googled 'Transgender'. What on earth did transgender mean? I honestly had no idea. I'd never consciously heard the word before I saw Laverne on the cover of *Time*. My whole mind-set and heart attitude had been that I needed discipline and grace to deny my feminine traits and self, not information. I was, sadly, an evangelical of simple mind who leant towards fundamentalism. I had never really considered my own ignorance before.

An American Navy SEAL, one of the team who had helped plan the daring raid into Pakistan to 'take out' Osama Bin Laden, a soldier who had served for years in Afghanistan with exceptional bravery, had come out as transgender and transitioned to become a transgender icon, Kristen Beck. Kristen's story and pain resonated with me as I watched a documentary about her life. I related with her in a thousand ways.

My searching and research into transgender lives, my own life, was leading me to study biology, endocrinology, medicine, psychology, history, sociology and anthropology. Two terms were becoming familiar to me,

Dysmorphia, *the condition of acute discomfort with one's own body, a condition of acute anxiety; emotional, mental, and even physical distress.*

Gender dysphoria, *the condition of dissonance between one's physical sex and perceived gender identity and, a dissonance that can create acute emotional, mental and even physical distress. Perhaps more crudely and commonly expressed as 'feeling trapped in the wrong body'.*

It was a revelation to see my symptoms described in medical, clinical language. Now I knew what I had been suffering from since my earliest conscious years. The relief swept through my whole being in waves. Alone, when I was still and quiet, this knowledge provided a balm and a healing comfort to my soul, and I would break down and cry, so grateful to discover who I was, and had been all my life,

'I am transgender, it's okay – it's okay, I'm not a freak.'

Transgender, neither fully male, or fully female, somehow stuck between the two, with a body undoubtedly male and a soul that was undeniably feminine. What was I now supposed to do with this information, this truth? How was I supposed to live my life, find peace and break free from my addiction to the bike?

I was full of self-hatred towards all my feminine attributes. The reasons for the addiction were now obvious, no longer subconscious or unconscious. I was using the bike to medicate my pain, I was using my male persona on the bike and building site to hide, obliterate, all my feminine attributes. Being strong and ruthless on the bike gave me a male aura to hide within.

Whether intentionally or not, Danny had exposed my

heart, and my self-deception had been stripped away. At home I was becoming hyper aware of just how distant and absent I was as a husband, father, parent and friend to my family. I was in torment from dysmorphia and gender dysphoria. I was failing at every turn, emotionally I was disconnected, empty, spent. Internalised anger which would have otherwise destroyed me with depression and despair, I turned into a silent rage on the bike. For the first time in my life I could see my addiction clearly for what it was. I had not reclaimed my mojo, I had slipped back into the same pattern of addiction that had gripped me in adolescence. Physically I was stronger and faster on the bike than I had ever been, but in terms of my masculinity it was a hollow performance, a hiding from the truth. Mentally, emotionally and spiritually I was a burnt-out shell of a person.

Resolving to quit racing, I stripped down my race bike and sold off my race wheels. Maybe I could make up for the years I had been absent from home and reconnect with Pam and the girls at a deeper level. It wasn't going to be easy. Pam had retreated into a frozen stoicism and Charlotte and Lauren were in their teens, bonding with their friends, the last people they wanted to be around was mum and dad. They didn't want or need me, I was too late, the damage had been done.

I had to keep my building business afloat, the recession was still cutting my profits to zero, sometimes less. I felt like my only use, or purpose in life, was to put bread on the table, and I was struggling to do that. Pam felt like she was being dragged under, depression haunted her too. We could see the strain each other was under. Pam continually pushed me out the door and put me on my bike.

'There's no point you staying at home and feeling miserable too, go out and do what you love.'

She knew my bike was the only thing holding me together, she knew it was my 'fix'.

It was a bleak winter. Christmas day was hell. Everyone was wishing us, 'Happy Christmas!', even those who knew of our situation. It was like having acid poured into an open wound. Everyone around us seemed to be celebrating. We looked in from outside. Church was the hardest place to be of all, tradition, nostalgia, saccharine and a virgin birth. Was this the medicine we were supposed to be drinking? Where was the love?

I got a phone call, the offer of a large building project in Berwick, on the Scottish border. It was good money. I was already running a local build. It was an insane gamble, just me and a labourer to run two building projects, back to back, three hundred miles apart, but I was desperate, and not thinking straight. I felt close to a breakdown.

Setting the project up meant a few trips back and forth. The acknowledgement of my transgender identity had both given me hope and increased my despair, it was keeping me awake, night after night. Battling with overwhelming suicidal thoughts, exhausted, I simply gave up the fight with my feminine self. I bought clothes, make-up, a wig. Stopping in a motel along the A1, I drank a bottle of wine, and got changed. Looking in the mirror, I loathed myself.

'God, I'm detestable to you, and I'm detestable to me, but this is me, this is who I always have been. A total and utter failure of a man, unable to look after my own family, unable to help them in any way.'

Out of my mind with grief, I walked out of the motel into the night and the driving rain, and began walking up the hard shoulder, a verge, less than a meter wide. There was a garage about a mile further up. Walking in heels is not a skill I've ever mastered, even these one-inch heels felt precarious. Lorries roared past, drenching me to the skin even more than the rain, the occasional blast of a horn, as drivers, too late, saw me walking on the side of the road. The suction and tail blast of wind from the lorries as they skimmed passed, physically shook me.

The garage was closed. Shivering and numb, frozen inside and out, I begged for a bottle of wine. The guy behind the glass, cashing up, relented. Walking back into the oncoming traffic I was wrestling with suicide. Raging at God, tears rolling down my face. I wanted to die. I wanted a lorry to hit me and send me into oblivion, anything but living with this. I didn't want to kill myself, I didn't want to destroy my family any further, but if a lorry hit me, that was fine, it would be recorded as 'an accident'.

The rain lashed down. Back in the hotel, I drank the second bottle. Picking up the car keys I headed out again. I drove out onto the A1. Tears gave way to a numbness. I was blind drunk, barely in control. Would I drive into a motorway bridge? I longed for death, a way out. It was the early hours of the morning, I was spent, the raging subsided, I felt almost sober, clear minded.

'I don't want to kill someone else's husband, son, partner or wife, I need to get back to the hotel safe. I don't want to damage my own family any further.'

'You have to walk into the light.'

The voice was calm, tender, loving and clear. I knew the Holy Spirit was speaking to me. I knew what walking into the light meant, I had to get real and be honest about myself. I had to find a community who could help me, I knew too, that the church was not the place. I'd been around church long enough to know the score, I'd tried enough times to find healing in confession and prayer, and I knew the church was powerless to help. The church knew nothing about people like me. It just labelled us, judged us and put us in its neat and tidy boxes. I knew all I would find in church was judgement, ignorance and fear.

Seeking out the transgender community on Facebook, I found a group of transgender women, all about my own age. They shared their stories with me, patiently, kindly – suffering my endless interruptions, ignorance and insensitivity. Those early conversations were a mind-blowing revelation, each phone call, each long messaging session, I was hearing my own story flowing from other people's hearts and lips. The love, the care, the patience, the kindness and the sensitivity of everyone I spoke to broke me wide open. I would put the phone down afterwards and weep with relief, with the knowledge that I was no longer alone. I had friends who understood me. None of them were churched, or Christian, as far as I knew, but they couldn't have been more kind.

Away from home, secretly I began to dress again, to express who I was. In doing so, I discovered, not the anger of God, but rather, God's love. Was God healing me? On the one hand I was finding a peace within myself about my gender identity, accepting my transness, but on the other I was riddled with guilt and torment at deceiving my own family, my friends and the wider world.

I came home from Berwick to news that had gone viral. In an explosive article in the *Guardian*, Vicky Beeching, the worship leader from our church in Oxford, had come out as lesbian. Vicky had become one of the biggest names in the American church worship scene. It was a massive moment, not just for Vicky, but for the western church. How they responded and judged her, really revealed just who they were and what they stood for. I was thrilled for her, that she had found the courage to break free. I knew what being imprisoned felt like. Vicky's coming out, made my own seem both inevitable and imminent.

Her story gave great hope to our girls too. Charlotte and Lauren both expressed their approval, many of their friends were gay. One of the main reasons that both our girls had given up on church was because of the way they saw their gay friends being judged and treated in church. If God was that kind of God, they were not interested. If God judged gays, just for being themselves, then how did he see them? In their eyes, God seemed to have some real hang ups. I watched quietly as Charlotte and Lauren lovingly challenged Pam's homophobia.

Pam:
'At university, my best friends had been a lesbian and a gay man. I loved them unconditionally, but my gay friend especially. Their sexuality wasn't even an issue, it was their characters that impressed me and enriched my life, their humour was exuberant and bright, they were good people to hang out with, they lifted me up.

Now my daughters were bringing their gay friends home from school and I realised that I had become homophobic. How had it happened? I saw the beauty and the character and quality in my daughters' friends and my heart was undone; who had I become?

Decades in the conservative evangelical church had caused me to become homophobic, not just my horrific judgemental beliefs, but even my emotional responses were ugly and dehumanising, for me and those I judged. I had allowed myself to become indoctrinated. My daughters' friends exposed the depth of my irrational and religious prejudices, they taught me to love again, to love freely. It was a healing, my heart softened and my understanding caused me to reach out and love – unconditionally, without judgement.

Church is a homophobic, transphobic institution, in the main. To my shame I had allowed myself to become that way too. We happily live our lives judging others, and don't even realise or recognise our privilege. What if we had been born somehow 'other'?

I have operated in judgement all my life in so many areas. I have judged people for their wardrobes and their bookshelves, their parents and their parenting. Ultimately it is not the judgment of God, a religion, a church – it is mine.

Mine to acknowledge. Mine to own. Mine to deal with.'

I was facing a huge dilemma. I had begun racing a tandem with a woman who lived locally. Jan had been a national level mountain biker but had developed macular degeneration and was going rapidly blind. It was huge, Jan was battling despair, depression, medication and fear. Fear of a life being blind. The grief and loss for her was all encompassing. Racing was a lifeline for her. Fear and torment, the despair and depression were things I knew only too well. I was gutted to hear her story, so I stepped in to pilot her tandem so that she could keep racing.

On the bike we clicked, we bonded, we 'got each other'. Jan knew nothing about my own battle. The chemistry was unreal. In our first season we were just getting used to the tandem, each other and how to synchronise our efforts, but straight away the results were way beyond our expectations. We were flying. Jan had big hopes for the coming year, winning the National Championships was her goal. I had decided to quit from racing and had already sold most of my kit, but how could I let Jan down?

I told Jan I wanted to quit, but that I would give her my total commitment for one last year. Over the winter I trained harder than I had ever done in my life. As winter gave way to spring and the two building projects began to rise out of the ground, Jan and I started our first race of the season. With ice still on the ground, our lungs ripped wide open in the cold air and legs shredded, we demolished our previous best time. Over the year we only raced twelve times, but every time we raced, we went faster, smashing previous times on every course we raced. It was unreal – I had been racing forty years and I had seen and known people race for years and never get any quicker.

I'd borrowed the wheels from my training bike and put them on my old race frame. After each race with Jan on the tandem, with only five minutes recovery I'd jump on my bike and race again. I was going even faster solo, than we were on the tandem. I was high, on adrenaline, testosterone and endorphins. This really was something weird going down. Everybody must have thought we were doing performance enhancing drugs. I was at peak fitness and in the form of my life.

Jan won the National Disability Championship Circuit Race, beating all the Para Olympic squad. I decided to have my first tilt at the National Championships since I was sixteen. I came away with a fourth in the ten miles, a bronze in the twenty-five and a silver in the Circuit Championship.

I raced solo half a dozen times and smashed my previous best times at both ten and twenty-five miles. I was averaging thirty miles an hour and racing at national level again. Inwardly, however, I was broken beyond anything I'd known since my breakdown from opium addiction. On the bike racing, I was almost floating, hardly feeling the pain in my legs, lungs and heart. Indeed, the pain of racing was once more, nothing compared to the hell of my life unravelling and disintegrating. It was a very zen experience, and yet on the bike I felt strangely closer to God than I ever had done; there, my life came into clear focus and I could pray, even whilst racing maxed out physically. There was a strange sense of rightness, symmetry about it all. I knew it was my swan song.

I was still training and riding with Mick. He had left the Forces, opened a bike shop in town with his wife. I had done the shop refit for them, converting a warehouse into a modern showroom and workshop. I was watching Mick mellow, from the Forces hard man to reveal a man with a massive pastoral heart, deep sensitivity and compassion. His humour was a powerful screen which hid a vulnerability I could relate to. We rode for hours and talked lots.

Some days, at my lowest, with nowhere to go and no one to confide in I would sit on Mick and Kirsty's office floor and cry. They knew the pain, grief and loss we had been through as a family, but not my secret battles.

Mick and Kirsty had gathered a thriving, close knit and friendly cycling club, built around the shop. It was astonishing to watch it grow from nothing, and it was a real tribute to their devotion and dedication. There was a core of a dozen women of all ages who were riding together, forging close friendships, and they were mad keen to race. The women wanted some coaching, so I offered to help them in training and racing, not as a coach, but as a friend and encourager.

We did long winter training rides, we practised skills and drills, we talked about pretty much everything cycling. The enthusiasm, the keenness and the team spirit were infectious. Watching them and helping them prepare and develop for team time trials was magical. They were of such diverse age and fitness levels, and yet they were riding and gelling as a team far better than the men, even better at times than my own race team, and we had years of experience in the discipline. Then it dawned on me, it was all to do with the lack of testosterone and jostling egos (of which I was probably the worst offender).

I felt so happy being *part of* the team, training with the women, I felt such a peace and oneness. Memories came flooding back, of all my female friends at school. I remembered that birthday party when our house was filled with girls. The sense of belonging was profound – then the penny dropped; this is what I had been missing and grieving all these years. I was able to drop my aggressive male mask and defence, my life-long melancholy lifted when I was with them. I was able, for the first time in decades to be myself. I could be gentle, kind, sensitive, loving, affirming and caring, without the fear of judgement! The relief, as all this settled into place, in my heart and mind, was measurable. Another piece of my jigsaw fell into place. My inner life was slowly starting to make sense.

Back in Berwick I continued in the long conversations with my newfound friends. Every month they would meet, to catch up with each other, socialise, party, let off steam and celebrate life together. They invited me along. For the first time in my life I was dressed en femme and it was not secret. I felt confident, happy and free as I walked through the city. I didn't want to rush to the restaurant where everyone was meeting, so I sat in a small Italian bar in the plaza, sipped on a beer and watched out the window as the world walked by. The waitress was lovely, she chatted with me, warmly and accepted me just as I was. Folks sat around, not batting an eyelid at my presence. It was clear they did not give a fig, whoever I was. It was the most wonderful realisation, that I could exist as me, people accepted me! Fear rolled off me.

Walking past a huge building site, a couple of construction workers stood up from their work, and as I walked towards them, I watched them smirk, leer and grin, as I passed them, they released a string of profanities, expletives and curses after me.

'So, this is what it is like, to be hated within society.'

Standing in the entrance lobby of the hotel bar, I was still shaking with fear and anger at the abuse I'd just received. I was grateful they had been at work, in uniform, stood behind a six-foot mesh fence. Had they been out on the drink, I think they might have beaten me to a pulp. I scanned around trying to search out Mia, Nikki and Mel. I pushed through the crowd.

Mia was easy to find, even in flats, she stood above the crowd. She had been so kind to me in messaging, texting and over the phone, and here she was, more beautiful than her photos, more engaging, witty and compassionate than I had imagined. Mel found us, and introduced herself, stunning and geeky, funny as hell. I knew I would like her from the conversations we'd already had. A triathlete and like myself, fit as a whippet, with the same quiet confidence. Nikki was so pretty, so attractive, it was impossible to tell she had been born male. Nikki and I had a similar upbringing and story, she was a few years ahead of us all in her transition, she had been a pillar of strength to me over the months. She had also inherited a deep faith from her grandfather who had brought her up.

They were all, without exception, sensitive, caring, brilliantly witty and self-deprecating. Over a meal and those ordinary, every-day discussions, I realised that to be transgender is perfectly normal. I even found myself, laughing at myself, the pain and the stigma was being broken off. It was one of the happiest weekends of my life. I had found my tribe, my family, and they adopted me, welcomed me in as one of their own.

We danced into the early hours. In male mode I had to be drunk in order to dance, I always felt awkward, exposed, embarrassed and stiff as a plank. Here, sober, I felt free as a bird. I danced out of pure celebration and joy, at being alive, at being me. In male clothes I had always tried to hide, be anonymous in the crowd, and if I ever had to wear a suit, a shirt and tie, it felt like a torture and a torment, and always had. Here, in a dress, heels and make-up, it felt the most natural thing in the world.

I paid for another night in the hotel, I couldn't face going back to the building site. Saturday, I got dressed in jeans and a summer top, and wandered down for breakfast. The hotel staff were warm and friendly. Some of them chatted as they served, their kindness, acceptance and affirmation reduced me to tears again.

Sitting outside the Italian bar, I ordered a coffee. The same waitress served me, she came and sat down at my table in the sunshine. Did I mind if she smoked? For fifteen minutes on her break, we chatted about family, Italy and work. I was still reeling inside, with the realisation people actually liked me, even though I was trans. Standing up to go, she smiled. Walking away, she turned, embarrassed, 'Ciao, and by the way – you look lovely.'

Driving back to the building site, 150 fifty miles north, I cried most of the way. I did not want to go back to macho-land, not now, not ever. I loved the gentle, quiet, sensitive, loving, empathising me that was emerging, like a butterfly from its ugly, male cocoon. That was another thing I had learnt in my research; the butterfly is the symbol of the transgender community, the perfect metaphor of transition, transformation, and metamorphosis.

I was becoming certain that God, and the Holy Spirit were leading me in this journey of self-discovery, but as I grew more sure of who I was, the conflict with the world, the expectations of family, friends, church and community grew more desperate. The feelings of guilt at deceiving Pam, the girls and my friends intensified.

One Sunday evening, longing to have some guidance from God, I accompanied Pam to church. She still had no inkling of the suicidal battle raging within me. I lay face down on the stone-cold floor, the worship washed over me. I wept with despair. Someone at the front shared 'a word, a picture'. They had found a brooch, lost on in the grass at the edge of the pavement on the way to church, it was a jewelled brooch – a butterfly. They had held it in their pocket, all the way to church. They wanted to share this, because they believed 'God might be speaking' to somebody through the story of this lost butterfly brooch.

Love, the presence of God, had already arrested me. The Holy Spirit whispered into my heart,

'I know you feel lost, but I knew where you were all the way through, I have you, I'm holding you, in the palm of my hand. You are safe in my pocket.'

I was that lost and found butterfly brooch. I felt love wash through me, over me, and embrace me.

There was a time for open prayer, for the church to pray and minister to one another. Richard walked over. We had led homegroup together a few years before. He and his wife Kathrine inspired me.

'I think I have a word for you, but it's not an easy one, take it away and pray about it, I might be totally wrong, I have this picture, of a seed, a seed being dropped to the ground, and it's falling into a big deep crack in the concrete.'

God's truth exploded inside me. Jesus' parable of the seed, dropped into the ground and bearing fruit, was one of the most central truths of my personal faith.

'Unless a seed falls to the ground and dies, it cannot bear fruit. But if a seed falls to the ground and dies, it will bear fruit, it will be fruitful, 30, 60 even a hundred-fold.'

In that moment I knew God was in this transformation I was going through, and more than that, God was confirming my place and role within the transgender community. Love flooded me, filled me – people talk about the Glory of God, I was tasting it, feeling it, love all around and within me. I knew in an instant the glorious truth of Richard's words.

God had dropped me into one of the most broken, hardest to reach people in the world, the transgender community. It was not that they were hard, it was that the church had spewed them out, cursed them, cut them off and demonised them. Many in the community had turned their backs on the church and on God because they had no desire to be abused anymore. God had broken my heart over the transgender community.

My labourer had taken a weekend off in London. I'd spent the weekend en femme with my trans friends in Leeds. I'd been happy, relaxed and at peace. We'd eaten out, talked and danced late into the night. Back in Berwick, walking alone into the house that we were extending and refurbishing, I stood in the hallway and started to shake uncontrollably. Looking at the sheer enormity of what we had undertaken, I felt like I was drowning, inadequate and broken by the massive project. I knew I was drained, physically, mentally and emotionally, close to burn out and a breakdown. These were the first tremors, the warning signs, I knew what was coming. I'd survived one nervous break-down, I didn't think I could survive another. Sick with weariness I climbed the stairs and sat on my mattress on the floor, staring at the walls. Sobs and convulsions engulfed me, my body and emotions trying to tell me they'd had enough and couldn't take any more.

I couldn't exist as me in secret much longer. I was facing some stark choices; thoughts of suicide were relentless, perhaps I should run away and leave my family, transition and start my life all over again? No, I couldn't walk out on my family. I knew a breakdown was imminent, I had to reach out and ask for help – that meant telling people who I am – walking into the light, 'coming out', the thing I feared most. I'd reached the end of the road.

Next day, I got up early, pulled out my laptop and began to write. I wrote for nearly twenty-four hours solid, twenty pages in all. I rewrote, edited and rewrote till I was sure that I had written the truth, in love, as best as I could. It was the most painful, difficult letter I have ever written. I saved it.

The drive home at the end of the week was three hundred miles of dread and anxiety. Fear turned my insides to liquid.

I thought I was about to lose my wife, my children and everything I had worked years to build; my work, friends, reputation, community. I waited till the girls had gone to bed and opened my laptop for Pam to read my letter. We held hands and cried.

Pam.

'As I focused on the screen, I felt a crushing weight come over me. As I read, I could see it had brought Paul a measure of peace and understanding and so I figured that made it good news. I felt numb, I could see that Paul's world had stopped and would not restart until I had given my response.

I had absolutely no idea what I was taking in, even less what the implication of what it all would mean. The term 'transgender' was new to me, I had no idea what it meant for us, but in that moment my priority was to affirm to Paul. Whatever this meant, we would face it together. I truly meant it, and I think I really did believe that we could find somebody who would be able to solve the problem … and if not that, then God would "sort" it.'

Pam's response floored me. I had been expecting total rejection. Her love, if anything, seemed more real than ever before. I had always known I had never been able to fully love her, not because I didn't try, but because I knew there was a part of me that was frozen, locked away, but I'd never known what it was. Now I knew.

I found myself crying all the time. Tears came easily, too easily, watching people hurting made me cry. When I went out en-femme and someone was kind to me, even the supermarket cashiers who called me 'love', with sincere warmth, their kindness would set me off in tears. The years of hardness, the mask, the pretence was being slowly peeled away. I cried with the relief of finally being free. I cried because of the pain I knew I was putting Pam through. I cried because I longed to transition, physically, I longed for hormones and surgery, to put an end to a lifetime of dysmorphia and gender dysphoria. It was as if my body was awash with hormones, I was so sensitive and so open emotionally and spiritually, I was raw, naked, it was almost impossible to think or see straight.

Pam:
'I was desperately playing catch up, trying to understand what had befallen us. I couldn't bring myself to tell anyone. Research made for uncomfortable, painful reading, and what I learnt led me to my knees, pleading with God to "take it away". I alternated between hope and despair, numbness and fury as I railed at God for the trap I found myself in. As the weeks turned into months, I began to see that in just being honest, Paul was beginning to experience a new freedom ... even happiness. It was all I had ever wanted for him, but I had no inkling of the price I would have to pay.'

A lifetime of volcanic anger that had festered in my heart, rooted in self-hatred, started to dissipate and dissolve. Explaining to Pam the power that dysmorphia and gender dysphoria had over me, my entire life, she prayed for me, with me.

'You have to stop hating yourself.'

After months of strained silence between us, we now found ourselves talking in depth whenever we could face the pain. We had years, decades, to catch up on. Our greatest problem was that me being me, presenting as feminine, was too great a shock for Pam. If I dressed, I would watch her response, it was as if I had stabbed her with a knife, my being transgender wounded her, every time she saw me. I interpreted that recoil as her repulsion of me. It was too difficult to even be in the same room together. I felt like killing myself because of the hurt I saw I was inflicting upon her, and her repulsion of me made me want to run away and hide. It felt like our marriage was in ruins. My self-hatred only increased with my failure as a husband.

Pam:
'The day had to come when I had to surrender my understanding and dream of marriage – to take in its place something I neither wanted nor understood. The tears flowed like I had never known before and I truly wondered if they would ever stop. The grief of letting go of something I had invested nearly 30 years of my life in was total. I felt mocked, humiliated and utterly alone.

I had reached an impasse. We had reached an impasse … for every step Paul took out of shame, I took one in; the fear of being judged, the fear of social stigma, the fear of people talking behind my back. Shame and solitude held me in those early months. I struggled so hard with my own shock and disquiet, I couldn't bear to impose even a fraction of that onto others, so I retreated into a cave of my own making. I couldn't face the opinions of others when I didn't even know my own mind. Much less could I stomach their awkwardness or pity. I wasn't interested in people's advice or direction … I desperately wanted to know what God thought, but my bitterness drowned everything out.

As I struggled to regain some handle on life, with two daughters to be there for and a job that demanded emotional resilience, I utilised my lifelong default towards stoicism. It enabled me to survive, I was mechanically meeting the daily demands of life, but inside I was still reeling, grieving. Little things would set me off … photos of friends, smiling couples, celebrating their wedding anniversaries on Facebook, posts of families all happily enjoying a meal or time together. As I scrolled through all the congratulations, the complimentary and positive comments, in those moments, I hated them for their "normal", happy lives.

Our silver wedding anniversary came and went without a word. It was one of the bleakest days of my life.'

Our greatest worry was Charlotte and Lauren. We knew, my life would have to remain a secret from them, until such time as we both knew they were ready and strong enough to cope with the reality of who their dad really was. Now was not the time to tell them.

Dressing, presenting as feminine, being myself caused the dysmorphia and gender dysphoria to dissipate and disappear. I felt free, happy and alive instead of tormented, depressed and hopeless. I called my sister, Sylvia; could I come and stay, and oh, by the way, I am transgender, can I visit en-femme? Over the years, with family, church and life, Sylvia and I, once so close, had drifted apart. Dad's death had brought us together again.

I drove to Sylvia's one Thursday evening. We embraced and began to unpack my story. For me it felt like being reunited to the sister I had lost as a young child when I buried my feminine self. All the years of feeling estranged were washed away and we bonded closer than ever. For the next four years, we lived as sisters, as if we always had been, always should have been, it seemed easier for both of us.

Living en-femme in Sheffield with my sister, Thursday to Tuesday, once every month, was my 'coming home'. I lived entirely en-femme. Here I found myself, here I found the peace I had been longing for all my life. Staying with Sylvia was the beginning of a deep and profound healing. Sylvia created a safe space, a place of security that enabled both Pam and I to grow, work through the damage in our marriage that my coming out had caused. The long weekends I spent in Sheffield gave Pam a chance to breathe, process and come to terms with who I really am, and have always been.

Pam.

'It was always a relief to see Paul drive off. From Thursday to Monday I would hide in activity and pretend life was normal. Monday evenings came round too fast, I didn't want to face the truth of what my "marriage" had become. The sight of Paul dressed as a female complete with feminine mannerisms assaulted me and scrambled my emotions into an uncontrollable mess of distress and confusion that was brutal and total. My partner, chosen in no small part for his rugged and macho appearance, had been hijacked. Was I seriously supposed to welcome this imposter? My shock and revulsion mixed with an anger which I could barely contain. Was my whole marriage built upon a lie that had finally been admitted to? This new character played before me seemed to mock me, the loser. My man, my husband had gone, the secret was out and life could never ever be the same again.'

Pam was praying for my healing, and for her that only meant one thing, that God would heal me of having this feminine soul, restore me to being wholly male, masculine to the core. I was open to that possibility, but I also genuinely feared it. As far as I could understand, that would mean God cutting out my heart. Maybe God would give me some kind of superhuman will power to crucify myself all over again. Thirty-five years of rigorous self-discipline, devotion to God, fasting and prayer had failed to make any difference to who I was. I had loved and served God with my whole being. Church had kicked my soul from pillar to post. Here I was, still standing.

My only desire and prayer in life had been to follow Jesus. I had given God everything I had, my whole life had become rooted and anchored in Christ. If it hadn't, I don't think I would have survived the church.

I had taken two steps walking into the light and out of secrecy. Both had been an incredible, beautiful encouragement to me. The transgender community had given me hope, and significant healing, as they shared their lives and stories with me, and Pam had not rejected me. It was time to drag out the list that I had written in my mind, all those nights I had lain awake in suicidal anxiety. Top of the list of safe friends to tell were my two best, and closest, Christian friends.

I phoned Alison the same week. She listened, she prayed for me over the phone. I would call her every now and then; I didn't want to burden her, she had enough worries of her own. Every time we spoke it was clear she thought I needed to repent, she didn't actually put it like that, but everything she said made me feel I was in the wrong and that she was trying to fix me. She encouraged me to go and see a counsellor from an organisation called Living Stones. I challenged her and told her she needed Jesus' healing every bit as much as me. I didn't hear from her for another two years.

I asked my best friend Bob over for a meal. We went to a quiet Indian restaurant, and I poured out my heart, told him my story. He listened, said all the good loving things, you'd expect a best friend to say. Leaving the restaurant, we hugged and he said, 'Goodbye'. I never heard from him again.

1964 – 2017
The Curse

L iving for fifty years imprisoned by society – living to fulfil everyone else's expectations of me – left me wondering what was left of my true spontaneous self; the personality that had become submerged, annihilated in the desperate need to become a male worthy of society's acceptance. It hadn't been a prison sentence; it had been fifty years in Total Isolation, a solitary confinement. It had been me who had locked the cell door and thrown away the key. I had never had the chance to live as myself, to express myself, to be feminine and happy; this was the sentence that society had forced, by violence and hate, upon me. It left me overwhelmed with grief and sadness, and even more tears.

I had stepped out into freedom, the thought of God 'healing' me, scared me. It seemed too cruel. After fifty-five years I had finally discovered who I really was, I had only just begun to live again, the thought of this being taken away from me, seemed a very real possibility. My heart was softening more every day. God had re-opened tenderness, gentleness and sensitivity, the doors and windows of my soul, the love was pouring in.

The personality I had tried to crucify was all about sensitivity, tenderness, gentleness, kindness, giving, sharing, vulnerability. I had such a love of colour, touch, feel, for fabrics, fashion, clothes and artistic expression that could only be described as feminine, all things I had obliterated in my male and drab existence of fear. Mothering and sistering, being, felt more natural than the endless striving of masculinity to be strong, resilient, dominant; the endless doing and competitive striving of masculinity.

Everyone sexualises gender and gender expression, assumes that gender expression is all about sexuality. To me, it seemed the smallest part. Was it about feeling like a woman? I don't know what a woman feels like. It was more to do with being myself, being honest, authentic and true, revealing what is inside of me. If that happens to be feminine, so be it and so what.

Fifty years of repressing personality had done untold damage, but I felt the joy of discarding the grave clothes of my male existence and with them, the fear of social rejection. I found, standing in that freedom, able to be myself, I no longer cared what anyone thought of me. I was beyond caring. Fifty years of suffering and misery was over. The world was going to have to get used to me. If there was a healing God needed to do, it wasn't in delivering me from a feminine identity; the healing was in the restoring of it. Joy was flowing from my heart in a way I had never experienced before, the melancholy that had permeated my soul for a lifetime, cleared and dispersed like fog in the sunshine and knowledge of God's love, and no one could take it from me.

The desire to transition was a daily, constant longing. Most my transgender friends that I was close to, women my own age, were in the process of transition. I was watching the effect that hormones were having on them, as their bodies changed shape, their skin softened and their feminine inner selves emerged and flowered into womanhood. I was deeply jealous of the femininity they were breathing out. It was way more than physical; it was contentment that hummed and sang in their souls. Love radiated and sparkled in their eyes. They had come fully alive. Butterflies.

Looking at my own body, it was muscled and ripped, from a life of cycling, running and graft on the building site. I had a large Adam's apple, square jaw, big nose, broad shoulders and big hands, I was, in appearance totally male. My own male body had always revulsed me. My skin was hard, leathered, worn and wrinkled from a lifetime spent outside under the sun. As far as being physically feminine was possible, I was aging rapidly, I felt my life was over. I was heart-broken, totally shattered. The ugly caterpillar.

Dysmorphia and gender dysphoria were crippling me. I was unable to 'flip the switch' anymore, I could not stop being me, the truth was out, it felt like I had opened a Pandora's Box. I had managed to live all my life with suicidal thoughts and compulsions, I think partly because I had been able to 'flip a switch', and go into total denial about my own, inner reality, and partly out of a duty to love and please all those around me.

Burying pain was a life skill, both off and on the bike. Gender dysphoria and dysmorphia had been the source of all my addiction. Suicidal ideation, suicidal thoughts still tormented and oppressed me, I could not turn them off.

Lying awake at night I realised, looking back over my life, that my cycling had kept me alive. It was my medication against despair and depression, it was my escape. Self-harm on the bike helped me manage the violence of my repressed inner life.

The fear of God healing me, and taking away my transgender being, and the distress of aging made me long to have some memories of my true self, the feminine me, that I could cherish in old age. I imagined old age, sitting alone in the nursing home, rocking away to myself. If I had some photos of myself on the wall, or in an album, at least I could look at them and remember the woman I was, the woman I might have been, and the woman who never got to live. I would take her with me, into old age, memories to cherish, even if God did heal me. It sounds pathetic and

I'm embarrassed to admit all this, but it was a very powerful grief, and a very real sense of loss, that I was battling with. I had discovered the truth too late, too late to be able to do anything about it; transition for me seemed an impossibility.

Looking through the photos and selfies of my friends, I knew some of them had been to see life-coaches who specialised entirely in helping transwomen look and feel more feminine in their own skin. Many of them provided a make-up tuition and took photos so that you had a record of the session. I decided to get some photos of my feminine self before God snatched it away.

I drove down to Winchester to see Kerry. We'd spoken on the phone, she sounded caring, kind, sensitive and professional. I'd seen photos of some of her clients, and I liked her style and skill with make-up, hair and fashion. The sense of shame and guilt I felt on the drive down was overpowering, by the time I arrived, I was frightened, embarrassed and tongue tied. The desire to run as I knocked on the studio door was causing my whole body to shake in tremors.

Kerry's warmth and friendliness were disarming. She chatted easily and settled my nerves and fears, she talked me through every stage of make-up application, cleansing, preparing the skin, primer and foundation. She showed me the best brushes, powders and tips on how to use them. I'd brought my own dress and changed in the dressing room. Then she sat me down and talked me through how to get the best from my hair, and the best brushes to use. It was a short masterclass in how to make the best of what you have – in my case, not much.

As we were talking, and as she applied my make-up, my soul was in total turmoil. Here I was, a father, a husband, a full-blooded male – in everyone else's eyes but my own. I had been a missionary and a pastor, a preacher and church leader. I felt like Jonah in the belly of the whale. I had run as far away from God as anyone could.

'A man in women's clothes, detestable to God!' These thoughts and feelings were crashing through me, even as Kerry said,

'There, finished. You look fantastic! Have a look in the mirror, while I sort my camera.'

Stepping in front of the full-length mirror, instead of the man in a dress, and my clown-like make-up, I looked at myself, and saw, for the first time, the woman I should have, could have, been, I felt a tsunami of love hit me, in crashing waves. Love was flowing through me, over me, around me, in me. I started to cry, the tears welling up in an unstoppable fountain, somewhere, from deep down within. Relief, relief and joy.

'… and streams of living water will flow from within.'

I knew the Holy Spirit was all over me and within. Everything I am describing happened in a second, milliseconds, moments. Kerry stood there, camera in hand, bewildered,

'Are you okay, honey, what's wrong?'

Tears are gushing, pouring out like a river.

'Nothing, honestly, I'm fine.'

As the Holy Spirit washed through me, I heard God whisper into my heart,

'Chrissie, I love you, just as you are.'

The tenderness, and the power of those words, broke me wide open, and I crumpled to the floor, sobbing. A vision opened in my heart, my mind, my spirit – memories as clear and real as watching a YouTube video:

I was walking up the stairs of our old squat in Kingston Road, I was cold, weary and wrung out, after dealing, and then that suicidal journey on the train back to London. I opened the door and saw Lizzy and Jeff, together in our bed. All the emotions and feelings, were as real as the day it happened, the shock, the homicidal rage, the sudden calm, closing the door on them, and walking down the stairs in a state of total devastation.

I heard the Holy Spirit, speaking gently, into my heart.

'Chrissie, the moment you closed that door, in your commitment to love – desiring to do them no harm, you opened a door into your own life, you released a murderous hatred upon yourself. You have hated yourself, for your failure as a man, ever since.'

Then the vision shifted to another scene, it was those days in Earls Court,

I was walking the street, as a transvestite, a prostitute.

I shuddered to see the memories, and the pain of it, the guilt, remorse and shame, choked me,

The Holy Spirit whispered to my spirit.

'Chrissie, today, right now, here in this place – I am setting you free. Free of the self-hatred, free of all uncleanness, free of the shame and guilt that has tormented you ever since.'

I collapsed into the loving arms of Jesus, I was there once again, washing Jesus' feet with my tears. Love and gratitude came welling up with an unstoppable force.

Kerry was kneeling on the floor next to me, watching helplessly as her client was having some kind of emotional melt down. She put a hand on my shoulder, said not a word. I knew she understood something had been unlocked in my soul.

Heaven had come down and kissed me.

I've been around long enough, I've experienced enough of heaven and hell, to know which is which. I've been set free of life-long torments before. I've had an exorcism, for goodness sakes! I survived and lived through the aftermath, and the healing that follows and flows from deliverance. I've prayed for others, and seen them released, in a moment, from ties that have bound them all their life. I knew I had just been through one of the biggest, deepest deliverance sessions of my life, a sovereign work of God, with no human agent but Kerry, who was totally unchurched. There, stood in a 'dressing service'

for transgender women, God had come and set me free from evil spirits, the 'shadows' of the soul, disturbances of the psyche, call them what you will – it was real.

I was looking forwards to enjoying the fruit of this new freedom and a deeper, fuller, more intimate relationship with God, and it had got suddenly very real, up close, God was in my face, and on my case. As I drove home, my heart rejoicing, I knew Pam was going to experience the first fruits of this deliverance. The self-hating, moody, sullen, easily angered husband she had tiptoed around all these years, was gone, dead.

How did I know – for the sake of my fundamentalist, Christian critics and friends – that what I had experienced was not some kind of demonic counterfeit? I am my own most severe critic, and need no help in that. Right-wing conservative and lunatic fringe Pastors, were pumping out YouTube videos, accusing transgender people of being demon possessed, 'Satan's children'.

I knew I had met with God, because love, joy, peace, gentleness, goodness, kindness, faithfulness patience and self-control were becoming easier and easier to manifest in my life. The fruit of the spirit is love, joy, peace, patience, kindness, goodness, gentleness, faithfulness and self-control. The way to test the fruit of any so-called experience of God, is in the quality of character that emerges from it. Let's be honest, many people claim ecstatic encounters with God, and often their character remains, every bit as bitter and broken as before.

The guilt I carried as a father was intolerable. As my own battles had increased, I had become unable to offer the love and support my family needed.

It felt like I was in the same place as King David when he was face down before God; he had committed adultery with Bathsheba and then murdered her husband, now he was pleading with God for the life of his son.

I had not committed adultery or murdered anyone, but I carried the guilt of being a useless husband and father. I felt like I had destroyed marriage for Pam, all her hopes, all her dreams, all that she had given and paid to come this far. I honestly believed in my addiction and absence as a father that I had neglected and damaged my own daughters. I loved them each with all my heart, but I had been unable to follow through by being present in their lives when they most needed me.

One night, in the midst of this despair and darkness, a scripture dropped into my consciousness, from out of nowhere. I hadn't read my Bible for a couple of years; in fact, I'd hardly read my Bible since our church imploded. I was sick of religion and religiosity, I just wanted to love Jesus. I didn't need or want more Bible knowledge; I had to learn to live what I had learnt so far. I wanted God, not religion.

'Return to me, says the Lord, for I have torn you, I have injured you, but I will now heal you. On the first day, I shall bind up your wounds, on the second day I will revive you, and on the third day I will restore you, and you will dwell in my presence.'

It was the early hours of the morning; Pam was sleeping fitfully by my side. I didn't want to wake her. Slipping as quietly as I could from our room, I crept past the girls' rooms, and sat in the cold of our dining room. Pulling out the Bible concordance and wiping off the dust, I looked up the words,

'For I have torn you.'

They were from the little book of Hosea, one of the minor prophets, sandwiched between the Old and the New Testaments. Sometimes you read these ancient scriptures, and it's just lifeless words on a page, other times they come alive, and resonate within you. I had no reason to recall these verses, and now they were speaking to me. The Holy Spirit was bearing witness with my spirit, God was breathing a promise into me.

'I will revive, heal and restore you that you may dwell in my presence.'

God was speaking to me through these words. These words spoken by a man who had seen the heart of God, eight hundred years before Christ appeared. My heart leapt; my spirit was stirred. I felt God was promising me; that we would each be restored, restored as a family too! Not immune from further suffering, but restored into an intimacy with God, with perfect love.

Scripture is a strange thing, it is both inert and lifeless, yet within it, both folly and wisdom abound. The stories are sometimes literal, historical and true. Other times they are mythical, allegorical – yet somehow these stories all contain truths. This is the power of faith, or is it just wishful thinking? For me, it was an encounter with God, who stepped into our suffering and wanted to walk with us through it. We had tasted death, we had lived in the absence of God, we had tasted Easter Saturday to the full. God was breathing into my spirit, resurrection, new life, hope, dreams and vision for the future.

For me, the Bible will always be a book of healing. I know others like to use it as a weapon, but the choice is entirely ours. I shared these verses with Pam. We held them close to our hearts and prayed.

'For I have torn you, but I will heal you.'

Death had seemed to be a real and imminent possibility to me, and yet Pam and I now had a sense of peace, where before we had only known despair. My suicidal ideation had gone. The deliverance I experienced in Kerry's studio was a lasting, ongoing experience – a deep healing.

We had finished the building project in Berwick, and the one near our home. I had made not a penny from either. The depth of the recession was biting in. My labourer had been a total legend and almost carried me through the past nine months. I launched into the biggest project of my life, building two new houses in town. We demolished the existing bungalow, cleared the site. I'd marked out the foundations, ready to bring the digger in and commence the build.

Inside I was stressed out of my mind, the dysphoria and dysmorphia were worse than they had ever been. I was also struggling to walk. A pain had flared in my hip. Walking a hundred meters, was so painful, it reduced me to tears, and I'd need to sit down. On site, I was beginning to have palpitations and anxiety attacks. I could feel the early warning signs of breakdown coming back. The rejection from Christian friends had been a devastating blow. All I wanted, was to transition, to become fully female, and leave the ugliness of toxic macho land behind. The conflict between providing for and protecting my family and the desire to escape my male existence and transition was proving too much for me to manage.

The crippling pain in my hip, was nothing compared to the pain and intensity of my dysmorphia and dysphoria. I broke down on Pam.

'I cannot go on any further, if I try and carry on with this build, I am going to have a total breakdown.'

Pam agreed, it was time for me to stop. I had been driven, all my life. Now it was time to stop and face the pain. To work out how to deal with it. We would get by, financially, somehow.

The couple I was building for were Christians. Obviously, they were concerned, I had dropped a bomb on them in pulling out, and I was racked with guilt about it. They were encouraging me to carry on. They both gave me 'words' – 'God words', prophetic words and pictures, encouraging me to take anti-depressants that would help me through. They had no idea what I was struggling with. Their words wounded, and angered me, I did not need to take drugs to numb my pain! They were prophesying over me the exact opposite of what God was asking of me; I needed to let God help me, to learn how to deal with this pain, even to make friends with it, if need be. God does not deliver us from suffering, he walks with us through it.

The consultant looked at my x-rays: severe arthritis and a disintegrated hip joint.

The Healing Retreat that Pam had booked me in on came round. I was dreading it; a weekend of confession, confessing my transgender self, and then the insufferable torment of being told to repent, then maybe God would heal me? I was pleasantly surprised; I spent the entire weekend soaked in love and prayer. The four days flew by. I didn't feel any significant healing.

Driving home, memories started to surface from my subconscious, I was watching the YouTube video run again. I knew the Holy Spirit was showing me something significant:

I was four or five or six, no more. I had been with my best friends, my two sisters from next door. I had on a miniature nurse's uniform, blue, with a white nurse's apron and a nurse's white hat from their dressing up cupboard. The hat and apron adorned with the red cross. The girls had brushed up my hair and I had on some red lipstick, the same colour as the cross.

The memory was crystal clear as the video played in my heart and mind:

Feeling so proud, I had run home, into my dad's studio to show him my uniform. I longed to be a nurse when I grew up. To look after people when they were ill, and care for them, make them better, all I'd ever wanted was to be able to love people better. My dad's face froze, John and Peter just laughed, Dad shouted at me loudly, angrily,

'Get out, go and get changed, right now!'

My father's anger destroyed me. My father never got angry. He was such a gentle, peaceful man. I was devastated and ran to

my room, tore the clothes off and cleaned my face. I took the girls'
uniform back and dumped it on their bed and walked out. I loved
my father, adored him. He was my life and security. I knew he was
really angry with me. I knew I had let him down. I knew I was a
disappointment to him in that moment. I knew what I was doing
was wrong because it hurt him.

He never mentioned it, ever again. He came home, cooked tea,
as if nothing had happened. I buried my pain, the hurt and every
desire and feeling I had to be myself and express myself. A boulder
of grief and shame rolled across my heart.

I remembered it as clearly as the moment it had
happened. How do these Spirit to spirit revelations happen?
I was driving the van safely, all the way through, but the
reality of the memory and encounter was undeniable, I was
filled with a ball of grief in my chest. I could feel it rising in
me, it felt like a choking, lead weight, a ball of barbed wire,
a physical pain and emotional, spiritual distress. It sat there,
like a cold, dead stone of locked emotions and feelings, over
my heart, all the way home.

I knew too, in that moment, my father had, totally
unintentionally, cursed me – shamed me, bound me up, he had
paralysed a fundamental part of my being and personality.
From that day on I did not dare show my feminine self to the
world, instead I buried it in guilt, shame and self-hatred. It
became my secret tormented double life, so I developed into
a split personality.

Home with the girls, we chatted a bit. Lauren came and sat
and had dinner with us, then retreated to her room. I talked
Pam through my weekend. I told her about the memory that
had surfaced on the drive home. We agreed to have a prayer
time, after we had gone to bed and hopefully the girls would
be asleep.

Lying in bed, I could feel the ball of barbed wire,

embedded in my flesh and soul. I knew with a lucid clarity that it was a spirit of shame. These things were familiar to me, after so many years, I knew how they worked. I talked Pam through the prayers of deliverance. I felt too weak to pray them myself. It was gone midnight; we were both shattered. We asked the Holy Spirit to come and anoint this time, a sacred time of healing. Pam laid her hands over the pain in my chest and commanded shame to leave my soul. The ball of barbed wire was accompanied by feelings of utter grief and desolation, the oppressive weight of shame filled my consciousness. As Pam prayed and commanded shame from my life, the ball of grief and barbed wire seemed to tear at my chest, not wanting to leave my body.

Pam and I commanded the shame from my life, and then I started to dry retch and vomit, I could feel this ugly presence rising in me, I vomited and gagged, and then it was gone. I knew it was gone. Pam knew it was gone. The curse had been broken off. We prayed the Holy Spirit to fill me afresh with love and peace. I felt raw, empty, drained. Evil shadows had lifted from my soul.

Shrek and Donkey are walking through the sunflowers, Donkey is needling Shrek, in his Eddie Murphy voice, getting under his skin, wanting him to be more Ogre-like, more macho aggression.

Shrek is trying to explain his sensitivities.

'Ogres are like onions.'

'What they smell?' says Donkey.

'NOOO!'

'They make you cry!'

'NOOO!'

'Ogres are like onions! They have layers.'

It is all too deep for Donkey, as they head into a field of maize.

God was peeling back the layers of my life, uncovering layer after layer of brokenness and trauma. I was worried, by the time God was finished, there would be nothing left of me.

Alison had told me to go and see a man she thought might be able to help me. He was a recommended counsellor for the Living Stones healing ministries. I caught the train to London. I stopped at a bank, and took out the £50 he charged for his services. A little man with grey hair and horn-rimmed glasses opened the door. He asked me a few questions, I told him my story. I told him, that I knew I was, without doubt, transgender, and had been all my life.

He was straight in with his theory and opinion. He opened his Bible and took me straight to Deuteronomy 22:5, that ancient Jewish law:

'If any man wears a woman's clothing, or any woman wears a man's clothing, they are detestable to God.'

He read it out loud, slowly, as if to help me understand. He looked at me piercingly, over his horn-rimmed glasses, as if expecting me to squirm.

I was caught in the ancient sins of worshipping Ashtaroth and Baal. I was guilty of the sin of sexual idolatry. He was sincere, kindly and firm in his convictions. What I needed to do, he said, was repent, and bring my whole being to God, to trust God to give me the strength to live by the Spirit, not the flesh. I would have to live the rest of my life with this 'thorn in the flesh'. He encouraged me to find my identity in Christ, to lean on Christ as my strength. There was grace at the cross, he said. We must crucify the flesh, he said. It all sounded strangely familiar. The hour was up, it was clearly time to leave, he had someone else due. I gave him his fifty pounds and got the train home.

I was deeply hurt by his ignorance. I was angry that he'd charged me fifty quid to sit and listen to it. He was a charlatan, a 'snake oil' salesman, who preyed on the weak, the confused and the vulnerable. Back home, I looked him up, to see his qualifications. He had none. I sent him an email, and questioned if he had any formal training of any kind, in any discipline or professional field? I reminded him that it was against European Law to try and counsel anybody out of either their natural sexuality or gender.

I got a clipped, one-line e-mail back. He had retired from ministry and counselling, and he had no energy at this time, to discuss the matter with me any further. Five years on, he is still practising, charging his fifty pounds an hour for conversion therapy and quackery.

I rode out into the Gloucestershire Wolds, alone; just me and God. I wanted to give the Holy Spirit time to search my heart, to sift and sort me. I knew there was a lot more healing to come. No video this time, just the memories.

I remembered David my first vicar; David the Priest, David the man of God. He was a good, and a kindly man, but now I was troubled; the counsel and prayer I had been given by the counsellor in London that week of 2016, was almost an exact re-run of what David had spoken over my life in the spring of 1982.

David had read Deuteronomy 22:5 to me in just the same way. The similarities in the two conversations and counselling sessions, some thirty-five years apart was uncanny, a coincidence, or something God had wanted me to see? Then, I had been a very vulnerable young adult, in recovery from a total breakdown, mental illness and severe drug addiction. Now I was more informed. I knew the difference between a transvestite (someone who dresses for reasons of sexual fetish), and someone who suffers gender dysphoria and dysmorphia. I had a lifetime experience of following Christ behind me.

I realised David had shamed me and cursed me. Sincerely and in ignorance, but he had shamed and cursed me, none the less. A curse; words or actions that seek to bind up, choke, muzzle, limit, restrict or cut off the life and spirit of another. We tend to think of curses as something medieval or primitive, but any of us can curse someone, cut them down, make them feel useless, inferior, stupid, small. Curses can stick, wound and bind us up. This realisation, the revelation of it, made me livid.

The recent counselling session had at least brought the curse into the light. David had abused me, from his position of power and authority and profound influence over me, as a priest. He had spoken words over my life, words about a subject he actually knew nothing about. I had been cursed by an ignorant Priest, at the very start of my 'Christian' life. The foundations of my faith were rotten to the core. I had been bound up, locked in chains of religious prejudice, ignorance and indoctrination.

It took me a long time to forgive David, for the damage he had done to me. Far from bringing me healing, he had piled upon me condemnation and shame. I realised that way back then, few understood the reality of transgender identity. Everyone, particularly the church, saw it only as a sexual deviation. The foundations of my 'Christian' life were rotten, defective, built upon an ancient Jewish law of condemnation. All my church life I had tried to live and build on this lie and curse. I had tried to build my marriage upon these rotten foundations, and the rot had infected my marriage and my parenting. It had nearly killed me and destroyed my family; I knew that as a deep conviction within my heart; he had inadvertently crippled me spiritually. I had been spiritually abused.

For a couple of years after this, I could not see a priest, a vicar, a dog collar, without a violent inner anger and revulsion, the force of which always caught me off-guard. I still recoil when I see clerical dog collars – the damage has been done, a trauma in the soul, thirty-five years wrestling with guilt, shame and a destructive suicidal ideation, caused by one ignorant man; a priest.

David's prayers and counsel, the curse of them, had led me into a Christian life of denial, repression, suppression, in Christian language, a life-long attempt to crucify myself.

My father's shaming and cursing of who I was as a child, and the Reverend David's shaming and cursing of me as a vulnerable young adult, even though done in ignorance, and perhaps fear, had resulted in my life of addiction, denial, repression, self-destruction and shame. I never knew the power of the curse, not whilst it was withering my life away. I had been blind to these hidden chains. Now, in the joyful freedom God had given me, I could see exactly what had happened to me.

With this revelation the shame, guilt, condemnation, self-hatred and self-loathing vanished from my life, instantly. All my life, I had been an Eeyore, shrouded in a cloak of melancholy, despair and depression. All those years as a church goer, I'd never consistently been able to bring forth the spirit of joy in my life. As a believer, I had always been haunted. Finally, I was able to me myself; transgender – the joy was beginning to flow naturally from deep down within.

Why do such curses stick, and bind us so tightly? Curses only stick because people already have great influence in our lives. Parents, teachers, Pastors and Priests, authority figures, can bind or curse our spirit. Sometimes we have willingly given them authority in our lives, but often not. Spiritual abuse is every bit as real as mental, emotional, physical and sexual abuse.

Close Christian friends I had told about my identity had dropped me like a hot potato, and walked away. I needed friends I could confide and trust in, I couldn't walk through this storm alone. If church wasn't going to walk with me through this, then I needed to find help elsewhere.

I was training regularly with one of the women from the race team. Charlotte is one of those all-round beautiful people, who will call a spade a spade, who will fight your corner, and tell you when you are being a muppet. She worked for the police, and often on our rides, she would offload her burdens. Steph trained with me too, she was a para-medic. I knew part of my role in encouraging and coaxing the race team, was to try and look after them when they needed it. Being there, in total confidence for them, when they needed to offload after painful and gruesome days and weeks, was the least I could do.

Charlotte called me, to see if I wanted to do a fifty-mile loop, a ride out to one of our favourite cafés. We met up, and before we could ride, before I had chance to think too much and change my mind, I blurted out my truth. She didn't bat an eyelid, and in her ever-calm and pastoral manner, loved, listened and asked the occasional relevant question. She was more than informed about my struggles. She was dealing with young trans children in her everyday work. Charlotte has been one of those faithful friends who stood by me through my worst days.

Mick and I were still training a lot together. He was working through his own battles, not least depression and PTSD from his time in the military. If I needed someone to have my back, I knew Mick was the man. He had all the qualities you need in a friend; faithfulness, an awesome sense of humour, a pastor's heart and broad shoulders. Whilst I had seen the sensitive side of his personality start to emerge since leaving the RAF, he was still 85 kilos of testosterone fuelled Grade One Alpha Male. I wasn't sure if he would love me or kill me if I told him I was trans. I was genuinely frightened, not of rejection, but at the thought of losing yet another close friend.

Mick was shocked, visibly so, when I told him, but he took it all in his stride. To his credit, he swallowed any preconceived ideas he may have had, and walked, or cycled the journey, alongside me, learning as we went. He has stood by me and has my back. His friendship through the bleak days kept me sane, even smiling. Mick can rip you, even when you are down, he knows humour is a saving grace. So many times, he has lifted me up, when church has dragged me down.

Sometimes I look at church, and how we seem to practise 'disposable-friendships'. I wonder, is this what God really wants? People leave our churches, and we forget them, they are no longer part of our club, or our concern. We spend everything on 'Welcome', and nothing on following up those who go missing. We live a parochial life building our small empires. Faithfulness in Christian friendships does not seem able to transcend our church allegiance, the ghetto mentality. At the most painful times of my life, Christian friends cut me out their lives, love seemed distinctly lacking. I walked out on church, but I never walked out on my friendships, I always tried to keep them alive. I've watched pastors and priests ditch good, long-standing friends when they have dared to be honest and come out as gay or trans. To me, that demonstrates the exact opposite of what I see Jesus doing in including the marginalised, the weak, the poor and the oppressed; it is an ugly religious spirit, not the love I see and know in Christ.

I'm reminded of the parable of the Good Samaritan; so often priests, pastors and Christians pass by, 'on the other side of the road'. Even in my own hometown, Christians cross the road when they see me, rather than having to stop and talk to me. I feel genuinely sorry for those who have walked away, for those who have crossed the road, to walk by on the other side. Yet they remain convinced that it is they who are the good Samaritan?!

As transgender, it has become so clear, that the many in the church do not want us, or our gifts, to be part of their team. They don't want us as trans, leading and serving their churches, in any way. Many prominent Christian leaders are attacking our right as transgender to exist, they are working hard to legislate against transgender youth, the most vulnerable of all. These Christian leaders have no real knowledge or understanding of our broken reality. The loudest voices in this clamour to shut us out of church have been from within the Church of England. They are trying to curse us, bind us up, silence us and cut us off from fellowship and communion at the table.

2016 – 2021
Advocacy

Leelah was only seventeen, it was around midnight when she headed out onto Highway 71. She walked a couple of miles into the oncoming traffic in the cold and dark night of 28 December 2014. At 2.30 am she stepped out into the road and an oncoming lorry.

Her suicide note appeared, posted automatically at 5.30 am. Within hours it had been read 80,000 times. It reached me the following day. I had only just, finally admitted, accepted, to myself, that I had been transgender all my life. It was the only key that fitted the padlock that chained my heart.

She ended her note with one last request:

'My death needs to mean something. My death needs to be counted in the number of transgender people who commit suicide this year. I want someone to look at that number and say, 'that's fucked up' and fix it. Fix society. Please.'

Her parents, Carla and Doug, were devout Christians. They had refused to accept Leelah, from the first day she 'came out' aged fourteen. They took her out of school, removed all her access to social media and her friends. They put Leelah through conversion therapy. Even in her death, they dead named her. They threw away the suicide note she had left them. The Police had taken a copy. After a year of investigation, Leelah's death was finally logged as a suicide. I understood their pain as parents, but I had already come to see and understand it was rooted in too binary an understanding of both scripture and gender, both science and scripture revealed a much greater truth.

The tragedy was, they had wanted Leelah to conform to their desires, their dreams, their beliefs, they could not accept their own child for who she was. I carried Leelah, every-day, in my heart. I vowed her death would not be in vain. I had survived puberty and adolescence. I had survived my own suicide attempts. I knew some of the pain and grief Leelah had lived and died with. I was still living it.

Chatting with Mia one day, she poured out her heart. Mia was Serbian, her church was the Serbian Orthodox Church, a church she felt drawn to for its ancient and rich tradition and culture, and the beauty of its art and icons. She was too frightened to return to her church; known for its transphobia, the fear of rejection was too great. Her situation really cut me up. I too felt estranged from church and isolated. The church was too prone to judging us, before they ever tried to understand us, they were all too happy to talk about us, but seldom with us.

I had been so troubled, and so burdened by Mia's fear of going to church, I felt deeply moved. My next weekend in Sheffield, I put on my favourite dress, and went in search of a church. For eighteen months I made a small Baptist church my home. I tried to deny the obvious; the Pastor and his wife were both homophobic and transphobic and manifestly passive aggressive towards me. Like most conservative evangelical churches, they kept their transphobic beliefs hidden, secret, only known amongst the leadership. I saw how they dealt with a young trans guy – it was ugly. I moved on. No one ever followed me up to ask why.

I'd begun to meet and make friends with LGBTQIA Christians. Many had been kicked out of their churches and church schools for being gay or lesbian, some even rejected by their own Christian families. These people were much further down the road than me, they carried their scars, the trauma and wounds of religious rejection and spiritual abuse, with a real grace and dignity. Talking with them, I began to realise how badly hurt by church I was. The realisation began to sink in, I was carrying the trauma of spiritual abuse.

I was still staying with Sylvia for five or six days every month, and Sheffield began to feel like my hometown. In Sheffield I found a down to earth humility, a friendliness and openness on the street. Everywhere I went I made friends, at the bus stop, in cafés and shops. I grew to love the city and its people.

Walking had become very difficult; my hip joint was crumbling away and was inflamed with severe arthritis. Living with Sylvia, living entirely en-femme, I found I was able to walk for miles, relatively pain free. I hadn't increased my use of painkillers whilst in Sheffield; if anything I was forgetting to take them and using less. The peace, joy and confidence I found in being me, feminine, Chrissie, able to express myself, I felt free and fully alive and it diminished my awareness of the severe and constant crippling pain in my hip, from major to minor!

I'd even taken to going to one of the gay nightclubs in town, it was a friendly safe place where I could dance to my heart's content. After fifty years of what felt like living in prison, at last I was free. I was letting off steam, I was celebrating being alive, being me, I danced into the early hours, so happy I barely felt the pain that usually crippled me. At home I was struggling to walk a few hundred yards, even from the car park to the shops.

This dramatic, tangible reduction in my hip pain was the most powerful experience, undeniable, repeated, month after month. It convinced me of the rightness of my decision to live as transgender, en-femme. Happiness permeated my whole being, like never before. Sylvia and this city, created a safe space in which I could both heal and grow.

Pam.
'It was so hard sifting through the debris of my dreams and hopes for our marriage. I dissected the components of our marriage relationship surgically and looked at in the cold light of day, almost detached and emotionless from the reality and pain we were both daily enduring and inflicting upon each other. What if Paul had suffered a life-changing accident or illness? Our situation certainly came within the category of life changing. Had Paul become paralysed I would not have hesitated to remain there for him, adjusting to the different dynamic that would have to be learnt. Many too would no doubt lend their support and express their sympathy, at least in the early stages. But this! – was I expected to stay?

The sad irony was that all I had ever wanted was to see Paul happy – to try and play my part in lifting that "brooding melancholy sadness". Now, perhaps his commitment to being my "husband" was actually standing in the way of that happiness? For me as a full-blooded heterosexual woman with a leaning towards testosterone-fuelled, hairy males! What was I to do with that? I feared feeling drawn to other men, and started to feel awkward with them, almost reverting back to being a gauche adolescent girl. I was a woman and I wanted to be loved by a man. So how much did I really want Paul's happiness? Because there was going to be one hell of a personal cost to pay to secure it.'

A whole summer had passed since I had pulled out from building the two houses in town. In the couple of years since coming out to myself, the realisation of my feminine identity, I'd been unable to stop crying. Tears flowed at the most insignificant things. I was a total emotional mess as the power of my release and healing sank in. I was no longer imprisoned or entombed in a secret hell, and the deliverance tasted so sweet. I was feeling things that I had not been able to feel for five decades! A whole dimension of my personality had been buried alive, locked away, I had become detached and disconnected from my own core identity, it was as if I had gained the acceptance of the world, but had, in the process, lost my soul. No wonder I had never been able to fully love Pam. A whole aspect of my personality had been frozen.

Tears flowed in unstoppable torrents, I no longer cared, I could feel them washing all the toxin and pain from my heart, from my body, from my mind. My heart was softening, becoming tender and sensitive. The empathy I felt for others, in their pain, was crushing. Jesus, man of sorrows, finally made sense, he felt all of our pain.

The problem was, I could not think straight, not in any rational, objective way. The only solution I could see or contemplate was to physically transition. Pam was adamant, that if I wanted to transition, we would have to separate. For me, separation was not an option, I loved Pam with my whole being. Maybe I hadn't been very good at loving her, I had failed her in a thousand ways, but I had always tried to give both her and my daughters my very best.

I booked an appointment with the Gender Identity Clinic. After a harrowing interview process that ripped me apart and left me feeling raw and vulnerable for days, the psychiatrist concluded my mental health was not just good, but strong. I was however clearly suffering with acute dysmorphia and gender dysphoria. I was cleared to start the pathway of gender realignment; hormones, laser treatment and surgery. I told him I didn't want to destroy my marriage and family by transitioning before my family were ready for me to do so, but that I was desperate for counselling. He told me there was nothing he could do for me, there was no counselling available.

☆

One weekend, keen to visit my step mum after Dad's death, I threw a travel bag of clothes in the car, and said goodbye to Pam. As I got in the car, I felt the Holy Spirit quicken my heart. I knew, even as I was driving, that whilst I was away, I was going to resolve, and find peace about my transition. Ever since coming out, my heart had been torn in two. Conflict between loyalty to Pam and my daughters, the need to be a husband and father for them; to provide and protect, and the need to end the dysmorphia and dysphoria had made my life hell. This divided heart needed to choose, one way or the other … to transition or not?

Over the weekend, the fog of emotional overload, cleared and lifted. Instead of conflict, there was a peace. What had felt like surges of oestrogen fuzzing and fusing my mind and emotions, was replaced with a clarity of thinking, an objectivity which I had not had in more than two years. Normally I am a very detached, cold, calculating and clinical thinker. I analyse and sift information, facts, observations, data, and even my own feelings and thoughts. It had been a totally disorientating thing to lose control of both my feelings, and my ability to process so rationally. It was as if the two halves of my brain had swapped places, the cold and clinical detached me, had been replaced by a sensitivity and feelings that swamped me. My feminine orientations and strengths had taken over the driving seat of my life.

Over the weekend I began to sift through the rubble and ruins of my life, of our married life. Pam and I were feeling huge strain. Church were of no help at a time like this, we knew no one would understand. We did not understand ourselves, we had to bring our brokenness to God, alone. I was nearly sixty.

The NHS was buckling under the austerity of the Tories, and despite heroic efforts was unable to fulfil its duties. It would probably take me in excess of five years, minimum, to get to the point of surgery following the NHS gatekeeping, pathways and protocol. My transition would require finding a new career. I was unqualified in anything – just five O levels to show for a lifetime of labours. I would have to transition socially, financially, mentally, physically and emotionally, by which time I would be nearly seventy, and complications in gender assignment surgery far more problematic. We could not afford for me to go through private medicine to transition. My hip replacement would likely mean the end of my building career and earnings potential.

I sat in my father's studio. Everything was left, just as it was when he had died. On his easel sat an unfinished painting of a large Iris, a pale creamy colour, stamens and petals, a soft and gentle feminine vulnerability. I was looking at the painting I had made of a lily in junior school, a strange symmetry of my life turning full circle. Tears welled up and started to flow down my cheeks. Losing my father had been a devastating blow, yet perhaps it had set me free from his power over me? I had never wanted to hurt him, disappoint him or let him down, I had loved him all my life and longed to make him happy; in that, I had never been able to express my true self. Now I was free. I wiped away the tears, my life was in clear focus.

As a family we had been through fifteen years of bereavements, losing our parents, financial hardship, the girls' illnesses and the trauma of losing our church family and friends; we were exhausted, broken, traumatised and in a sorry state. Charlotte and Lauren both still seemed very vulnerable. I could not drag my family through another five to ten years of trauma as I attempted transition. I had no option but to give up all hope of transition. Maybe that was it, like my father's painting, staring at me from the easel, my life would forever remain, unresolved, incomplete, unfinished.

Sunday evening, I said goodbye to my stepmum. It had been a special time together. Since accepting my trans self I had become so happy and relaxed in female company. I made my peace with God – I would give up all hope of transition. I cried most of the way home. My feminine self was now secure but facing a lifetime of being stuck with this male body, an almost daily torment. There was the relief of having made 'the decision', and the peace of knowing God would help me through, and then the awful unspeakable pain and grief of letting go of a lifetime's longing, letting go of the hope of a physical transition.

I really would have to lean on God. I was limping, in more ways than one. Yet out of my wrestling with God, I now enjoyed an intimacy and unbroken peace of communion and union with God, that I'd never tasted before. The Holy Spirit felt like my new best friend, and I was hyper-sensitive to grieving the Holy Spirit. My old life was dying, I was tasting resurrection life, real, intimate, lasting and true. All the toxicity of my old male self, that false persona, was falling away.

If I could not transition, I set my heart to fighting for the lives of all the trans kids who would follow on behind me. I did not want a single one of them to go through the hell my life had been, to suffer from the ignorance, prejudice and bigotry I had tasted all my life. I would live my life for them, to include them as Jesus would have included them. A life of studying and being aligned with black and liberation theology finally made full sense. I did not want to become some kind of placard carrying, ranting activist, but I determined I would be an advocate for transgender youth to my dying breath. I felt the full pleasure and seal of God's approval and peace. My path was set.

☆

Finding a safe church for my friend Mia was still my major mission. I visited a mega-church in Nottingham. It was easy to drop in on the way back home from my sister's in Sheffield. Slipping past the welcome team, I hid in the toilets to calm my nerves. My hands were shaking as I brushed my hair and freshened my lipstick. Walking into the vast auditorium, about a thousand people gathered for worship, I was quaking with fear, one almighty panic attack. I had come to Trent because of the worship. I wanted somewhere, a safe space, in which I could get face down before God and worship with all my heart, freely and without interruption. I sat down in the very back row, the 'sinner's seats', closest to the doors, in case I needed to run.

The woman sat alone at the other end of our empty row of seats, shuffled over.

'You're new, here aren't you?'

She reached out a hand,

'Hi, I'm Gill, I'm the church secretary.'

The worship started, a black woman sang out, that glorious, uninhibited gospel, her voice soared over the drums, bass and guitars. The Holy Spirit fell on me like a waterfall, I got soaked, drenched. I knelt on the carpet, wedged between mother hen and the plastic seats. I washed Jesus' feet with my tears and forgot all my worries and cares.

Gill asked why I had come to Trent. I explained all about Mia. She introduced me to the Senior Pastor. Helen was all heart and ears. We arranged to meet for coffee, next time I came to church.

Pam and I braved a new church just down the road. I wanted to live an open honest, life; I told the Pastor I was transgender. Less than year later, I was summoned to the Pastor's house.

In front of one of the elders he began to shout in anger at me, 'You have no right to speak like that in MY church!'

Yet neither he, nor the elder could explain what I had said that was wrong. I had pleaded with the church not to look at him, or the 'prophets' to lead the church, but to look to Jesus as head of the church. His response was a 'gagging order'.

I had no doubts I was being silenced because others in the church 'had found out' that I was transgender. Only months later the pastor ran off with the prophetess, and left his children and wife of thirty-six years. The church is no more. Either I have the gift of discernment, or the Holy Spirit was trying to gently warn the church?

Four decades in church. Four times I'd watched a man take over and rule the church, devastate and destroy church. Forty years of church, continual micro-aggressions, slap downs, cold shouldering, abuse and church tragedies. I still have the T-shirts and bear the scars. I am one of the survivors. I tell these stories for a deliberate reason; it is only with the retrospect of history – our stories – that church will ever have the chance to learn. No one holds these church leaders to account, it's time to stand up and call them out, and let our stories be heard.

I sat in the café, attached to the vast warehouse that the church used for worship. The place was thronging, heaving with life. Despite being Senior Pastor with her husband Tom, to a church that had three thousand people on its books, Helen gave me her undivided attention, asked questions, sat and prayed with me. We tried to grab a half hour over coffee in the café each time I came to church. I was humbled, broken and awed by such a practical demonstrative love. Sometimes you meet Jesus, in the people who love you, serve you, nurture you and nourish you.

I made Trent my home church. Helen had opened her heart to me. For a senior pastor, to give me, a stranger and transgender, so much of her valuable time, really was a powerful healing for me. A lifetime of repeated wounds from church leadership had spiritually disabled me.

Every time she saw me, Helen would say,

'What do you want?'

It was a question that both rattled and challenged me. At one level, I didn't want anything, other than to be loved and accepted. On another level, I knew that the ignorance and fear surrounding us as transgender, was often deepest within the church. My experiences, living in Sheffield, proved to me that many, if not most people in the world did not mind or care that we were trans. Some of the loudest voices in society, opposing our existence, were coming from the church. I wanted a church that would be a safe place, a home, for kids like Leelah, for Mia and me.

On television celebrities like Piers Morgan and Jeremy Clarkson were openly mocking us, vilifying us, using us as punchbags, inciting the world to join with them in despising and hating us, as transgender. In the press, papers like the *Times* ran several articles a week, which were subtly and deliberately massaging and manipulating the truth to create a steady drip, drip, drip of transphobic fear and hate. Old school feminists like Germaine Greer, Julie Bindel and Julie Burchill, had declared 'open season' against the transgender community and were doing their best to stir up fear and hate against us.

The Pope had likened transgender people to the threat of nuclear weapons, considering us to part of a dark movement to 'annihilate humanity'. The revered theologian Bishop N. T. Wright posted a letter in the *Times*, mocking, deriding and demonising us. It really revealed the ignorance, pride and unconcealed prejudice and bigotry of an out of touch, embittered old man, living in his ivory tower, throwing stones from his palace of glass. It was a letter that wounded me deeply. I had a big place in my heart for the Church of England. That it was now turning on me was a bitter blow. Were they just trying to divert public attention away from the sexual and child abuse scandals that threatened to sink the Church of England? As transgender we were a convenient and timely scapegoat for both politics, religion, celebrities and the media. They put us down and elevate themselves. They sit in their seats of judgement as if they were thrones.

Transphobic hate crime had soared. Trans friends were being assaulted and abused on the streets. We were reeling, struggling under the backlash. These were bitter days for the transgender community. The atmosphere within the trans community was one of very real anxiety, fear and dread. It took a lot of courage to even walk out of our own front doors. It felt like even just existing, being visible, was a powerful act of resistance. In America we were seeing and hearing of black, Latino and indigenous transwomen being brutally murdered every week.

January 2017, against this backdrop of social ignorance, fear and hate, a young transwoman, a post-grad, an academic at Oxford University, took a bottle of cyanide from her lab and committed suicide. I knew her doctor, he was a lovely guy, I'd met him bike racing, he was a pillar in both the student and Oxford cycling community. Erin was only 22 when she died.

August 2017, only a few miles from me, a young trans boy, Leo Etherington, hanged himself in his bedroom. He was only 15. His school had refused to acknowledge his transgender identity or allow him to use his own name. Two tragic unnecessary deaths, that rocked our community. Both only a few miles from my home. These are not isolated suicides; they are happening too often. What needs to be spelled out, loud and clear, simple and plain is this basic truth:

We do not become suicidal because we are trans, we cannot help being who we are. We become suicidal, because we are rejected and shamed, by our own families, by our communities, by society, and, perhaps worst of all, by the church.

Shame is the single greatest motivator in both suicidal ideation and suicide attempts. Shame that family, community, society and tragically, the church place upon us, because of their ideologies and theology.

'Helen, all I want, all we want, as transgender, is to be heard, listened to, believed and understood. We want to feel safe, in society, we want to feel safe in church. I don't know what you, or your church believe about me. Your theology, your policies regarding me as transgender, are secret. That makes me feel unsafe.'

Leelah's words were pounding in my heart:

'My death needs to mean something. My death needs to be counted in the number of transgender people who commit suicide this year. I want someone to look at that number and say, 'that's fucked up' and fix it. Fix society. Please.'

We sat hugging our coffees; Helen opened up, she moved from being senior pastor, in control, to being human, being all too real, vulnerable and totally honest, her tears flowed. She looked at me through eyes that were all compassion, sorrow and empathy,

'Chrissie, I don't know what I believe – I don't understand what being transgender really means.'

Helen had battles of her own she was fighting. Her vulnerability made my heart ache. If I had loved Helen before, I couldn't have loved her any more than I did in those moments of her jaw-dropping honesty and humility. I wanted to hug her so much. I was a mess. Here was a senior pastor, relinquishing control, being human, totally vulnerable. Tears welled up, and I broke down in tears.

'I don't fully understand what being transgender means either, maybe I never will – but we are fighting for our lives.'

Helen had opened her heart to me – to us – but she followed through with more than words. She offered to host a training day for the church staff. Could I put together a group of transgender people who would be willing to share their experience, their lives and their faith with them as a staff team, so that they could learn more as a church leadership about what it meant to be transgender. It was Leelah who had called me to a role of advocacy, but it was Helen who first recognised it.

It was an incredible day. One of the largest, most successful churches in the UK opened their doors to us and rolled out a red carpet. It really was an expression and overflow of Tom and Helen's radical inclusive love as Senior Pastors. Amongst the staff present were the Senior Pastoral Care Pastor, the Homeless Pastor, worship leaders, the Youth Pastor, Gill and Helen. Speaking for the transgender community was Steph; Christian, sixty, transitioned, a member of the Metropolitan Police, founder of the Police Transgender Association. Rach, who was not Christian or churched, in her forties, part way through transition, ruthlessly, candidly honest, and such a fun speaker. Nikki was supposed to join us, but she had just been diagnosed with cancer.

It was a no questions barred day. The love in the room was palpable, touchable, real. Tears flowed, hearts were broken wide open, both for us as trans, and them as church staff. I ached with the absence of Nikki. They showed us around the vast complex of buildings and the many ministries that church ran. The staff cooked us a meal, and we sat into the evening, chatting and drinking wine. It was a wonderful day of healing, just being welcomed and heard. For me it was a dream come true. A chance for the church to see, that we as transgender, were only human, broken and humble, just like them.

Steph, Rach and I stayed over. We wanted to enjoy the morning service. I stood in the entrance lobby, looking for Rachel. Helen saw me standing all alone, a stranger in the crowd, she grabbed my hand,

'Come on, Tom is away, come and sit next to me.'

She dragged me, not letting go of my hand, to her seat at the front of church. I wanted the ground to open up and swallow me. The front row seats were for leadership! I was shaking with fear. I shut my eyes, lifted my hands in worship, focused on Jesus, and tried to forget where I was; stuck at the front of a mega-church, visibly trans, and a stranger, being stared at by hundreds and hundreds of people.

After the service, feeling shaken, I said to Steph, 'What on earth, was all that about, being sat at the front of church, like a guest of honour?!'

'You were exactly where God wanted you to be – visible. You need to learn, God is not judging us, God is judging the church, when they sit, in judgement over us. God will use your presence, our presence in church, to expose people's hearts, ignorance, fears and prejudices – ignorance is formed of lies, we incarnate Christ and expose the fears, the ignorance and the prejudices at the heart of the church.'

Nikki died a few weeks later. She had been self-medicating, taking hormones, oestrogen, and they had found insane levels of oestrogen in her blood, which had probably led to the cancer. She was the most beautiful trans women I had met, not just physically, but in her spirit too. She really was one of life's angels. She had given me hours of her time, listening, explaining and comforting me as I came to terms with who I am.

Nikki had been unwilling to wait years, to go through the laborious and soul-sapping, NHS 'gate-keeping' processes. Dysmorphia and dysphoria had made her desperate to transition and become physically female. She couldn't have been more feminine in her being and personality. I was heart-broken to lose her. Every year, I read back through our long-messaged conversations. I planted a rose for her, in our new garden.

'Nikki, I love you. Rest in peace and rise in glory.'

As transgender, we have everything to fight for. The gatekeeping within the NHS, and the politics behind it leads to women like Nikki self-medicating. As Nikki had warned me, it is high risk without medical oversight. Losing Nikki only strengthened my resolve to advocate for transgender acceptance in every area of society.

Helen and Tom stood down from their roles as the senior pastors of Trent. They had devoted twenty years of their lives helping build this church that loved the poor, the hungry, the homeless, the addict, the stranger, the refugees and immigrants who flooded to their doors. It was a humbling church to be a part of.

They gave it all up, to start all over again, with nothing. They weren't clinging to their position or titles, they weren't climbing the career ladder of church success, they were demonstrating something far more powerful, they were following Jesus, not the money, security or kudos. They moved to Derby to start a new church. For me they epitomised servant leadership, not paying lip service to the notion, but living it. Downwardly mobile, servant-hearted leadership, always washing our filthy feet and wiping away our tears. I had no option but to follow them; love always wins.

It seemed that this call to advocacy was to be very much, and primarily, within the conservative evangelical church that had formed my life over the past forty years. For me, loving Jesus was inseparable from loving the church, and loving the scriptures that reveal him. When you love, you are left wide open to abuse, and that has been my experience of church over the decades, yet it did not stop me loving the church. It was a painful place in which to find myself when so many Christians were speaking out opposing our rights and existence as transgender, but that makes the need for advocacy even more urgent.

As a life-long empathiser and pastor, my relationships within the transgender community were clearly revealing that vulnerable transgender youth were led into self-harm, suicidal ideation and suicide attempts because of rejection, being judged and shamed, not being accepted or affirmed for who they are. I knew the reality of this in my own bitter experiences throughout childhood and growing up in a hostile and aggressive world. Not a month seemed to go by in the community, without me being directly pastorally involved with people who had either attempted suicide, or had lost a loved one to suicide. The church had played a major role for the worse in many of these people's lives. They felt judged, looked down on, pitied and rejected. For some, like Leelah and Lizzy (Lowe) it had been too much. My heart was broken wide open by the pain and suffering I was sharing in.

If this church needs a better understanding of transgender people, then I was well placed to negotiate the ignorance and prejudices within it. It was a no brainer for me, and I knew the Holy Spirit was all over me whenever I stepped through the doors of a church. I'd never felt such confidence in God before. Even standing in worship alongside Christians who were clearly uneasy in my presence, I felt the love and affirmation of God flood my heart – their fears, prejudice and rejections only made God's love all the sweeter.

☆

One has no option but to love the church if one has set one's heart on following and loving Christ. He commanded us to love each other! My old life of the flesh, the self and its rights and pride, found it shattering when Christians wounded me. The Bible verse that has sustained through my darkest times also led me to understand the depth to which we must die before we experience resurrection life, or eternal life pouring through us, empowering us to rise above fear, ignorance, prejudice and hate.

'I have been crucified with Christ, and I no longer live. The life I now live, I live by faith in Christ, who loved me and gave himself for me, and Christ lives in me.'

We cannot crucify the very depths of our sinful nature, with its ugliness and negativity, its desire for revenge, (or at the very least a grovelling apology from those who have wounded us!). Someone else has to drive the nails in, and often it is the religious who wound us the deepest. It was the religious who crucified Jesus.

Eventually I learnt to give thanks for those who had wounded me the deepest, for they have helped expose this crooked heart and allowed it to rise above revenge and self-pity and exercise forgiveness. With that, also comes the recognition of how deeply I have wounded those I love the most.

'Father, forgive them for they know not what they are doing.'

That is the power of love, the power of the resurrection life that transforms us in the very deepest place of our lives, where ego is enthroned and God has little influence. When we find ourselves forgiving those who have hurt us most, then we know we have let Jesus take his place at the centre of our lives. It is the greatest love of all, Christ in us, and forgiveness freely flows. Unforgiveness had once been the most bitter and deepest rooted, toxic poison in my life, but through being wounded, and primarily by church, its ugly destructive power is gone. It has been the hardest lesson of my life, an ongoing lesson.

☆

My love for the Bible had grown cold. I knew only too well that I stood condemned by the ancient Jewish law within it, so I laid the Bible aside. The encounter with God and my experience of God, stood in Kerry's studio, dressed en-femme had been perhaps the most healing encounter with God of my life, the Holy Spirit had washed me, flooded me, floored me, and set me free from guilt and shame, a lifetime of suicidal ideation, and I was a very different, happier, more content person for it. Peace and joy had become lasting fruit in my life rather than fleeting experiences of momentary respite from the melancholy and deep despair. My personality had become lighter, brighter, more buoyant and far less vulnerable to rejection and the moods of despair that had been a hallmark of my life up till then. The problem was my experience of God now seemed to be in direct contradiction and conflict with my understanding of the Bible.

In my research I had stumbled across a Christian website that talked much about the eunuchs and their story throughout scripture. When I heard the word eunuch, something in me resonated, I instinctively knew, as I had when I first heard the word transgender, that the eunuch's mysterious identity held a clue and was a path to understanding myself and my relationship with God.

The Holy Spirit led me back into the Bible. I was hungry and thirsty to learn, eager to enter into the mystery of the eunuch's story, knowing I was going to discover the truth. Eunuch was just a label, a term of reference that encompassed a vast spectrum of human experience, from those whom today we call Intersex, to those castrated as young boys to become sex slaves or servants, even officials who rose to great power in ancient royal courts. The Romans included within their legal definitions of eunuch those who were impotent and also those with no natural desire towards women, whom today we might call homosexual. As I studied eunuchs in the ancient empires of China, India, Assyria, Babylon, Persia, Greece and Rome, these stories in the Bible came to life and breathed a message of profound hope into my heart. In these very real and human stories of brokenness, abandonment and rejection, I identified with the eunuchs. They stepped off the pages of this inert book and came to life in my heart and mind.

The narrative arc of the eunuch flowed from the ancient Jewish law, where they were condemned and outcast as unclean, rejected as impure, deviant and defiled, through to the words of the prophet Isaiah, where they are exalted and honoured. In the book of Esther their lives are laid bare, and are foundational to the teachings of Jesus, who includes, affirms and exalts the eunuch, to the explosive story in the Book of Acts, where Philip baptises a black eunuch on the road to Samaria, welcoming them into the church.

In that moment, reading about the baptism of the Ethiopian eunuch, I realised that the ancient Jewish law that had condemned me all my churched life – *'If any man wears a woman's clothing, or any woman wears a man's clothing, they are detestable to God'* – was in fact no different from the law that condemned the eunuchs: *'No one who has been emasculated by cutting or crushing can enter the assembly of God's people'* (Deuteronomy 23:1)

It too was washed away in the waters of the eunuch's baptism. They, and I were now free of the law, under grace and saved by a love too deep to fathom.

I had been cursed by a priest, using this single verse to condemn me. Now the curse was well and truly broken.

God welcomes the eunuch, once condemned by law, never able to enter the 'fellowship of God's people' in worship or prayer, family or community, into the church with open arms. Here I found more evidence for God's acceptance of transgender and non-binary people than I ever believed was possible in the Bible. God had opened the eyes of my heart and mind to see God's radical affirming, inclusive love.

These eunuchs' stories revealed God's heart toward those who are broken beyond recognition. Broken in their gender, in that they don't conform to a binary of either male or female, even broken in their sexuality that they may be confused, lost and brutalised by their oppressors. If I identity with one group in the Bible, it is with neither Israel nor the church, but with the eunuchs. I saw God looking beyond those who feel righteous, whole and complete in their gender and sexuality, to love, include and minister to those who do not conform, to those of us who are intersex, transgender, eunuch, to those of us whose gender and sexuality is non-binary.

These stories made those loud voices in the church that seek to invalidate and argue against my existence all the more, ugly and absurd. They want to police my identity, as they want to police the identity of the eunuch, but it is a futile hope, a legalistic and religious attempt, devoid of either empathy, grace or reality, their argument a construct of their religious minds and systems of control. When you have spent years immersed in the transgender community, when you have spent years studying the identity of eunuchs throughout history and across every culture, you discover Christ is very much active in loving, affirming and embracing the eunuchs, intersex and transgender.

Those in the church who chose to judge, reject or pity us? The loss is theirs, for Christ lives in us and celebrates our lives. Theirs is but an argument, ours is an incarnation. When you have experienced God's love, and when you have experienced the Holy Spirit breathing love, truth and freedom into your soul through the Bible, then someone who comes with a mere argument against you is of little consequence.

We have returned to the church we were married in, the church we belonged to, financed and served for fifteen years, in search of a spiritual home and a people who would accept me as I am, transgender. To our shock we discovered five male members of the senior clergy had signed a letter to the House of Bishops, demanding they withdraw their welcome to us as transgender, offered in the form of a liturgy to be used to celebrate our transition. I am still awaiting their explanations. Their theology regarding us as transgender is secret, hidden, and their power feels heavy- handed, dictatorial, ugly and oppressive to many of us who are transgender, and who have faith and love for the Church of England as a broad church that seeks to encompass all. This work of advocacy is far from over, and this story far from finished. I'm going nowhere. We'll probably still be here when they have all moved on, picking up the pieces of the lives they condemn.

Pam:
'Our marriage has always been costly, and still is; when I married Paul, I married into the poor, the weak, the homeless and the marginalised, they were there as a witness at our wedding and the banquet table afterwards, a foretaste of heaven.

When Paul confessed his real identity to me, I thought I had undone the years of indoctrination from church, but I was quickly faced with the ugliness of my own heart again. I was repulsed by him, her, they, I was transphobic. It wasn't just because he was my husband, but it was twice, three times, a hundred times worse – because it was my own husband! I didn't want to be repulsed by him, her, them, but I was, deeply.

298

Our marriage either had to end, or I had to learn, and unlearn, fast. I faced a stark choice, with no way out; to judge, or to love? I discovered it's far harder to love, listen and change, than it is to judge. How has God undone my fears and deep-seated phobias? How have I changed from being the one who judged and felt so virtuous and righteous, to being one who loves?

Paul/Chrissie has exposed the depth of my ugliness and propensity and preference to judge, rather than open my heart and open my mind to listen, to learn and to grow, to become more fully human, caring and kind. It's not about the outward appearance, it's not about the clothes, the make-up or hair; it's about the heart. It's about character. If God judges, then God does not look or judge us upon our outward appearance, but for our heart attitude and the content of our character.

I have discovered the cost it takes to listen and love, to embrace those we do not understand. To love is to be made vulnerable, to love is to admit our own weakness and brokenness, we are after all, only human, not "other". We all have hearts that bleed and skin that is pierced so easily.

I have watched Paul/Chrissie tear down the toxic male persona behind which they have hidden all their lives; a protective shell against the judgement, ignorance, hate and fear of this world, and even of their own family, church and community. I see now, how trapped they were. The person that has emerged is more truly honest than anyone else I know.

Instead of the unexploded bomb, the dormant volcano I once tip-toed in fear around, I have a partner who is peaceful, gentle, good, kind, long- suffering, gracious, and at long last, after years, decades of my prayers – joyful, the melancholy has gone.

I have listened, I have watched, and I have learnt much. I am ashamed of the judgemental person religion had moulded me into, but it was only working with the raw materials of my own pride and self-righteousness, I own my part in that.

We make of our religion so many sacred cows, doctrines, rules, unspoken laws, but for me, the most sacred thing is when someone is brave enough to expose their broken heart and tell their story.

That; the vulnerable human intersection of our broken lives, is the sacred, holy place in which God dwells. I am lucky enough, blessed enough to live with such a one.

Again and again and again I watch and listen as they make themselves vulnerable, share their weakness and brokenness, and in so doing create a safe space and time in which others can begin to share and heal.

The greatest tragedy is that I see the suffering and the pain of one whose heart is broken by the judgements of the church, not so much for themselves, but for their community and for the vulnerable and fragile transgender kids who are growing up in a world that loves to hate on them. Chrissie in so many ways stands for, and represents all those the church turns away.

I am married to one who reflects the expansive and inclusive love of God to all, through their eyes I have learnt to see, listen to and hear those who live on the margins, helping me to see those who I would otherwise have overlooked. I am married to one who doesn't so much talk about Christ, but seeks to incarnate the love of Christ; they don't do charity handouts, they have always invited the weakest, the most broken and the most vulnerable into their hearts, their life and our home and marriage.

They are the partner I married. Our marriage, the "rules"? We are redefining its nature day by day, but its essence shall always remain the same; love, the love and faithfulness we both see reflected in Christ.

I would have it no other way. I am blessed.'

Resources

This book, my story has covered some deeply painful memories and realities that touch the lives of many who are trans or non-binary. The first, the biggest, and sometimes the most painful step we will ever take is that of asking for help, walking into the light, 'coming out'. Isolation and shame is the biggest killer in our communities. Please don't struggle on alone and in isolation. Reach out, talk to someone you can trust. Be willing to ask for help, there is no shame in being weak, or recognising you need friends. Here are a few resources that may be of help to you, a friend, a partner, family member or child.

Christian Transgender groups, The Sibyls – a UK-based confidential Christian spirituality group for trans people and their partners and supporters.

http://sibyls.gndr.org.uk

Diverse Church – caters for LGBT+ Christian youth, 18-30 years.

https://diversechurch

Open Table network – ecumenical Christian worshipping communities across UK, offering safe and sacred space for LGBT+ Christians.

http://opentable.lgbt

Resources

UK Organisations that offer support to adults with a trans partner, friend or adult family member.

www.depend.org.uk

Gendered Intelligence. Specialises in supporting trans people under the age of 21, their parents and carers; provides trans youth programmes and trans awareness training for all sectors, including schools.

www.genderedintelligence.co.uk

Gender Identity Research and Education Society. (GIRES) – aims to improve the lives of trans and gender nonconforming people of all ages by working with them, drawing on the latest scientific research, and delivering training to public and private sector organisations.

www.gires.org.uk

Mermaids. Largest UK organisation supporting gender non-conforming young children and their families.

www.mermaidsuk.org.uk

Stonewall, London based and Proudtrust, Manchester can help you find an LGBT youth group in your area.

https://www.stonewall.org.uk/help-advice/whats-my-area.

https://www.theproudtrust.org/foryoung.people/lgbt-youth-groups/where-can-i-find-a-youth-group/

Trans Lifeline provides trans peer support for our community that's been divested from police since day one. We're run by and for trans people.

United States (877) 565-8860

Canada (877) 330-6366